Other books by Ken Dychtwald:

Bodymind
Millennium: Glimpses into the 21st Century (with A. Villoldo)
The Keys to a High Performance Lifestyle
Wellness and Health Promotion for the Elderly
The Role of the Hospital in an Aging Society:
   A Blueprint for Action (with M. Zitter)

AGE WAVE

The Challenges and Opportunities of an Aging America

Ken Dychtwald, Ph.D.
and Joe Flower

BANTAM BOOKS
NEW YORK · TORONTO · LONDON · SYDNEY · AUCKLAND

AGE WAVE

A Bantam Book / February 1990

PRINTING HISTORY

Tarcher hardcover edition published 1989

Library of Congress Cataloging-in-Publication Data

Dychtwald, Ken, 1950–
  Age wave : the challenges and opportunities of an aging America /
Ken Dychtwald and Joe Flower.
      p.   cm.
  Reprint: Originally published: Los Angeles : J.P. Tarcher; New
York : distributed by St. Martin's Press, 1988.
  Includes index.
  ISBN 0-553-34806-X
  1. Aged—United States—Social conditions.   2 Aging—Social aspects
—United States.   3. Self-realization.   I. Flower, Joe.   II. Title.
[HQ1064.U5D93   1990]
305.26'0973—dc20   89-15071
                                                               CIP

Published simultaneously in the United States and Canada

Bantam Books are published by Bantam Books, a division of
Bantam Doubleday Dell Publishing Group, Inc. Its trademark,
consisting of the words "Bantam Books" and the portrayal of a
rooster, is Registered in U.S. Patent and Trademark Office and in
other countries. Marca Registrada. Bantam Books, 1540 Broad-
way, New York, New York 10036.

PRINTED IN THE UNITED STATES OF AMERICA

BVG 01

To Maddy . . . wife, friend, lover, partner, soulmate

Contents

Acknowledgments

I would like to extend my deepest thanks and appreciation to a number of people who have made a special contribution to this project:

My dear and wonderful wife Maddy, who loved, inspired, and believed in me during the darkest nights of this project—and there were many.

To Casey Kent Dychtwald, from whom I drew the greatest strength during the final year of this project, when I needed it the most.

Joe Flower, a unique and fantastic character—sent from heaven to save the day and bring this book to life.

Pearl, Seymour, and Alan Dychtwald, who have always surrounded me with love and encouragement, and from whom I will always draw confidence.

Sally and Stan Kent, Richard, Linda, David, and Joel Kent, Frieda Gordet, and Annea Neuss, my terrific second family.

My wonderful friends, Jaymie Canton, Marc Michaelson, Diane Zinky, Kenny and Sandy Dorman, Jessica Brackman, Tara Bennett and Danny Goleman, Barry and Loren Schneider, Mark Goldstein, Phil Polakoff and Nancy Pfund, Rick and Brooke Carlson, Willis Goldbeck and Anne Kiefhaber, Jean Duff, Joan Kaplan, Jessica Brackman, Frank and Caryn Wildman.

Fred Rubenstein, Jim Bernstein, Bob Hurel; and earlier—Bill Newman, Frank and Claire Wuest, Don Mankin, Will Schutz, Jean Houston, Goodwin Watson, Eugenia Gerrard and Gay Luce for caringly guiding me along the way.

Robert Butler, Maggie Kuhn, Helen Ansley, Landon Jones, Carl Eisdorfer, and Gloria Cavanaugh for inspiring me to deepen my understanding of the aging of America.

The Age Wave, Inc., family of friends, colleagues, critics, and playmates who have assisted me in developing the point of view that this book reflects: Mark Zitter, Bruce Clark, Jean Sheppard, Gail Brodkey, Michael Farmer, Alice Farmer, John Houck, Karen Hirtzel, Dick Hartz, Wayne Marks, Cathy Anderson, Praline McCormack, Bud Pence, Ruth Falk, Sue Adler, Sandra Journer, Steve Taylor, Joan Levison, Tracey Mendoza, Marney Dempsey, Jan Leonard, Neil Steinberg, Michael Blum, Cathy Calloway, Charlene Norman, Debra Gutierrez, Donna Berger, Edith Fuller, Edith Pettaway, Evelyn Willson, Francine Kuykendall, Janice Hoaglin, Janis Dvorin, Jud Walker, Judy Peck, Michele Pollard, Paul Airoldi, Peter Oprysko, Robert Harvey, Rudolph Ashford, Stephen Murphy, Sue Bach, Tony Robinson, and Voncia Williams.

Sandy Mendelson, Judy Hilsinger, and Brad Minor for believing enough in the Age Wave to support its publication.

Laurie Bagley, Jeanine Hinkle, Kathy Goss, Molly O'Lone, Lynette Padwa, Hank Stein, Mary Nadler, Toni Burbank, Robert Welsch, and Liz Williams for their masterful research, editing, and book development assistance.

Jim and Elizabeth Trupin, my literary agents, for having the patience to wait ten years while I completed this project.

And most of all, my publisher, dear friend, and fellow traveler, Jeremy Tarcher.

—K.D.

I would like to extend my sincere appreciation and gratitude to:

Judy Berger, for suffering with me through the thousand peregrinations of the project.

My children, Noah and Abraham, for reminding me constantly of the beauty and continuity of the stages of life.

My parents, Bart and Fran Flower, for giving me the love of the music of words.

Laurie Bagley, for her research assistance.

Molly O'Lone, for effort beyond the call of duty, for her skills in researching and interviewing, which produced many of the anecdotes, quotes, and profiles used in the book, and for saving my office and notes from a flood.

Robert Carroll, for his research help.

George Leonard and Rick Foster for their inspiration and counsel.

The Age Wave, Inc., family, for their support.

Jeremy Tarcher, for his unstinting enthusiasm and personal involvement in the project.

And most importantly, to Dr. Ken Dychtwald, for the opportunity of being involved in an historic and mind-expanding project.

—J.F.

Introduction

This story begins in the winter of 1973. I was then 23 years old and living and teaching at the Esalen Institute, the heart of the human-potential movement, in Big Sur, California. I was completing my doctorate in psychology while simultaneously putting the final touches on my first book, *Bodymind.* At that point in my life I was researching strategies and techniques by which people could enhance their creativity, physical vigor, and mental capabilities. All my life I had heard that most of us use only 5 percent of our potential. I was hoping to find the key to raising that percentage.

My friend Dr. Jean Houston, president of the Foundation for Mind Research, had recently put me in contact with a most extraordinary woman, Dr. Gay Luce. Gay was planning a grand experiment, a kind of academy of holistic health and human development, and she was looking for someone to help her create the curriculum.

The challenge was intoxicating. I immediately took steps to wind up my work at Esalen, and I spent the next several months developing what I thought would be an ideal program. My mind raced with the possibilities: I would include techniques for enhancing all aspects of physical functioning (for instance, yoga, martial arts, proper nutrition, and aerobic exercise), along with methods for improving mental skills and inner awareness (such as meditation, visualization, and biofeedback). Since we would be working in groups of between 15 and 20 people, I dreamed up an assortment of encounter and sensitivity-training processes that would help create a mood of trust and intimacy among the group members. And, of course, in the spirit of 1970s California there would be a great deal of interpersonal sharing and risk taking to help people break old and limiting patterns of behavior.

I then prepared to move to Berkeley, California, where the project would be headquartered. I had just finished making all of my moving arrangements when Gay called and said, "I've changed my mind."

I was stunned. "But you can't change your mind! I've already created a terrific program, and I'm all set to move!"

"Please," she said, "hear me out. I've become very concerned lately about my mother. She's in her seventies and hasn't been feeling well. In caring for her, I've realized that although there are a lot of programs to help young people feel and function better, no one's doing anything for old people. If you're game, I'd like you to consider rewriting the entire program for people over 65. Let's create a human-potential program for senior citizens!"

I was appalled by the idea. This definitely did not sound like fun. Like many other 23-year-olds, I thought of older people as unattractive, set in their ways, and difficult to relate to. Besides, since most of the human-development strategies I'd planned were geared toward younger people, I wondered if they could even have an effect on people who were, I knew, "over the hill."

I quickly rejected Gay's proposal, although I did agree to think it over for a few days. When I did, my imagination started to churn. What would it be like to practice yoga and share feelings with septuagenarians? Could you take a 70-

year-old body and help it to become more supple, flexible, and relaxed? Could you take an individual who had been alone and socially isolated for years and somehow bring back a feeling of intimacy and pleasure in dealing with other people? Would it be possible to create an environment in which the people I thought of as being the least changeable could, in fact, change? And if people could grow and improve themselves at 70 or 80, what would that say about people in their thirties and forties who claim that it's too late for them to change?

Before I knew what had hit me, I'd been bitten by the challenge.

That was my introduction to gerontology. Before that week, it had never occurred to me that I would wind up spending the core of my adult life searching for a new image of aging in America. But during the 15 years since then, the study of aging in America has drawn me in over and over again, each time in new and different ways.

The SAGE (Senior Actualization and Growth Exploration) Project, as our program was called, became extremely successful. We found that physically rigid people of 70 and 80 could become much more flexible. We found that many elders who had seemed distant, or even mentally dysfunctional, were simply bored and had turned inward. We found that people who were loners became open to the group experience, to making new friends, to romance. We found that many of the problems of these older people were problems of confidence and self-esteem, problems that were exacerbated by a gerontophobic culture. Once they started feeling better about themselves, some of them decided to go back to school or work, some became volunteers in the community, and some formed new relationships and even fell in love. Before we knew it we had a breeding ground for highly spirited, highly vigorous, turned-on humans who happened to be 60, 70, or 80 years old.

During the 1970s, this program (which was eventually funded by the National Institutes of Health) became the national model for several hundred other human-development and wellness programs for the elderly throughout the United States, Canada, and Europe.

My five years as co-director of the SAGE Project brought me an unexpected result. I thought that what I was doing was teaching older people how to live well, a presumptuous thought for a person so many years younger than they. But in spending 40 to 50 hours a week with long-lived humans, people who were close to death but full of life, I learned the depth of experience and seasoning in the spirits of these people. I began to see not only what I could teach them but also what they could teach *me*. And, most profoundly, I became aware of the similarities between them and me, of how young grows into old. Participants told me that in me and my friends they could see themselves at earlier times, and I became increasingly able to catch glimpses in them of myself in later years. Over time, a haunting realization came to me: the elderly are not "them," they're "us."

Then came a second fascination with aging, one that has become somewhat of a professional obsession. I wondered if any of the social, economic, and physical difficulties and problems that older people suffer were preventable. I noticed that many of the older people who were lonely had never quite learned the skill of making new friends in their later years. Many of those who were bored had long before resigned from challenging social and intellectual involvement. Many who were struggling with the hardships of fixed incomes had not been poor earlier on but had simply not managed their finances well.

And I observed that a lifetime of disregard for personal health usually led, not to a death sentence, but to chronic disease, a kind of extended-life imprisonment. It was obvious that many of the painful, punishing illnesses of old age could have been prevented.

I began to see that aging was most definitely not something that begins on the 65th birthday. Rather, the way we care for ourselves, the way we engage our social relationships, and the kinds of activities we're involved in throughout our lives lead us straight to the door of who we will be in our later years.

If so, I wondered why in the world we don't start thinking about the whole life process when we're younger, when there's still so much time to shape a healthy, productive future. I was convinced that if during youth and middle age we could instill in our lives a sense of how to create a meaningful, rich, and active old age, we would have a higher likelihood of actually achieving it.

By the early 1980s, as a result of the success of the SAGE Project and of several of my books, I found myself being invited to lecture at many conferences on aging, to serve on scientific and academic advisory panels, to appear on local and national television, and to consult with a wide variety of corporations interested in the challenges and opportunities of the aging of America.

At that time I began the research and study for this book. Until then, my primary orientation had been toward the way individuals relate to their own aging processes. The wider social focus required by this project made it clear to me that many age-related problems and challenges were so common that they might be part of some larger social phenomenon.

As I interacted with national policymakers, corporate leaders, and media personalities, I quickly learned something very interesting about how Americans want to think about aging: they don't. Aging, like other "taboo" issues, was not discussed at polite social gatherings, not written about in popular books, and not displayed in advertising. It seemed incredible to me that aging could be such a neglected issue when there were so many older people. The psychologist in me could recognize denial when he saw it. As I probed deeper, I was shocked by the degree to which gerontophobia had permeated our culture.

This gerontophobia was not only being expressed in our social values and popular media, it was ingrained in the texture of our man-made physical environment as well. I noticed that we had designed America, top to bottom, inside and out, to glorify the size, shape, and style of youth—from the height of the steps and the intensity of lighting in public buildings, to the age and style of the models in advertisements, to our embarrassment about our birthdays, to the fact that only 3 percent of the characters on television are over 65, while in reality this age group represents 12 percent of the population. We live in a youth-oriented—perhaps even youth-obsessed—nation. In thousands of ways we have learned to like what's young and dislike what's old.

Against this background of avoidance and negativity, I became increasingly excited about what I saw as a really big story: the absolutely predictable arrival, in our culture and in our time, of a demographic revolution that has no precedent in history. The very thing that we had blanked out of our cultural life was about to overwhelm us. Our young country is growing old. But are we prepared? The answer is no—at least, not yet.

However, in recent years a handful of innovative leaders, associations, and companies have begun to take notice of the problems *and the opportunities* that the aging of America will bring. In response, in 1986 I formed Age Wave, Inc., which has become one of the country's fastest growing information and communications firms.

At Age Wave, Inc., we're convinced that increases in the number, power, and resourcefulness of older Americans will render obsolete many of our social and business assumptions about what it means to be an older adult and to serve older adults. By working in partnership with many of America's leading associations and corporations in various fields and industries, we are committed to fostering a factual and positive new image of aging in America.

Age Wave's team of demographers, researchers, educators, business consultants, and media and communications experts has collaborated with many progressive companies and groups to assist them in understanding and meeting the social, lifestyle, and consumer needs of America's growing older population. Our list of clients includes American Express, CBS, Coopers & Lybrand, Gillette, Time Inc.,

McGraw-Hill, Avon, Bank of America, Institutional Investor, Blue Cross/Blue Shield, Marion Laboratories, the Young Presidents' Organization, and the Chief Executives Organization. But the work has just begun.

In the coming years, American culture will shift from being focused on youth to being increasingly concerned with the needs, problems, and dreams of a middle-aged and older population.

The coming "age wave" will challenge and shake every aspect of our personal, social, and political dynamics. How we will alter ourselves in response will be an issue of mounting concern; indeed, it may prove to be the single most controversial issue in the twilight of this century.

How strange that while we have spent the past 10,000 years trying to live long and grow old, now that we are having some success we don't know what to make of it. Our nation has yet to figure out a positive and hopeful way to think about itself growing up. America is having an identity crisis, one that can be resolved only through the adoption of a dramatically new image of aging.

In my capacity as an author, public speaker, and consultant on aging, I have had the opportunity in the last 15 years to study and interact with literally hundreds of thousands of men and women throughout America about their feelings, fears, and hopes for their later years. My great hope is that this book, which represents the culmination of these years of research, reflection, and writing, will begin to tell the story of what is to come: a hopeful, vigorous, and productive aging America.

KEN DYCHTWALD, PH.D.
Emeryville, California
December 1988

CHAPTER 1

The Rising Tide

A young country is growing old.

The nation that was founded on young backs, on the vigor, strength, impetuosity, and hope of youth, is growing more mature, steadier, deeper—even, one may hope, wiser. America is aging.

Most of the future remains unknown. But this much of the future is already written: more of us are growing older together than ever before, and the impact of that collective aging will change every facet of our society in the coming years.

The upheavals are not just going to happen to society, or to policymakers, or to social demographers. They will happen to you. They are probably already happening to your parents or older friends and family members. Whether you are 20, 55, or 70, the Age Wave will change your life in ways you might now find hard to imagine.

- You will live longer than you might now expect— possibly much longer—as future science brings the

aging process under control. It is likely that you will grow old more slowly than did members of previous generations, with greater health, energy, dynamism, and direction. You may even benefit from long-sought-after breakthroughs in life extension that will allow many people to live to 100, and some even to 120. And as science learns more about the aging process, you will be able to take advantage of the continual discovery of new drugs, foods, therapies, and health programs that will cause your body to age at a slower pace.

- **You will change the way you love, whom you love, and how long you will love them.** Marriage will change, as "till-death-do-us-part" unions give way to serial monogamy. In an era of longer life, some people will have marriages that last 75 years, while others will have different mates for each major stage of life. You may find yourself falling in love later in life, and in more unusual ways, than you now expect. Older women will deal with the shortage of older men by turning increasingly to unconventional relationships, such as dating younger men or sharing a man with other women.

- **You will change your conception of family life and the ways in which you relate to your parents and children.** The child-focused, nuclear family will become increasingly uncommon and will be replaced by the "matrix" family, an adult-centered, transgenerational family bound together by friendship and choice as well as by blood and obligation.

- **The physical environment you live in will change.** Because the man-made world we inhabit is now designed for youth, the form and fit of everything will be redesigned. To fit the pace, physiology, and style of a population predominantly in the middle and later years of life, the typeface in books will get larger, and traffic lights will change more slowly, steps will be lower, bathtubs less slippery, chairs more comfortable, and reading lights brighter. Neighborhoods will be safer, and food will be more nutritious.

- **You may never retire, or you may retire several times.** You may stop working one or more times in your thirties, forties, or fifties in order to go back to school, raise a second (or third) family, enter a new business, or simply to take a couple of years to travel and enjoy yourself. You may go back to work in your sixties, seventies, or even eighties. You may find that the traditional framework of life—with youth the time for learning, adulthood for nonstop working and raising a family, and old age for retirement—will come unglued, offering you new options at every stage. A cyclic life arrangement will replace the current linear life plan as people change direction and take up new challenges many times in their lives.

- **You will find yourself part of a new intergenerational struggle that will dwarf the generation gap of the sixties.** Several generations, each with its own powers and interests, will be competing for limited resources. Age wars will take place as the old refuse to retire and make room for the young in the workplace, as middle-aged and older Americans come to dominate politics, as the young find the burden of supporting the older generations to be crushing, and as the baby boomers approach a later life in which they rightly suspect that they will have to do without the traditional benefits of pensioned retirement.

THE TURNING OF THE TIDE

Throughout history, our nation's growth and development have been influenced by a variety of social, political, and technological shifts. But underlying all of these changes has been one relatively constant factor, the age-related composition of our culture. Now, for the first time, this axis has begun to twist and tip.

Three separate and unprecedented demographic phenomena are converging to produce the coming Age Wave.

The senior boom.   Americans are living longer than ever before, and older Americans are healthier, more active, more vigorous, and more influential than any other older generation in history.

The birth dearth.   A decade ago, fertility in the United States plummeted to its lowest point ever. It has been hovering there ever since, and it's not likely to change. The great population of elders is not being offset by an explosion of children.

The aging of the baby boom.   The leading edge of the boomer generation has now passed 40. As the boomers approach 50 and pass it, their numbers will combine with the other two great demographic changes to produce a historic shift in the concerns, structure, and style of America.

THE SENIOR BOOM

In 1776, a child born in America could expect to live to 35, on the average. At the founding of the Republic, the median age of the people who suddenly found themselves American was 16. A century later, life expectancy was only 40, and the median age was 21.

As a result, Americans in earlier times didn't give much thought to how they were going to handle their old age. Middle-aged people didn't worry very much about how to care for their aging parents, because most of their parents were already gone. And couples didn't wonder how they might relate to each other after the kids had grown up and left home; in the middle of the last century, the average "nest" could expect to be "empty" for no more than 18 months before one or both of the parents were dead.

As a nation, we weren't concerned about such financial transfers between generations as Social Security and Medicare, since there was no mass population of elders. There was no attempt to create retirement housing for the aged; there just weren't enough older people. And, of course, American industry didn't focus on the mature marketplace. There simply wasn't one.

For years, high mortality rates and equally high fertility rates kept our nation young. The graves at Gettysburg more often than not cover the bones of boys who were no older than 15 or 16. The builders of the railroads were poor young people. The cowboys of the Western plains were usually in their teens and twenties, and they often died young—not from rustlers' bullets but from tuberculosis, pneumonia, and exposure to the elements. And most of the immigrants who were herded through the cavernous halls of Ellis Island were young men.

During the past century, extraordinary breakthroughs in health care have been eliminating many of the diseases that used to keep us dying young. In the developed parts of the world today, breakthroughs in medicine and public health are raising the prospects of longevity. Smallpox, the cause of terrifying epidemics throughout history, is gone. Cholera is almost nonexistent in America. The death rate from tuberculosis, the leading cause of premature death a century ago, has been reduced by over 99.9 percent. Measles and streptococcal infections have been changed from killers to childhood annoyances. Pneumonia and influenza are no longer fatal in and of themselves; their deadliness has been confined to people already enfeebled by trauma or great age. Whooping cough and syphilis, once major epidemic diseases, now kill fewer than 1 in 200,000 people. Typhoid and diphtheria no longer kill Americans. Even AIDS, which is expected to claim nearly 2 million lives worldwide in the next decade, pales in comparison both to the bubonic plague, which during the fourteenth century killed 20 million Europeans—one of every three—and to the influenza epidemic that claimed 20 million lives worldwide in 1917–19.

In the decades since 1900 we have added 28 years to the average life expectancy in this country. A child born in 1989 can thus expect to live to be at least 75. The median age has climbed to 32, and it is projected to reach 36 by the turn of the century. The first generations of long-lived humans have already arrived: two-thirds of all the men and women who have lived beyond the age of 65 in the entire history of the world are alive today.

The Census Bureau projects that life expectancy in 2040 will be 75 years for men and 83 for women. The National Institute on Aging, a division of the National Institutes of Health, projects 86 years for men and 91.5 for women.

In sum, in a little over 200 years America has experienced a doubling in the life expectancy of its population. For the first time in our history, we are creating a mass society of healthy, active elders.

Throughout most of recorded human history, only one in ten people could expect to live to the age of 65. Today, nearly 80 percent of Americans will live to be past that age.

A Nation within a Nation

In 1890, there were only 2.4 million Americans over 65, representing less than 4 percent of the nation's population. It took 30 years for that number to double to 5 million. By 1960, the number of Americans over 65 had more than tripled to 16.5 million; since 1960, another 13.5 million have been added. Now, in the late 1980s, there are more than 30 million Americans over 65—some 12 percent of the population—and this group is increasing by nearly 6 million every decade. In the last two decades, the over-65 age group has grown more than twice as fast as the rest of the population. In the last hundred years, while the population of the country

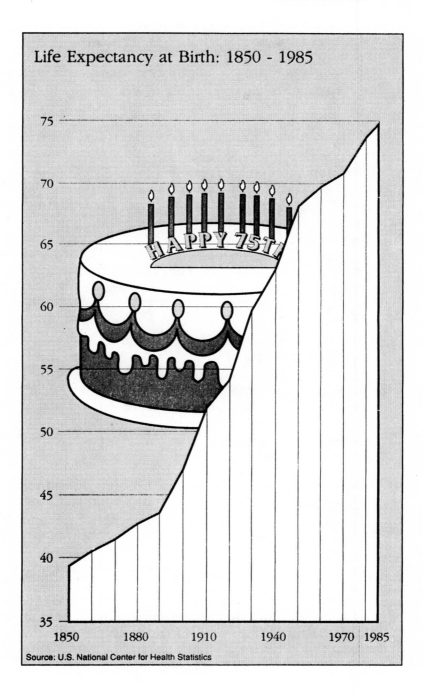

Life Expectancy at Birth: 1850 - 1985

Source: U.S. National Center for Health Statistics

has multiplied 5 times, the population over 65 has multiplied 12.5 times.

In July of 1983, the number of Americans over the age of 65 surpassed the number of teenagers. We are no longer a nation of youths.

Furthermore, a great many Americans already live on the far side of the life-expectancy curve. More than two-fifths of the 65 + population have passed 75. The over-85 group is the fastest-growing segment of the population. At the turn of the century there were only a few hundred thousand Americans over 85; today, there are 3.3 million, and it is estimated that there will be close to 20 million by 2050.

Most mornings on the "Today Show," Willard Scott congratulates somebody on his or her 100th birthday. Such birthdays are not rare. If Scott were to congratulate all of the centenarians in the country in 1988, one each morning, it would take him 180 years to do it! There are currently an estimated 45,000 Americans over 100. That number has doubled in the last decade alone.

The Census Bureau projects that there will be more than 35 million Americans over 65 by the turn of the century, accounting for nearly one-seventh of the population. By 2040, the National Institute on Aging projects that 87 million Americans will be over 65. By 2080, there are expected to be 5 million centenarians.

With continuing improvements in lifestyle and medical technology, the over-65 population in 2000 is likely to be close to 40 or 45 million, representing as much as one-fifth of the total population.

In the years ahead—that is, in our lifetimes—science will continue its attempts to push back the current limits to life expectancy. Gerontologists and medical researchers continue to debate the true limits of the human life span, but there is evidence that its upper natural range may lie somewhere between 120 and 140. The Rand Corporation, a future-oriented

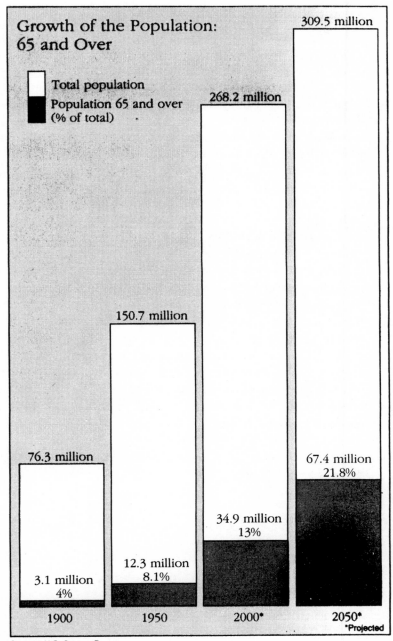

Growth of the Population:
65 and Over

Total population
Population 65 and over
(% of total)

309.5 million

268.2 million

150.7 million

76.3 million

67.4 million
21.8%

34.9 million
13%

12.3 million
8.1%

3.1 million
4%

1900   1950   2000*   2050*
                                        *Projected

Source: U.S. Census Bureau

think tank in Santa Monica, California, projects that by the year 2000, massive improvements in health care, disease prevention, pharmacology, genetic engineering, bionics, and organ transplantation may have raised the average life expectancy at birth to upwards of 90 years. Currently, Japan has the highest life expectancy in the world: 75.2 years for men, and 80.9 years for women.

It's estimated that if some new technology could eliminate all heart disease, the average life expectancy would rise by about ten years. Another five to six would be added if we could prevent all strokes, and yet another three years if cancer could be eradicated. While our great-grandparents would have called themselves blessed indeed to see 60, many Americans now hope and even plan for a healthy and active ninth or even tenth decade.

As it discovers the power and resources of elders, America will in effect be discovering a nation within a nation, one that is already populated by printers, lawyers, master machinists, architects, and entrepreneurs. The members of this group, already tempered by time, are as smart, eager, and ready for life as people half their age, and possibly a little less confused. This generation of elders is bolder, more powerful, more savvy in the marketplace, more socially outspoken, and more politically forceful than any previous generation of elders on Earth.

There have been baby booms before, but there has never been a senior boom.

THE BIRTH DEARTH

It seems as though babies are everywhere. Magazines tout articles about "boom II," "the boomlet," or "yuppie puppies." Cars sprout "baby on board" signs. Child care has become a major issue for American corporations.

But this "boomlet" is an illusion. The rise in the number of babies in recent years is due entirely to the enormous number of women of childbearing age. In fact, there has not been, and is not likely to be, any repeat of the postwar baby boom. The births that would even-out our population scale by adding more young people are simply not occurring. In fact, although there are twice as many women of childbearing age today as there were in the previous generation, they are having only half as many children. Compared to members of most earlier generations, fewer boomers have gotten married, stayed married, or had children. Those who have had children have had fewer and have done so later in life.

An estimated 20 percent of baby boomers will have no children at all; another 25 percent will have only one.

The boomers are not even replacing themselves. In 1986, the latest year for which figures were calculated, the fertility rate of American women (that is, the number of children each woman would have in her life if the present rate of birth were to continue) hit 1.8, less than half the rate of their mothers, 27 percent lower than the rate in 1970, and less than one-fourth of the fertility rate in 1800—in fact, the lowest rate ever recorded in America.

The shift from a birthing to an aging culture has been gathering momentum for some time, both in America and in other modernized nations. Except for the fairly singular exception of the post–World War II years, the combination of declining fertility and declining mortality has been a centuries-long phenomenon throughout the developed world. As Third World countries develop, nearly all are experiencing the same reductions.

A number of factors come together to produce cultural aging, including the following trends:

- As the economy moves from an agricultural to an industrial and then to a postindustrial service and information base, children become an increasing economic hardship. In a nonmechanized agricultural economy, with its great need for cheap, unskilled labor, a large number of healthy children is not just an advantage, it's an economic necessity. In a skill-based industrial or postindustrial economy, each child represents tremendous long-term costs with no economic return.

- As the world becomes rapidly urbanized, the cost of space for each new child rises. While this extra space was relatively cheap on the farm, it is very expensive in the city.

- As more women enter the work force, the cost of supporting each child increases. Mother must either forgo a paycheck to stay home and care for the children, or she must spend a good part of her paycheck on child care.

- As the divorce rate goes up, adults spend a smaller portion of their lives in stable relationships into which they feel they can bring children.

- As concerns over pollution and the threat of nuclear war grow, people feel an increasing disquiet about bringing children into the world.

America in the birth dearth is showing postboom stretch marks. Gerber Foods, which once flourished under the slogan "Babies are our business . . . our only business," dropped the last part a few years ago when it was forced to diversify into new product areas, including clothing, shampoo, and life insurance. Between 1971 and 1979, *Parents'* magazine saw its circulation drop by 33 percent. More than 9,000 of the primary and secondary schools of the 1950s and 1960s, vast prefab learning factories for the baby boom, have been closed down or recycled, many of them as adult-education centers. After skyrocketing from 23 million in 1950 to 37 million in 1970, the elementary-school-age population dropped by 6.5 million between 1970 and 1980. In Cupertino, California, a typical suburban school district, enrollment plummeted from 23,000 in 1970 to 10,300 in 1986, and the number of schools dropped from 42 to 22.

In short, the baby boom has been replaced by a baby bust. The combination of increased longevity and low fertility is turning the hourglass of America upside down.

The era of the United States as a youth-focused nation is coming to an end, and it will not be seen again in our lifetimes.

THE AGING OF THE BABY BOOMERS

The combined effect of the senior boom and the birth dearth in America will create a nation that is increasingly concerned with the needs and desires of its middle-aged and older citizens. This has already happened in many other modernized nations, such as Sweden, Great Britain, and France. Today, with only the above two events affecting the balance, the United States ranks eighteenth in the world in the percentage of population over 65, trailing nearly every country in Europe.

When life returned to normal after the Second World War, births rose dramatically in many parts of the world. This phenomenon was due partly to the soaring economy and the widespread feeling of hope brought by the war's ending, and partly to the fact that when the boys returned home, couples made up for lost time for romance. In most countries, this birth spurt lasted for three to six years. But in the United States, Canada, Australia, and New Zealand, for reasons that demographers still debate, the boom lasted for nearly two decades.

Fully one-third of all Americans—76 million people— were born between 1946 and 1964. Likened by demographers to "a pig moving through a python," this generational mass has dominated American culture for four decades. To the extent that America has been a leader in world culture, the boom generation has enormously influenced life on the rest of the planet as well.

At each stage of their lives, the needs and desires of the baby boomers have become the dominant concerns of American business and popular culture.

The 25 Most Longevous Nations

		Percent of population over 65
1.	Sweden	18
2.	Norway	16
3.	United Kingdom	15
4.	Denmark	15
5.	West Germany	15
6.	Switzerland	15
7.	Austria	15
8.	Belgium	14
9.	Italy	14
10.	Greece	14
11.	Luxembourg	14
12.	France	13
13.	East Germany	13
14.	Finland	13
15.	Hungary	13
16.	Netherlands	12
17.	Spain	12
18.	United States	12
19.	Ireland	12
20.	Bulgaria	12
21.	Portugal	12
22.	Faroe Islands	12
23.	Uruguay	11
24.	Czechoslovakia	11
25.	Canada	11

Source: U.S. Bureau of the Census, International Data Base (1987).

When the boomers arrived, the diaper industry prospered. When they took their first steps, the shoe and photo industries skyrocketed. The baby-food industry, which had moved 270 million jars in 1940, ladled out enough strained meals to fill 1.5 billion jars a year by 1953. The boom kids created an insatiable demand for the sugar-coated cereals and toys hyped on Saturday-morning cartoon shows. Cowboy outfits, very popular with toddlers in the 1950s, rang up sales of $75 million per year. As the boomers suffered scraped knees and runny noses, a massive pediatric medical establishment arose, and Dr. Spock became a national figure.

When the boomers hit school age in the early to mid-1950s, many schools went into double sessions. More elementary schools were built in America in 1957 than in any year before or since. There was a boom not only in teachers' colleges and in the school-building, textbook, and desk industries but also in the market for Hula Hoops, skateboards, Slinkies, and Frisbees. Television shows for and about kids—from "The Mouseketeers," "The Little Rascals," and "Captain Kangaroo" to "Ozzie and Harriet," "My Three Sons," and "Father Knows Best"—became central to the television industry. We had become a child-focused nation.

As the boomers became teenagers, the bulge in the school system edged up through the grades. Between 1950 and 1975, the high-school-age population doubled. Following the trend, more high schools were built in America in 1967 than in any year before or since. As teenagers, boomers bought unprecedented quantities of soft drinks, movie tickets, and records; they pleaded with their parents to flaunt their middle-class affluence by buying them television sets, cars, and personal phones. Teenage girls accounted for one-fifth of all sales of cosmetics and toiletries, while boys spent $120 million per year on hair oil, mouthwash, and deodorant. In 1964 alone, teenagers spent over $12 billion, and their parents spent another $13 billion on them. The boomers gobbled vast quantities of fast foods, making millionaires of the founders of McDonald's, Jack-in-the-Box, and Kentucky Fried

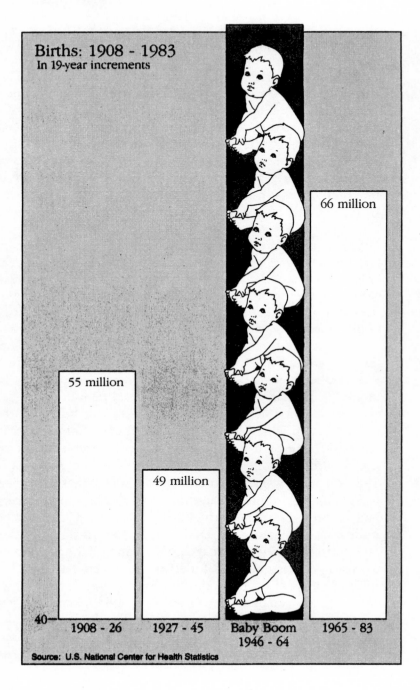

Births: 1908 - 1983
In 19-year increments

66 million

55 million

49 million

40—

1908 - 26   1927 - 45   Baby Boom   1965 - 83
1946 - 64

Source: U.S. National Center for Health Statistics

Chicken by kicking these franchise chains through year after year of 20 percent annual growth.

Then the kids went to college. The number of college students rose from 3.2 million in 1965 to 9 million in 1975, and 743 new colleges were opened to help absorb the glut. *Rolling Stone* was the new publishing success, and rock and roll flourished. With the popularization of marijuana, the U.S. Tobacco Company's profit from Zig-Zag roll-your-own cigarette papers rose by 25 percent every year for a decade. The Gap, a store that sold mainly blue jeans and catered to the boomers, was founded in 1969 on an investment of only $60,000. Its sales were $600,000 in the first year, and within seven years it had grown to a 165-store chain with $99 million in sales.

Millions of boomers were experiencing the pressures and enlightenments that arrived with advanced education, a heightened awareness of international conditions, made instantly available by the mass media, and their first tastes of lifestyle freedom. During this period, social unrest and political rebellion erupted on campuses across the nation. Rebellion is, of course, common to all generations in their late teens and early twenties. But when 76 million young people are rebelling at the same time, it's a revolution. America should have learned a potent lesson about the aging of the boomers at that moment: when they arrive at any stage of life, the issues for them at that stage—whether these are driven by financial, interpersonal, or even hormonal forces—will become the dominant social, political, and marketplace themes of the time.

In the seventies, when the first of the boomers were moving through their twenties, their focus and priorities shifted from teenage rebellion to the challenging transition into young adulthood. With this maturation, a host of concerns about personal identity, self-esteem, lifestyle experimentation, earning a living, and the meaning and purpose of work became the compelling social themes. Introspective books such as *I'm OK—You're OK, How to Be Your Own Best*

Friend, Your Erroneous Zones, and *What Color Is Your Parachute?* became best-sellers. Personal growth itself became a growth industry as the boomers en masse sorted out the goals, philosophies, and skills of adult life. Not surprisingly, such programs as EST, Lifespring, Transcendental Meditation, and Silva Mind Control sprang up nationwide to meet the psychological and lifestyle needs of this group.

In the eighties, with the boomers moving into their thirties and focusing more intensively on careers and families, publications such as the *Wall Street Journal, Esquire, GQ, Money, Forbes,* and *Fortune* entered periods of record growth, while *Rolling Stone* and its imitators were forced to either retrench or fold. Day-care centers became a hot political issue as boomers became parents. Books about business and success, such as *In Search of Excellence, Megatrends, Iacocca,* and *Trump,* filled the best-seller charts. Wall Street ballooned as millions of boomers became investors and managers for the first time. Just as the image of the hippie came to stand for much of what had made the sixties unique, the "yuppie"—another version of the boomer—came to stand for the eighties.

As the boomers grow older, they will continue to dominate the culture. When a few thousand people across the country share an opinion, read a book, or buy a product, that's interesting; it may even amount to a trend. But, again, when 76 million people do so, it's a revolution. From Barbie dolls and yo-yos to compact discs and Macintosh computers, from Yippie radicalism and antiwar marches to "Sharper Image" consumerism, this generation has by its very weight created industries, driven politics, made and broken heroes, and altered the very look, feel, and style of American life.

The boomers are not aimlessly wandering through an unknown landscape of serendipitous life patterns. They are moving forward, second by second, inch by inch along the one-directional highway of the human life span. And because this generation is destined to be the force that most profoundly influences popular culture in our lifetime, as they grow up, America grows up.

If you can anticipate the movement of the baby boom generation's life-span migration, you can see the future.

Many social observers predict that concern for the elderly and issues of aging will explode around the year 2011, when the first of the boomers celebrate their 65th birthdays. But this massive generation will not wait until then to confront these concerns.

The boomers will change the nature of aging years before any of them reach the later stages of life. Long before they actually arrive, they will have begun to reenvision and reshape popular habits, styles, and attitudes toward aging to better accommodate their unique fancies and needs. There are several reasons why we will see a widespread interest in the issues of aging within the next decade.

First, the boomers will get serious about the challenges of growing older in America not only out of concern for themselves but also because they will have witnessed their own parents struggling through the later stages of life. The members of the "Me generation" will become the caregivers, parents to their own parents. As this enormous generation experiences this together, the challenge of how to relate to the aging of loved ones will become one of the powerful themes of the coming decades.

Second, as more older Americans retire and continue to live longer than the designers of Social Security anticipated, an increasing share of their financial burden will land on the shoulders of the boomers, who will be in their key earning years. This inescapable social and economic crisis will cause the boomers to struggle with the pros and cons of such age-related economic issues as "intergenerational equity," transportable private pension plans, means testing for Social Security, phased retirement, extended work life, and trans-generational cooperation.

Finally, the boomers have always influenced adjacent generations, both those following and those preceding them. Many men and women who are now in their late forties and early fifties, although not boomers themselves, have always felt comfortable sharing the values and lifestyle adventures of the boomers. These depression and World War II babies will, in all likelihood, be directly influenced by the new images of aging promoted by their younger brothers and sisters and even by their children. When the boomers propose a new definition of aging, as they undoubtedly will, their vote will be forcefully seconded by those already in the later stages of life.

The oldest of the boomers are now in their fifth decade. What will America look and feel like as the boomers migrate through their forties, fifties, and sixties? What will a mid-life crisis be like when it's multiplied by 76 million? What will happen when this generation decides that it doesn't like baldness and wrinkles? When it decides that dependence and senility are not desirable options? When it decides not to grow old?

Oil of Olay has used this attitude as a tag line in a recent magazine ad in which a thirtyish model declares, "I don't intend to grow old gracefully. I intend to fight it every step of the way!"

We would be unwise to forget that above all else, the boomers are the "youth" generation. They love their youth. They love the youthful vigor and vitality that have always been a part of their lives. In fact, we might expect that because they love their youth so much, they will do everything possible to take it with them into old age. In the years to come, entire industries will rise and fall in response to this anti-aging, pro-longevity obsession.

The boomers redefine whatever stage of life they inhabit. They have, in fact, already begun to rebuild the later years of life in their own, more youthful image.

We can already see evidence of this in the enormous growth of the fitness movement, which took off as the boomers hit their thirties—the decade of life in which one first begins to feel the pull of gravity. For five years after its appearance in 1982, Jane Fonda's *Workout* videotape outsold every other nontheatrical videotape. Sales of home gym equipment rose from $75 million in 1982 to over $1 billion in 1985. In the past ten years, 29 percent of all smokers have quit, and the proportion of Americans who exercise has risen to two-and-a-half times that of the early 1960s. The dollar value of membership in health clubs spiraled from $227 million in 1972 to over $8 billion by 1984. Whether the numbers chronicle the growth of megavitamin therapy, Herbalife products, face-lifts, hair transplants, or jogging shoes, they add up to one thing: the boomers would prefer to grow old youthfully. If they have their way, they will be the first generation in history to take 100 years to become 50.

The Age Wave is Coming

The senior boom, the birth dearth, and the aging of the baby boom are coming together to create a massive demographic shift, one which we refer to as the Age Wave. The numbers themselves will peak in the early decades of the new century as the baby boomers reach their fifties, sixties, and seventies. But the shift in attitudes, style, and meaning—the "social revolution" that the Age Wave brings—will begin to rumble and quake long before the first boomer turns 65.

The Population Reference Bureau, a nonprofit demographic study group in Washington, D.C., has predicted that by 2025, Americans over 65 will outnumber teenagers by more than two to one. According to the Census Bureau, by 2030 the median age is expected to have reached 41. By the year 2050, it's likely that as many as one in four Americans will be over 65. Many demographers consider these projections to be very conservative; by some estimates, the median age will eventually reach 50.

No one can know exactly to what extent these demographic changes will alter American culture, but the implications are staggering. Are we ready for a social transformation with such far-reaching and deeply felt implications? Are we prepared to grapple with the personal, social, and political changes to come?

- What will our nation feel like, what will be our pace and rhythm, as longer life unfolds and as we all become older? What kind of music will we like? What will be the new face of beauty when the "eye of the beholder" wears bifocals?
- As the boomers migrate toward late adulthood, with its concern for making a significant social contribution and leaving something behind for the future, will the activism of the sixties return in a more powerful, more organized form? When the boomers next encounter the American political machinery, will it be from the inside?
- With a society becoming both older and more active, how will we change the way we work and retire and the way we spend our time? Does it make sense to stop being productive at any particular age? Will economic realities and personal priorities end retirement as we now know it?
- Since the shifting sands of money and assets in America are largely determined by the shape of the generational hourglass, how will a longer-lived society change the financial world of investments, pensions, mortgages, wills, and taxes? What will replace Social Security and Medicare, systems that depend on people dying at a younger age than they now are?
- And what of our physical environment, designed to fit the shape, senses, and pulse of youth? How will the design of homes, cars, public buildings, and products change to accommodate our more "mature" physiological needs?
- What alignments and issues will shape the power politics of the coming years? Will political "age wars" erupt as the boomers find themselves paying more and more money into a Social Security system that few of them believe will

be there when they need it? Or as an increasingly adult population loses its interest in paying for schools and child-care centers? Will intergenerational equity become the major civil-rights issue of modern times?

To understand aging, we can wait the 25 years until the first boomers celebrate their 65th birthdays. Or, we can find glimpses of the future in the challenges and crises being experienced by today's middle-aged and elder Americans.

These people are the true social pioneers. Like "age scouts," they travel ahead into the later years to chart the uncertain territory of long life. In this book, we will often look to these frontiersmen and women of the spirit for their guidance, example, and inspiration.

Along the trail they blaze will lie our future.

CHAPTER
2

Retiring the Myths of Aging

The way you respond to the news of the Age Wave depends to a great extent on the way you think about aging. In China, it is believed that the older a person is, the more wisdom and knowledge he or she has. When asked, "How old are you?" a 55-year-old in China might cheat a bit and claim to be 59. But an American asked the same question would be more likely to respond with "I never tell my age" or to cheat a bit and answer, "I'm 49." In our culture we believe that the older a person is, the less socially attractive he or she is. Jack Benny was 39 for a long time.

You could interpret the news of the coming Age Wave in two ways. You could hear it as a forecast of a dark future, a slow descent into senility and ossification, a hardening of our arteries as individuals, and the slow death of our culture's vitality and creativity.

Or, you could hear it as news about a world of extended opportunities, of enhanced possibilities for living, of new freedom and new hope.

For most of us, the image we hold of aging is very negative, and very wrong.

Our attitude toward aging is reflected in the multibillion-dollar greeting-card industry. Recently, a large greeting-card company created a line of birthday cards it refers to as the "Black Balloon" collection—hardly a joyful image. Designed to communicate popular thoughts about the process of growing older, the cards include such zingers as these:

(front) Don't feel old. We have a friend your age . . .
(inside) . . . and on good days he can still feed himself.
or,
(front) You have just turned 30.
(inside) You will never have fun again for the rest of your
          life.
or,
(front) There are worse things than birthdays . . .
(inside) . . . like nuclear war.

At least in part, our images of aging are negative because of our glorification of youth. The image of youth as vigorous and powerful and sexy has as its shadow an image of older people as incompetent, inflexible, wedded to the past, desexed, uncreative, poor, sick, and slow.

When we ascribe to youth much of what is good about life and to age every trauma and sorrow, we create the image of a descending slope from one to the other. Every sign of growing older appears to us as a sign not of growing maturity but of increasing decay and closeness to death. The old age we dread does not come on us suddenly; rather, it comes in increments over the whole middle part of our lives. Starting at 30, our decade birthdays fall on us like hammer blows.

A long list of negative comparisons have become embedded in American culture:

- If young is good, older must be bad.
- If the young have it all, then the old must be losing it.

- If young is creative and dynamic, older must be dull and staid.
- If young is beautiful, old must be unattractive.
- If it's exciting to be young, it must be boring to be old.
- If the young are full of passion, the old must be beyond caring.
- If children are our tomorrow, then older people must be our yesterday.

Gerontophobia is ingrained in all of us, including the elderly. Several years back, a joint study conducted by the Louis Harris polling organization and the National Council on Aging uncovered a provocative fact: although all age groups expressed great misperceptions about what it means to grow old, the elderly are as misinformed and prejudiced about aging as any other group. For example, when men and women over 65 were asked whether they had enough money to live on, only 18 percent said that they did not. But when the same people were asked what percentage of other older people were struggling with poverty, they assumed that the figure was greater than 50 percent.

In her 1987 book *Disguised,* sociologist and design consultant Pat Moore performed an unusual and dramatic demonstration of age discrimination. For three years, as a graduate student and fledgling designer in her mid-twenties, Moore repeatedly put on elaborate makeup, wig, and wardrobe to turn herself into a woman who appeared to be in her eighties. Moore then wandered city streets all over the United States and Canada in her disguise. She found that she was routinely treated rudely, referred to disrespectfully as "sweetie," "honey," or "dearie," shortchanged by cashiers who thought she couldn't count her change, bumped into in the street by people who thought she was moving too slowly, and cut ahead of in lines by people who assumed she wasn't paying attention. Once, she was robbed and beaten badly by a gang of teenage boys. She comments, "Sometimes, even though years have passed, I still feel the results of having been beaten so badly. I can't help but wonder why teenagers were so willing to bash an older woman."

Moore learned that these overt acts of discrimination are an everyday concern for older people. But she brought another advantage to her experience besides her sensitive point of view: removing her disguises, she could repeat her social experiments as an attractive young woman. She returned to stores where, as a "little old lady," she had been treated rudely, shortchanged, or ignored. Encountering the same salespeople and making the same requests, she was invariably treated much better than she had been as an old woman. The difference was not brought about by personality, by something she said, or by the circumstances, but solely by the appearance of age. As Moore learned, gerontophobia can leave us uncomfortable, even angry, with the elderly.

The gerontophobia that pervades our thoughts and actions is made up of a network of negative myths about what it means to grow older. These myths, which will be listed and explored individually later in this chapter, block us from treating the elderly as human beings who are as fully alive, active, and vigorous as the young. And it's easy to forget that we ourselves may be among those hurt the most by our negative images of aging.

THE ELDER WITHIN

Each of us has a "child within," made up of all our fond as well as unpleasant memories from childhood. In a sense, we might also have an "elder within," made up of all the images, good as well as bad, that we possess about our later years.

If we envision these later years as a time of boredom, social isolation, and ill health, we may consciously or unconsciously aim ourselves in these directions. On the other hand, if the expectations we have of long life are filled with vigor, fulfilling activities, and social usefulness, we might similarly aim ourselves toward these more hopeful possibilities. This "elder within" becomes a personal and social blueprint from which we build our futures.

Seeds of this notion occurred to me many years ago when I was working as an educator and psychotherapist with the SAGE Project. I was struck by the fact that many of the older people with whom I was working would regularly comment that some young person reminded them of a friend they had known in their youth and were still in contact with. They told me that they noticed a great many similarities between what their older friends were like now and what they had been like many years earlier.

I asked them to reflect on what, if anything, they had observed over the years about how people grow older. What did they feel was the single most important ingredient in whether someone aged well or badly?

Invariably, they all told me that in their view, the most essential determinant of successful aging is attitude. Each of us has the difficult task of steering our own ship through the challenging waters of life. Although it's good to have a sound boat, with a good motor and comfortable sleeping quarters, your attitude is in control of the wheel throughout the journey.

Of course, there are aspects of our lives that we can't control. There are physical, financial, social, and political limits to what we can do and be in any period of life. But it may well be that one of the most powerful limits is inside us, in the visions we hold of tomorrow and next year, of ourselves as we grow older.

Once, when I was presenting a seminar on this issue, a woman whom I later discovered was in her eighties raised her hand, stood up, and called out to me, "Young man, with regard to this point you're making . . . I believe in the 'more-so' philosophy." And then she sat down. I did not recognize this word *more-so* from any of my philosophy courses or graduate studies, so I wasn't sure what to make of her comment. So I asked her, "Would you mind elaborating on this point?" And she said, "Well, if you're a jerk when you're young, you'll be 'more so' when you're older!"

According to Robert Wood, publishing director of *Modern Maturity* magazine, "Your personal identity, with all its special characteristics, will persist throughout your life. Identity is stronger than age in its effect on your sense of self as you grow older. You'll never lose this identity and become your grandpa: you'll always be you! So each of us should give serious thought to exactly who we want to be."

Our culture is deeply gerontophobic. We have a fear of aging and a prejudice against the old that clouds all our perceptions about what it means to grow old in America.

Many of us have already either consciously or unconsciously created a blueprint for ourselves of fearful and unattractive images of aging. When these personal images are gathered together, they represent an "age trance" in whose spell most of us are currently held. The most pervasive myths of aging keep us from seeing the current reality and cloud our ability to shape the future in a more positive fashion. Imagine the effect of an entire nation's building a cultural point of view from the values of such a prejudiced blueprint.

FREEING OURSELVES OF THE MYTHS

How might we break free of this gerontophobia? If we are to create a new, more positive image of aging, we must first uproot the prevalent negative myths and stereotypes that bind us:

Myth 1: People over 65 are old.

Myth 2: Most older people are in poor health.

Myth 3: Older minds are not as bright as young minds.

Myth 4: Older people are unproductive.

Myth 5: Older people are unattractive and sexless.

Myth 6: All older people are pretty much the same.

Examined one by one, these myths range from the merely disprovable to the downright absurd.

Myth 1: People over 65 Are Old

When you reach 65 you're old. It's time to quit. It's time to act like an old person. It's time to sleep late and watch TV all day, time to learn mah-jongg and perfect your chess game. The great moments of your life are gone, and you can't expect any more to come. You're out to pasture. You're done.

The marker at the entrance to old age reads "65." More than we realize, we have taken that arbitrary marker for reality. It has become a key transition point in the script we've written for our lives.

We use the age of 65 to calibrate our purpose and worth. A 33-year-old thinks, "I've turned the corner. Now I'm closer to the end than the beginning." A 58-year-old unconsciously thinks, "Seven more years." A 65-year-old thinks, "Time to punch out. Wrap it up. I'll grow a few roses, maybe see a few sights, and then it's time to die." There are many people nearing this point who are uncertain of whether they're supposed to stop or start.

Although a 65-year-old has an average life expectancy of 14 more years (11 for men, 19 for women), we tend to think of the over-65 population as a warehousing problem and a medical and financial dilemma rather than as a rich natural resource. But anyone who comes into regular contact with large segments of this population, as I do, knows how far from the truth that image is. For example, some time ago I went to Albuquerque for a conference on aging. The man assigned to pick me up at the airport was eager to show me his latest interest, so he did, right there in the baggage-pickup area. Break dancing. Moonwalking. All the little mechanical curls and glides that you would see on street corners in the Bronx. He was 72. This was definitely not an "old" man.

The same vitality is demonstrated in a thousand different ways, day in and day out, in lives across America—from the passionate political fighters of the Gray Panthers and the dozens of marathoners in their seventies; to the men of San Francisco's Dolphin Club, most of whom are in their sixties and seventies, who take an annual four-mile swim in the frigid bay on New Year's Day; to the growing legions of entrepreneurs who have established businesses, and in some cases even made fortunes, after they have "retired."

There are neither biological nor psychological reasons to connect the number 65 to the onset of old age.

Nothing happens on or around the 65th year of life to set it apart from the five or ten years just before it or just after it. That marker is partly due to the Social Security Act, drafted in the 1930s.

The creators of the act decided on 65 as "retirement age" based on the simple political realities of that time. Old-age programs of various state and foreign governments had set the retirement age variously at 60, 62, 65, and even 70. The New Deal Congress felt that placing the retirement-benefit age at 60 would make the program too costly to garner the necessary votes. Putting it at 70 would have cut out almost everyone, since life expectancy was then only 61.7. So 65 was a reasonable political compromise at a time when most people didn't live that long.

But our contemporary benchmark of old age had its roots long before the arrival of Social Security. Germany's "Iron Chancellor," Prince Otto von Bismarck, picked the first official retirement age in 1889 when he established the world's first state system of social security. He picked the biblical "threescore and ten," 70, and German officials later reduced that to 65.

Bismarck did not expect that the average worker would ever receive a pension, since life expectancy in Germany at that time was only about 45. The retirement age he chose was thus 56 percent higher than the life expectancy. If today's retirement age were 56 percent higher than life expectancy

—75 years—you could look forward to receiving your first Social Security check at the age of 117.

Even though life expectancy has jumped radically, we still cling to the anachronistic marker of 65 as a sign to slow down. The idea that 65, or indeed any specific age, means "old" is so pervasive that it is difficult to talk about older people without constantly reinforcing that very idea. It is time to redefine old age in a way that matches the style and tempo of the time in which we live. If it is necessary, for bureaucratic or legal reasons, to pick a number that marks the onset of old age, 80 or 85 would be more reasonable than 65. And, since people are growing old much later than they used to, that marker will continue to move higher.

In the not-too-distant future we will likely think of old age as setting in at around 90, or even 100.

The trend is evident already. When Gloria Steinem turned 50, one interviewer asked her how 50 felt. She said, "It feels a lot like what 40 used to feel like."

We are aging more slowly, socially as well as physically. When you reach 65, you will still be far from old.

Myth 2: Most Older People Are in Poor Health

Wheelchairs. Canes. Oxygen bottles. Pills. Sciatica and broken hips. Wheezes and coughs. Most of the elderly are frail and disabled. In advertising, old people should only be used to sell dentures, laxatives, painkillers, and medical-insurance plans.

As we age, even our doctors wrongly attribute all of our health problems to our accumulation of birthdays. The story is told of an 82-year-old man who visits the doctor with the complaint that his left knee is painful and stiff. The doctor examines it and says, "Well, what do you expect? After all, it's an 82-year-old knee."

"Sure it is," says the patient. "But my right knee is also 82, and it's not bothering me a bit."

Aging and disease are often intertwined, but they are definitely not the same. When asked what proportion of the over-65 population is in some kind of institution, whether acute hospital, convalescent hospital, mental hospital, or nursing home, most people would guess 20 or 25 percent. The correct answer is actually 5 percent, a figure not much higher than that for the rest of the population. And for that 5 percent, the average age at admission to nursing homes is not 65 or 70, but 80. Most older people are not ill.

A recent study by the Louis Harris polling organization found that far fewer older Americans report problems with their health than the public assumes, even the elderly public. Although young people guessed that 50 percent of the elderly were suffering from serious health problems, only a little more than 20 percent of the older respondents said that they were debilitated by health problems themselves. In fact, most responded that they were feeling quite well.

While older people may have chronic, controlled health problems as they age, they are not necessarily bothered or limited by them.

Of course, even the healthiest body ages. The process occurs throughout the body; its details are myriad, and it happens to us all. In time the body's cells begin to liquefy and its tissues to shrink. Skin tends to thin out and become less elastic. The heart gradually loses its power, the metabolic rate slows, and the bones become brittle. The eyes may develop cataracts and other defects, and the ears may lose the higher registers. The sense of balance becomes less sure.

But this process does not happen to everyone at the same age or at the same rate. A body that is properly maintained will show the effects of aging gradually and gently in the eighties, the nineties, and beyond. Aging is different from disease. A body that has been subjected to continual stress, that carries too much weight, that has been continually exposed to pollutants, that has seen years of poor nutrition, and that has not been exercised regularly will begin to show the effects of aging decades earlier. Recent research from the National Institute on Aging suggests that many of the problems of old age are not due to aging at all, but rather to improper care of the body over a lifetime. Eighty percent of the health problems of older people are now thought to be preventable or postponable. What many of us call aging is instead a lifestyle issue.

Osteoporosis, diabetes, and vascular disease are commonly thought of as diseases of aging. When a 90-year-old has them, that's what they are. But when a 60-year-old has them, they may be nothing more than the results of a body wearing out prematurely as a result of a lifetime of bad maintenance. With optimal care, it is possible to grow old with energy and vigor, in the absence of disease.

The myth that age automatically means decrepitude leaves little room for such people as diet-and-exercise guru Jack LaLanne. Throughout his lifetime, LaLanne has celebrated aging by demonstrating that with proper care and maintenance, the human body has remarkable powers of resilience, even in the years after youth. He marked his 40th birthday by swimming across the Golden Gate underwater, wearing 140 pounds of scuba gear. At 41, he swam from Alcatraz to Fisherman's Wharf in San Francisco—while handcuffed. Then he did 30 pushups. At 42, he did 1,033 pushups in 23 minutes on television. Every year the feats of strength got wilder.

In 1974, on his 60th birthday, LaLanne swam from Alcatraz to Fisherman's Wharf again, handcuffed. And with his ankles shackled. Towing a half-ton boat. On his 62nd birthday, he completed a mile-and-a-half-long swim in Long Beach Harbor, handcuffed and shackled, towing 13 boats filled with 76 cheering kids from the local Y. When he was done, his pulse was a mere 76. He repeated the feat on his 70th birthday, this time hauling 70 boats full of friends and reporters.

At 75, LaLanne still follows the routine he has followed for half a century. He rises at 4:30 in the morning, and by

5:00 he's pumping iron. After two hours, he heads to the pool for an hour of swimming and water exercises. Then he eats breakfast—typically, a shake made of apple juice, nonfat milk, a banana, and several packages of Jack LaLanne–brand protein powder.

Jack and his wife, Elaine, spend half of each year on the road, promoting the fitness gospel through speeches and special appearances. When he's asked about retirement, he says, "Retirement? No way! I don't care how long I live—I want to be 100 percent active and alive while I'm living. Most Americans, hell, they die at 40, and they bury 'em at 70. Who wants that? I want to be productive. I want to be able to help people every day of my life!"

LaLanne is far from alone. He merely shows what the body can do when treated right. Mavis Lindgren of Orleans, California, is still running marathons at 80. She took up running at 62, ran her first marathon at 70, and has run 48 more since then. "I like to think I can help other people feel better in their older years. I hope younger people will see me running and say, 'Well, if that old lady can run, I can at least get out and walk.' "

Arabella Williams of Escondido, California, took up water skiing at 70, and at 91 she's still winning trophies. Hulda Crooks, now 91, has climbed 98 mountains, including Japan's Mount Fuji, since the age of 65. She is known as "Grandma Whitney" for having climbed Mount Whitney, the highest peak in the contiguous 48 states, once a year for 22 years.

Lucille Thompson of Danville, Illinois, an 88-year-old, 4-foot, 11-inch great-grandmother, had begun to stoop and to feel the arthritis in her fingers. The exercises she was given at the local senior center didn't seem to have any effect. She started to look for something more physical, even though she had never done anything athletic in her life. One afternoon at the center, tae kwan do master Min Kyo Han and his students gave a demonstration. "The next day," says Lucille, "I went down and signed up." Her 55-year-old daughter did not approve, and her fellow students secretly bet that she wouldn't last two weeks. But after two years of daily practice, Lucille earned a black belt, along with the nickname "Killer." "The arthritis is gone," she says, "my heart rate has dropped, and my mind is more alert than ever."

Simplistic definitions of "sick" and "well" don't really apply in an aging America.

Traditional notions about old age and health will have to be rethought. Definitions that have more to do with functional abilities, levels of vigor and vitality, and an individual's own feeling of well-being will become the norm in the years to come.

In Sun City, Arizona, older people who use canes or transport themselves in wheelchairs don't like to be referred to as handicapped. The name they prefer is "handicapables."

In the coming decades, chronic disease is likely to be less common. As our attention shifts from acute to chronic diseases, as breakthroughs take place in genetic engineering, pharmacology, preventive health, bionic prostheses, and organ transplants, and as more people make the lifestyle changes that can prevent chronic disease, we will see today's years of illness compressed at the very end of a long, vigorous life.

Myth 3: Older Minds Are Not as Bright as Young Minds

At birth, our brains have all the cells they will ever have. These cells are slowly lost over time, so that older brains have markedly lower capacity. The aging brain becomes more rigid. As the body ages, the IQ drops, memory weakens, and the ability to learn or change all but disappears. A kind of senile mindlessness becomes the norm.

In 1984, a group of young medical students was asked how likely they were to lose their mental faculties as they grew older. After some discussion, they agreed that about 30 to 40 percent of the elderly population experiences signs of "senility." They were wrong, by a wide margin.

Of the 30 million Americans over the age of 65, only 10 percent show any significant loss of memory, and fewer than half of those show any serious mental impairment.

Most of the losses in mental capacity happen to the very old, not to people in their sixties, seventies, and early eighties, and are due not to age itself but to depression, drug interactions, lack of exercise, or one of many other reversible conditions. As we attack these problems with greater public awareness and proper care, the percentage of people who lose mental faculties as they age should decline greatly.

The idea that "you can't teach an old dog new tricks" permeates our culture. It confirms the stereotype of older people as mindless, rigid, uninteresting, unproductive, uncreative people who are simply waiting to die.

This myth has very deep roots. Before modern medicine, when older people were more vulnerable to the ravages of disease, the evidence supporting the idea that old age meant decrepitude seemed overwhelmingly obvious. But what was taken then as the direct result of aging was instead the result of a host of frequently misunderstood diseases, such as atherosclerosis, syphilis, cancer, osteoporosis, diabetes, and hearing problems. Even now, if an older person fails to respond or else responds inappropriately when spoken to, we may assume that age has taken this person's mind, when in fact the problem may be only a hearing difficulty.

Over the years, both scientists and popular writers have made credible the myth of loss of mental agility due to aging. In 1881, George Beard, an influential American psychologist, reported his findings on how aging affected the mental faculties in a popular book called *American Nervousness*. Studying the age at which great creative works had been accomplished, he reported that "70 percent of creative works had been accomplished by age 45, and 80 percent by age 50." Of course, his conclusion ignored the fact that in earlier centuries few people lived past those ages. Using vague and highly impressionistic data, Beard concluded that as people grow older, their mental faculties deteriorate considerably. He wrote: "The querulousness of age, the irritability, the avarice are the resultants partly of habit and partly of organic and functional changes in the brain."

By now, the scientific community has completely discredited Beard's conclusions. It is now recognized that in the absence of specific neurological diseases, aging by itself produces no diminution whatsoever in mental acuity until well into the seventies, on the average. From that point on, the only drop in mental functioning that can be attributed to the aging process itself is an inconvenient, but not incapacitating, loss of short-term memory. Brain-scan studies undertaken at the National Institute on Aging and based directly on metabolic activity have shown that "the healthy aged brain is as active and efficient as the healthy young brain."

Concern about aging is heightened by our fear that senility lurks in each of our futures.

In reality, there is no such disease as senility.

There are a few serious illnesses, such as Alzheimer's, that can produce the symptoms associated with "senility." Besides these few illnesses, there are more than 100 different conditions that can lead to such symptoms, and most of these can be treated relatively easily. According to Dr. Robert Butler, the founding director of the National Institute on Aging, "The belief that if you live long enough you will become senile is just wrong."

Dr. Marian Diamond, a prominent neuroanatomist at the University of California at Berkeley, is one of many researchers dedicated to disproving the long-held beliefs about aging. Diamond set out to track down the study that had led to the widespread belief that the brain loses cells with age. She conducted an exhaustive search and found no evidence of such a study. And her own studies have shown that no cell loss significant enough to influence normal mental functioning occurs in the normal aging process.

Much of what was once attributed to a loss of intelligence is now being recognized as the result of the way old people are often treated. It has been shown experimentally that people left in isolation become less social and less mentally active. If we were to take normal, functional adults of any age and isolate them, confine them to wheelchairs, and regiment and patronize them—treat them, in other words, the way many elderly are treated, especially in institutions—within a matter of weeks they would begin to act "senile": dependent, querulous, antisocial, irrational, and unintelligent.

Study after scientific study has shown that people who stay active and intellectually challenged not only maintain their mental alertness but also live longer. And they live those extra years in better health than those who simply retreat from engaging in social activities.

Across the country, adult-education classes are becoming inundated with older learners, people whose ability and creativity regularly astonish teachers who have grown up with the myth of the mindless senior. It is becoming increasingly clear that these "old dogs" are, indeed, capable of learning new tricks.

Chances are that if you continue to challenge yourself, your sharpness and understanding will increase with age.

Myth 4: Older People Are Unproductive

Older people have poor attendance at work, as well as lower productivity. They have less education to start with, old techniques and slow work habits that interfere with new learning, and rigid, stubborn attitudes. Older workers are not worth the investment of training and retraining them. They also have more accidents on the job.

The reality behind the myth is quite different. A series of recent surveys and studies has shown the following to be true:

Older workers have fewer avoidable absences than younger workers, and they have good attendance records overall. Following an exhaustive search of the available statistics and professional literature, gerontologist Pauline K. Robinson reported in *Generations,* the journal of the American Society on Aging, that "the factual record belies the expectation held by many that older workers would be absent more because of illness."

No consistent pattern exists to show the superior productivity of any age group.

Studies on this question have been conducted by the Department of Labor; the Senate Committee on Human Resources; the Conference Board, an independent research organization; and independent sociologists reporting in such professional reviews as *Journal of Gerontology* and *Industrial Gerontology.* These studies have looked at thousands of workers, from semiskilled piece-rate and assembly-line workers to office managers and salespeople. All the studies revealed that, except for a slight decline in productivity in jobs requiring substantial physical effort, older workers performed either as well as or better than younger workers.

Older workers are likely to stay with a company longer than younger workers and are thus more likely to repay an investment in retraining. An American Association of Retired Persons (AARP) study found that employees 20 to 30 years of age tend to stay with a company for an average of 3.4 years, while those 50 to 60 tend to stay for 15 years. A Bureau of Labor Statistics study showed that turnover rates are lower for workers in the 45–64 age group than for workers under 45. When the Great American First Savings Bank in San Diego began hiring older people as tellers instead of the usual 19–25-year-olds, turnover was drastically reduced. Naugles, a prominent West Coast restaurant chain, found that after its hiring policies were changed to concentrate on older workers, the turnover rate dropped from 400 percent per year to 80 percent.

Psychological skills, such as the ability to adapt and to find life satisfaction in a variety of situations, do not seem to be age-related. Although older workers are somewhat more resistant to change than younger workers, they can, and do, adapt. In fact, they are more accustomed to change than their younger counterparts, having lived through a greater variety of social and technological changes.

Older workers have fewer on-the-job accidents, especially in situations that require judgment based on experience and the expectation of hazard. Older workers, who make up 13.6 percent of the labor force, account for only 9.7 percent of work-related accidents, while workers between the ages of 20 and 24 account for 50 percent of such accidents. According to a recent analysis of worker-compensation case records by the Bureau of Labor Statistics, older workers are less likely to be injured on the job: the injury rate peaks in the 20–24 age group, drops off steadily with age, and then shows a sharp drop after 65.

Older people experience less job stress than younger workers, show lower rates of admission to psychiatric facilities, and have far lower rates of illegal drug use.

In more abstract measures of work competence, such as speed and intelligence, some interesting and subtle facts pop up. For instance, studies show that our general impression is true: older people perform most tasks, whether cutting with a knife, dialing a telephone, or remembering a list, more slowly than younger people. But other studies show that the loss in speed is often offset by greater abilities in other aspects of intelligence, such as fewer errors and wiser decisions.

The small declines in short-term memorization abilities and mental quickness experienced by older workers are more than offset by the superior judgment and advanced "chunking" ability—the ability to organize information in useful and logical ways—necessary for finding solutions to complex, real-world situations.

If we look beyond our age-related prejudices, we see that history has given us countless examples of powerful, creative, and productive elders. For instance, Goethe completed *Faust* when he was over 80. Alexander von Humboldt worked out his great contribution to science, *The Kosmos,* from ages 76 to 90. At 71, Michelangelo was appointed chief architect of St. Peter's Cathedral in Rome. Over the next 18 years, until his death at 89, he personally supervised the creation of the vast main body of the church; during those same years he wrote some of his finest poetry. At 89, Mary Baker Eddy was still running the Christian Science Church.

George Bernard Shaw wrote *Farfetched Fables* at 93. At 90, Pablo Picasso was still in full creative production. Arthur Rubenstein gave a stunning performance at Carnegie Hall at 90. Pablo Casals was still doing concert tours at 88. At 91, Adolph Zukor was chairman of Paramount Pictures. George Abbott, the great Broadway actor, writer, director, and producer, brought *Pal Joey* to Broadway at the age of 53, *The Pajama Game* at 67, *Damn Yankees* at 68, *A Funny Thing Happened on the Way to the Forum* at 75, and at the age of 100, a revival of his first hit, *Broadway.*

As our gerontophobia is replaced by a more positive image of aging and as men and women continue to grow older more youthfully, studies of competence will reflect their increasingly vital, healthy bodies and minds. In the years to come, the statistics about how people work and create as they grow older will look better and better.

In the future older workers will be considered not worn out but seasoned, not out of date but able to learn, not ready to retire but open to a more flexible and productive work life.

Myth 5: Older People Are Unattractive and Sexless

Wrinkles are inevitable, and they are ugly. So are drooping breasts, sunken chests, mottled skin, and bald pates. None of these things are sexy. If you want to be sexy, you have to be young, or at least look young. Nobody gets physically excited about someone who shows signs of aging. Besides, older men are sexually inadequate, and older women aren't interested.

This myth dies hard. Go to the nearest bookstore and ask to see the nonfiction section on sex, romance, and intimacy for older people, or the fiction section on older romance. You won't find them. The movies, the daytime soap operas, the sitcoms, and even the commercials that feature romance and intimacy very seldom use older actors. With a few recent exceptions, the world of romance is pictured as a young world.

Studies show that Americans have traditionally believed that sexual interest and ability decline rapidly with age and are inappropriate to the old, and that sexual exertion is actually dangerous to the health of the average older man or woman. Like any other self-fulfilling prophecy, this one has proved itself. In the past, many older people gave up sex more or less voluntarily, if not while they still had a partner, then certainly once death or divorce had rendered them single again.

Current research is proving that men and women continue to feel sexy and sensual in later life.

While the statistics do show a slight decrease in sexual activity with increasing age, the facts are far from what the myth would have us believe. Researchers have recently explored these questions in depth for the first time, and what they have found shatters most of our preconceptions about older people and sexuality. Dr. Bernard D. Starr, a professor at Brooklyn College of the City University of New York and a research associate at the CASE (Center for Advanced Study in Education) Center for Gerontological Studies, and Dr. Marcella Bakur Weiner, an adjunct professor of psychology and gerontology at the City University of New York, reported their findings in the *Starr-Weiner Report,* one of the only reliable quantified studies ever conducted on the sexuality of older people. The study probed the lifestyles of more than 800 people between the ages of 60 and 91 from all parts of the country.

Among other things, Starr and Weiner found that

- 91 percent of older people approve of unmarried or widowed older people having sexual relations or living together;
- 97 percent like sex;
- 75 percent think sex now feels as good as or better than it did when they were young;
- 72 percent are satisfied by their sexual experiences; and
- 80 percent think that sex is good for their health.

The reality demonstrated in this and in other studies is that the great majority of older men and women are sexually capable, enjoy sexual activity, and in many cases now find greater pleasure in sex than they did when they were younger. As Harold Cox wrote in his book *Later Life,*

> Men and women in a state of general good health are physiologically able to have a satisfying sex life well into their seventies, eighties, and beyond. Kinsey found that four out of five men over the age of 60 were capable of intercourse and that there was no evidence of sexual decline in women beyond the age of 60. A research project at Duke University followed a sample of respondents for 20 years, and interestingly enough, Pfeiffer reports that 15 percent of the men and women studied showed a steadily rising rate of sexual interest and activity as they got older. Duke University's findings indicated that two out of three men are sexually active past 65, and one of five is still active in his eighties.

Many older people report experiences like those of Paul and Mary Costain, who were recently married in Bradenton, Florida, after each had been widowed for five years. According to Mary, "All my married life I was so inhibited about sex. What amazes me is that now that I am 71, my sexuality is finally beginning to blossom."

Paul reflects, "But it's a different kind of sexuality. When you're young, sexuality is heavily oriented toward proving yourself, a kind of immature showmanship. Now it's different. It's more loving, more playful, more of a nourishment between two people."

It is hard to ignore a wide range of changes in the ways in which we publicly portray our images of beauty and sexuality. Ten years ago it would have been difficult to imagine a television show like *Golden Girls* or a character like Blanche (played by actress Rue McClanahan). It would have been hard to picture movies like *On Golden Pond* or *Cocoon.* It would have been difficult to believe that Ford Models, Inc., the nation's largest modeling agency, would open a "Classics" division for models over 50, or that this would become the company's fastest-growing division. It would have been hard to imagine that such women as Jane Fonda, Diahann Carroll, Joan Collins, and Angie Dickinson would still be acknowledged as sex symbols in their fifties, or that *Ebony* magazine would vote Lena Horne one of the ten most beautiful black women in America—at 70.

Or consider this phenomenon: a few years ago, *McCall's* named the ten sexiest men in America over 60. The list included Paul Newman, 60 at the time; Lee Iacocca, 61; Norman Mailer, 62; John Forsythe, 67; Frank Sinatra, 69; Joe DiMaggio, 70; Ronald Reagan, 74; John Huston, 79; and Isaac Bashevis Singer and Cary Grant, both 81. It is doubtful whether such a list, with an average age of 70, could have been published in a major popular magazine even ten years ago. The editors probably would not have thought that anyone was interested or that the list would help sell the magazine. All of these men would be admired in any decade, but "sexy" is something different. Some of these people seem not only to have stayed as attractive as they were when young but to actually have become more attractive over time.

Filled as we are with the myths of aging, it can be difficult for us to imagine older beauty, but over the next few decades we will learn to appreciate its special qualities and characteristics as thoroughly as we have appreciated the beauty of youth.

Sex and romance, fueled by other changes in relationships, will continue into the later years—and may well
become deeper, fuller, and more satisfying than ever.

Myth 6: All Older People Are Pretty Much the Same

*If you've seen one old man, you've seen them all. A woman after a
certain age becomes "a little old lady" like all those other "little old
ladies." To say someone is a senior citizen is to say a lot about
them—what their political outlook is, how they spend their time, what
they are apt to want, what their financial situation is, and what
hopes and fears they have. Older people are a pretty homogeneous
group.*

Beneath many of the myths of aging runs the assumption
that there is only one way of being old, that all older people
think, feel, act, and look pretty much the same.

When we look beyond the myth, there is no age group
more varied in physical abilities, personal styles, tastes
and desires, or financial capabilities than the older population.

Today's older Americans are a symphony of cultural diversity. Many came to America during the flood of immigra-
tion in the early years of this century. Their roots might be
in Poland or China, in Ireland, Greece, or Japan. They are
likely to have less in common with one another than do their
children or grandchildren.

Some older people are dreadfully sick and waiting for
death. Some are physically fit and in training to run marathons. Some are abysmally poor and entirely dependent on
the government for food and shelter. Others have condos in
Vail and yachts in Tahiti. Some wait in breadlines for a warm
meal. Others buy and sell railroads, wheat futures, and Cha-
galls just to keep a hand in.

Some older people live rigidly conservative lifestyles,

while others live extremely radical lifestyles. In many instances, older people actually live freer, more experimental lives than their children and grandchildren do.

Some older people feel finished with work and are happy to putter in the garden, travel, and volunteer. The same routine would drive other older people nuts; they love their work and hope to keep doing it as long as they can.

Some older people live lonely, miserable, desperate lives. But we all know older people who are more socially active than they were when they were young—joining clubs, traveling, going to lectures and dances, visiting old friends, and making new ones.

Any age group has these divergences, these extremes. What is astonishing about the elderly is that the extremes enlarge, and the center diminishes. The elderly tend to practice a greater spectrum of lifestyles than any other age group. The later years of life give you the opportunity to become more yourself.

People in their later years become more, not less, diverse. And tomorrow's elders will be different not only from one another, but from today's elders as well.

When this tendency toward diversity is more fully understood, it will be catered to by the designers and producers of goods and services (as we'll explore in depth in later chapters). Commercial America has long thought of the elderly as a single block of people. To the extent that these people wanted anything at all, they were all assumed to want the same kinds of things. No one bothered to make anything special for specific segments of the older market. All this will change.

Moreover, the world is moving so fast that each successive generation is increasingly different from the ones that preceded it. In the past 50 years we have entered the atomic age, the space age, and the computer age; life expectancy has increased by more than 15 years; more than 80 new nations have appeared worldwide; and the global population has more than doubled. It is thought that 75 percent of the infor-

mation ever known in the history of the world has been
discovered in the last 25 years.

After all of these experiences, tomorrow's older people
will have little in common with yesterday's. They will have
traveled to more places, read a greater variety of books and
magazines, met more people, lived through more world
changes, experienced more sexual and lifestyle experimentation, lived longer, and taken part in a more powerful "elder-
culture" than any previous generation in the history of the
world. Who we will be in the future is even more surprising,
more malleable, and richer with the seeds of opportunity than
most of us now imagine.

TOWARD A NEW IMAGE OF AGING

Each of us has a point of view about growing old, an "elder
within," made up of all the images we possess about later life.
Many of these impressions were formed during our youth and
are based on our experiences with our grandparents and their
friends. The often unconscious impressions and expectations
we carry form the foundation for our future.

If the images of these "elders within" are negative, then
living longer could become an extension of the unpleasant
and unrelenting decline of all that is joyous and full in life. If
these images are positive, if our "elders within" are healthy,
involved, active, and full of life and learning, then the gift of
extended life might hold the promise of a dramatic and unprecedented expansion of our opportunities for growth, adventure, wisdom, experience, and love.

But if our culture remains gerontophobic as it ages, the
aging of America will be traumatic, both for America as a
culture and for each of us as individuals. Can we break free
of the "age trance"?

**If we cling to our myths and fears about aging, many of
the possibilities of the Age Wave will remain undiscov-
ered and unawakened.**

History has taught us that we tend to do and become what we expect to do and become. We fulfill our own prophecies. We have seen this happen over and over: one person will project a compelling vision, an image of a possible future, and a new future will take root and grow from that vision. Most of us can remember this happening when President John F. Kennedy declared that we would put a human being on the moon before 1970. It happened, too, when Brigham Young, searching for a site for his great Mormon city, pointed to the edge of a saline lake in the desert and said, "This is the place." Before the great runner Roger Bannister broke the four-minute mile in 1954, everyone "knew" that it could not be done. Once he had done it, and had thus changed the idea of what was possible, all great runners could soon run a mile in under four minutes. Bannister's breakthrough literally created a new vision of speed, one that has led to faster and faster performances. Perhaps we will live to see the three-minute mile.

And perhaps we'll soon see a positive new image of aging in America.

In the rest of this book we will explore how you as an individual and we as a nation can construct a new vision of aging for ourselves, in our relationships and families and in society at large. It is up to us to decide whether, as the Middle Eastern proverb has it, we are heading into the winter of our lives, or the harvest.

The Giant Wakes Up

Once a sleeping giant, older America is now awakening to its social and political power. In doing so it is throwing off the biggest myth, the sum of all the others, which states that the older American is unimportant, invisible, politically weak, socially discountable, and economically insignificant. Mature America is rapidly coming to terms with the gathering demographic forces that have already begun to shift the economic and political foundations of our society. And, great as they already are, those forces offer only the barest hint of the overwhelming political and economic clout that older Americans will exercise in the coming years.

As decision makers become aware that America's elders are growing more numerous each day, have more money than most people suspect and are willing to spend it, vote more regularly than younger people, and are willing to pound the pavement to make their viewpoints known, the power of older America will snowball.

NOTICING THE "NEW KID ON THE BLOCK"

One of the best tests of the growth of any social issue is the number of people who study it. In the first five years after the passage of the Social Security Act in 1935, only 14 scholars in the United States chose human aging and gerontology as the subject of their doctoral dissertations. In the 40 years between 1935 and 1975, only 337 academics pursued the study of aging in America. But in the past decade alone, there have been 2,035 such studies. In the decades to come, gerontology will likely be among the fastest-growing areas of study.

The explosive growth of interest in aging is mirrored in every statistic about the field. When the American Geriatric Society was founded in 1942, it had only 400 members; today, it has more than 5,200. The Gerontology Society has grown from 80 members in 1945 to more than 6,000 members today. More than 283 American universities and colleges now sponsor gerontology programs. Whereas serving the needs of older people did not constitute a professional field 50 years ago, today tens of thousands of men and women are devoting their lives to this endeavor.

Similarly, in recent years there has been an explosion in the number of newspaper and tabloid-type publications geared to the mature reader. There was 1 such publication available in 1973, 8 in 1977, 60 in 1985, and nearly 200 by mid-1988. The combined circulation of these types of publications is believed to currently exceed 7 million copies, which are read by nearly 20 million adults age 55+. Sixty percent of these senior publications are distributed free and are completely ad-supported.

According to Len Hansen, chairman of the Senior Publishing Group, a California-based advertising firm representing 87 senior newspapers, "Two of the biggest-circulation senior publications are *Senior World of Florida* and *Senior World of California.* Published monthly in Fort Lauderdale, Florida's

Senior World reaches 120,000 retirees in South Florida and the Treasure Coast. California's *Senior World,* in its fifteenth year as a monthly news tabloid, reaches 350,000 senior readers in six counties in Central and Southern California."

These publications target the active, older adult and include upbeat news on the subjects that Hansen believes are of greatest interest to their readership—"travel, health, finances, dining, entertainment, and senior profiles. Mature adults will read their own newspapers actively and thoroughly, and they react to a positive ad, a value message, and the right opportunity for them."

But it's not just the world of free newspapers that is waking to the booming mature marketplace; magazine publishers are beginning to catch the wave as well. According to Gerald Hotchkiss, publisher of *50 Plus,* his magazine's circulation has mushroomed, going from 170,000 in 1981, to 350,000 in 1985, to 500,000 in 1987. The growing success of this well-conceived adult-lifestyle magazine is due to the promotion of a message Hotchkiss describes as "Get off your duff and enjoy the best years of your life." In early 1988, *50 Plus* was purchased by *Reader's Digest,* which intends to change the title to *New Choices* to eliminate any mention of age.

In March 1988, a new women's magazine called *Lear's: For the Woman Who Wasn't Born Yesterday* was launched with much media fanfare. Allstate Insurance company publishes *Mature Outlook,* a general-interest, bimonthly magazine circulated to 1 million readers nationwide. And in July of 1988, *Modern Maturity*—the grandparent of all popular 50+ magazines—surpassed *Reader's Digest* and *TV Guide* to become the largest-circulation magazine in America, with 18 million subscribers and an estimated 30 million readers.

In response to the obvious increase in the interest and demand for publications geared to the mature reader, numerous new launches are planned, including the following:

- *Longevity,* a health-and-lifestyle-oriented publication that began as a newsletter and is being elevated to monthly-magazine status. *Longevity* is published by Bob Guccione, chairman and founder of Penthouse International.

- *Second Wind,* a bimonthly publication intended to be an upbeat general-interest magazine. The brainchild of Paul Green, president of Intercontinental Publications, and Robert Potts, former publisher of *Dun's Business Month, Second Wind* calls itself "the full life magazine."
- *Renaissance,* a monthly magazine billed as "the magazine for living well," will target affluent customers of regional banks. It will be marketed as a custom publication that banks can give as a gift to "preferred" customers older than 55.
- *Lifewise,* from the editors of *American Health,* was developed in cooperation with the National Council on Aging and is intended to be distributed to senior centers nationwide. *Lifewise* is geared to what Jay Berzon of *American Health* calls "OPALS" —older people with active lifestyles. (OPALS is a term coined by David J. Demko, Ph.D., of Demko-Finley & Associates.)
- A *Silver edition of McCall's,* which will target more than 1 million *McCall's* subscribers in the 50-to-64-year-old group and will be published bimonthly.
- *Memories,* launched by Diamandis Communications, Inc., formerly CBS Publications, a nostalgia-oriented, *People-*type magazine geared exclusively to the 40 + audience.

Industry insiders project that by the mid-1990s, every major magazine-publishing company will have a special publication geared to the middle-aged or older audience, something that would not have been considered as recently as five years ago.

The growth of gerontology as a profession and the parallel rise of 50 + related publications offer an index of the phenomenal growth of the older American as a rising social force. But the real measure of "gray power" can best be seen in its effect on American politics.

SOCIAL AND POLITICAL MUSCLE

During the past 25 years, senior-advocacy groups have grown with astonishing speed. Today, there are

- 20,000 seniors in the Older Women's League (OWL);
- 74,000 in the fiercely activist Gray Panthers, with chapters in 30 states;
- 2.2 million in the conservative National Alliance of Senior Citizens (NASC);
- 4.5 million in the 4,000 local chapters of the National Council of Senior Citizens (NCSC), founded by the AFL-CIO during the fight for Medicare and widely credited with defeating the lobbyists of the American Medical Association (AMA); and
- 30 million members in the American Association of Retired Persons (AARP), which has seen its membership skyrocket since its founding in 1958. As a national club, AARP is second in size only to the American Automobile Association.

If AARP were to become an independent nation, it would be the thirtieth-largest nation in the world, with a population only slightly smaller than that of Argentina.

According to current projections, the association will have 33 million members by 1993—three years before the first of the 76 million boomer become eligible for membership.

In the 1987 Congress alone, AARP racked up successes in getting pension-reform legislation amended into the tax bill and in helping to end mandatory retirement based on age. It also tripled its legislative staff (to 125), and it now has 20 lobbyists working full time on the federal government and another 20 advising volunteer lobbyists at the state level. And, of course, there are AARP's 350,000+ active volunteers.

According to John Rother, AARP's legislative director:

> The political power of AARP rises from the fact that we can speak for those 30 million members and from the fact that we have volunteers working in every state at the local level. But the biggest source of power in this age is information. For instance, in 1983, when Congress was debating whether or not to freeze Social Security benefits, we hired a consulting firm to do an economic-impact study. The study showed that the freeze would eventually drop a half million seniors below the poverty line. This study was the single most important factor in influencing Congress not to freeze the benefits.

The power of information was underscored by Eric Schulman, Rother's counterpart at the National Council of Senior Citizens.

> We are a "blood-and-guts" group focusing on political and legislative issues. Our power comes from our grass-roots network. Congress knows we can deliver the votes.

> Our single most effective tool is the Congressional Voting Record, in which we score the legislators by how often they voted the way we think they should. We mail this record to a half million people a year. We get tremendous pickup in the newspapers. We get countless calls from political candidates. The record becomes a focal point of campaign debate. If a senator or representative gets a low score, it forces them to focus on the issues. It forces them to do research and come up with justifications.

The growth of this kind of activism, from AARP to NCSC to the Gray Panthers, is unrivaled by any other population segment or special-interest group. What the gray lobby wants, it usually gets. Following is a sampling of the impressive legislative victories that older people have brought about during the last 25 years:

1965—Medicare and Medicaid enacted

1965—Older Americans Act establishes the Administration on Aging

1967—Age discrimination in employment made illegal

1972—Supplemental Security Program guarantees all older Americans a minimum income

1972—Social Security indexed to inflation

1973—Federal Council on Aging established

1978—Age of mandatory retirement for most workers pushed back to 70

1981–82—Efforts to cut Social Security and Medicare benefits defeated

1983—Social Security reform pulls the system back from the brink of bankruptcy

1986—Mandatory retirement at any age eliminated for almost all workers

1988—Catastrophic health insurance under Medicare passed

The numbers in the federal budget show the same growth in the clout of the elderly. Before 1935 there was almost nothing in the budget that could be identified as earmarked for the elderly.

In the most recent federal budget, subsidies for housing, meals, medical care, pensions, Social Security, and other benefits for the elderly came to nearly 28 percent of the budget, equal to the amount spent on defense.

For example, the Older Americans Act—a vehicle for the distribution of federal monies to people over 60—was first funded in 1965 at $5 million. It received over $1 billion in the 1988 federal budget. Under the aegis of the federal Administration on Aging, 670 Area Agencies on Aging have sprung up nationwide to administer programs for citizens over 65. Since the Nutrition Act became law in 1972, the number of nutrition programs for the elderly across the country has grown to over 11,000. Medicare has changed from a $35 billion to a $91 billion program in just the last eight years.

According to the Urban Institute, a Washington, D.C. research organization, by the turn of the century the percentage of the federal budget that pertains to spending for the elderly will have risen to 32 percent. If programs continue at their present levels, this percentage will have increased to a staggering 63 percent by the year 2025.

Beware the "Truth Squads"

In 1984, Slade Gorton, a Republican senator from the state of Washington, voted for freezes in cost-of-living adjustments (COLAs) in Social Security and Supplemental Security Income and approved reductions in Medicare and Medicaid. His position bothered a lot of older people.

In 1986, when Gorton was running for reelection, senior citizens' lobbying groups put up thousands of signs along every major commuter route in the state, attacking Gorton's record. They printed flyers by the hundreds of thousands that proclaimed, "Slade Gorton Is No Friend of Social Security." They took out radio ads in which older people complained about Gorton's voting record. A senior group, called "The Campaign for a Pro-Senior Senate," sent out a "Truth Squad" in an RV for a 1500-mile, 17-stop trip to talk to senior groups and media statewide.

But Gorton fought back. He brought in John Heinz, chairman of both the Republican Senate Campaign Committee and the Senate Select Committee on Aging. Gorton hoped that Heinz's public blessing would bring in the senior vote. The two men publicly spoke, shook hands, and posed for pictures through five campaign stops at senior centers around the state. Gorton made an extra effort to get the press to cover this special campaign swing, and the media were there in force.

But the Truth Squad was there at every stop with picket signs, banners, and scorecards comparing Gorton's voting record with that of—John Heinz. "All we want," one protester told Heinz, "is someone who votes like you." The seniors easily saw through Gorton's ploy.

The press loved it. It made the evening news: shots of Gorton putting up a brave front, surrounded by pickets, with Heinz off to the side, looking chagrined.

Gorton lost the election. In its day-after analysis, the Seattle *Post-Intelligencer* pointed to Gorton's problems with the elderly as one of the major issues that had cost him his seat. Eric Schulman, director of research/legislative liaison for the National Council of Senior Citizens (NCSC), said flatly, "Slade Gorton lost his job because of his views on Social Security."

Gorton was not alone. Schulman and other election analysts identified at least five close U.S. Senate races in which direct campaigning by older Americans had tipped the balance. Social Security became a major issue in Florida, where 24 percent of the voters are over 65—a higher proportion than in any other state. In the closing days of Senator Paula Hawkins's campaign to secure her seat against Governor Bob Graham, the NCSC held press conferences denouncing her voting record. Hawkins lost the race.

According to Graham, "The political significance of the growth of the older population goes far beyond voting blocs. The needs of our older citizens will increasingly dominate the political agenda of the future."

The growing power of older Americans is a political fact of our time.

A quarter century ago, the political future of a Slade Gorton could not have hung on an issue concerning the elderly. Before the National Council of Senior Citizens formed around the fight for Medicare, few would have thought of older people as a potent political force. And before a playful New York news producer dubbed Maggie Kuhn and her followers "the Gray Panthers" in the early 1970s, few could have pictured older people demonstrating, chanting, carrying picket signs, knocking on doors for their causes, getting press attention—and winning their points.

Poll Power

Part of what underlies the growth in concern and expenditure for older Americans is that not only is this group growing in number, but its members vote in much greater numbers than younger people do. In the November 1980 national election, for instance, fully one-third of those who voted were 55 or older. Voters aged 55 to 64 took the participation prize: 71 percent of them went to the polls, barely edging out the 65-to-74-year-olds, 69 percent of whom voted. In contrast, the figure for those 18 to 20 was only 36 percent. In the 1984 elections, the oldest groups voted at nearly twice the rate of the youngest groups.

The shift became even clearer in the 1986 elections, when the proportion of older voters grew, while those for all other age groups shrank. For the first time in American history, the oldest group of voters (65 and over) outnumbered the youngest group (18–24).

In addition, the average age of American voters has climbed to 47, while the average member of Congress is now 50. As a result, whether or not they realize it, voters and politicians may be more likely to focus on issues pertaining to the second half of life and less focused on concerns of the young. This may already be happening. During the Reagan administration, payments to the elderly rose by 35 percent. At the same time, Aid to Families with Dependent Children was cut by 19 percent and school meal programs by 41 percent between 1981 and 1984. According to Russel Edgarton, president of the American Association for Higher Education,

"The aging of the population tilts the landscape of political life toward the aged and away from children. It makes it harder to mobilize resources to invest in our future through our children. For example, schools are funded on the 'remainder' method—we give them what's left after we've paid for everything else—and an aging population puts a lot more stress and strain on state and local budgets." Senator Daniel Moynihan has commented that the United States "may be the first society in history in which a person is more likely to be poor if young than old."

Still, a great deal of gray ballot power remains latent. As has been pointed out by Dr. Robert Binstock, a political scientist at Ohio's Case Western Reserve University and editor of *The Sociology of Aging*, "Older persons do not vote in a monolithic bloc any more than middle-aged or younger persons do. There is no sound reason to expect that a cohort of persons would suddenly become homogenized in its political behavior when it reaches the 'old-age' category."

This point of view is echoed by Dr. Hugh Heclo, professor of government at Harvard University, who says that "the elderly don't vote as a bloc any more than any other age group." He believes that the elderly are not necessarily more conservative in their voting preferences, but rather that they vote along lines that are almost identical with the voting patterns of the rest of the population. The only difference is that with aging there seems to be a greater involvement in the voting process.

The idea that people automatically become more conservative as they age is proved false in the statistics of almost any election. Studies have shown that as people grow older they tend to keep the same basic political stance they have held all their lives, so older Americans only show up as a political bloc on issues that concern them directly as older citizens. But such issues will show up with increasing frequency and force over the next decades and will draw older voters in even greater numbers into the political process.

Few candidates or issues offer a clear-cut choice on the basis of age alone. But when an issue arises that concerns older Americans as a group—such as Social Security, long-term care, mandatory retirement, or property taxes (which concern older citizens more because their home equity is often very high compared to their low mortgage payments) —this latent power can become ferocious.

The late Howard Jarvis, one-time industrialist turned political gadfly, is an example: "I was all retired, ready to do some traveling. I was 71; I'd had enough of all the hassle. I had sold my company and was ready for a long, restful vacation in Hawaii. But first there was this little meeting my neighbors wanted me to attend. It had something to do with property taxes." That meeting was the founding of the United Organization for Taxpayers. Jarvis emerged from the meeting as head of the organization, with the bit in his teeth. Loud, argumentative, and tenacious, Jarvis led what eventually became the nationwide taxpayers' revolt of the late 1970s and early 1980s. His partner in that revolt, Paul Gann, the leader of most of the campaigns in other states, and many of the troops they led were over 60. This tax revolt was an early example of the kinds of struggles that will erupt in the coming decades whenever a single issue galvanizes older Americans as a group.

Because many older Americans are retired and thus free of the time constraints of working people, they contribute more than their share to the nuts and bolts of political work; they stuff envelopes, walk precincts, and attend caucuses. The majority of the people in those tiny political caucuses in Iowa that exert such extraordinary influence in choosing our successive presidents are over 50. Most of them are retired farmers and their wives, who have the time to sit and visit with senators, governors, and vice-presidents who would be president, challenging them on domestic and foreign policy and getting commitments about the security of the Medicare and Social Security programs.

In 1987, AARP set up seminars across Iowa to train its members in the fine points of the political caucus. They were swamped by more than 2,000 older voters, one-third of whom had never attended a caucus before. On caucus night,

National Public Radio's Linda Wertheimer commented repeatedly on the large number of AARP buttons on the lapels of the gathered voters.

Nearly all of the 350,000+ older men and women who offer programs and activities at AARP's more than 4,000 chapter offices are volunteers. Think of the power of such a massive, experienced, and well-connected work force whose members are driven by a high level of commitment.

In the coming years, the aging of the boomers will boost the strength of the mature voter with each passing election. The boom generation cut its teeth on activism. If the boomers decide to wield their increased power when they reach more mature stations in life, their clout in local and national politics will be enormous.

When the boomers advance into their fifties and sixties, they will become the demographic group that sets the political agenda and dominates election outcomes.

The growing social, political, and economic power of the older American over the past decades would have been hard to miss. But large as that change has been in legislation, economic shifts, and in the popular culture, it is but the turn of the tide. The full flood is yet to come. The giant has just begun to awaken.

According to Dr. Neal Cutler of the University of Southern California's Andrus Gerontology Center, "In 15 years there won't be anybody as powerful as the organized elderly."

AGE WARS OR AGE QUAKES?

The waking of the giant is not without its disturbances and problems. As a result of the rapid increase in the power and clout of America's older citizens, a battle is brewing that threatens to divide the nation and set generation against generation for decades to come. These intergenerational conflicts could make the generation-gap tensions of the late 1960s seem tame in comparison. Conflicts could center on issues of emotional turf, the rules of parents and children, or privilege and status. But more than anything else, such conflicts will be about the distribution of our nation's resources.

The headlines announcing the beginnings of these intergenerational challenges have begun popping up around the country. On the cover of the March 1988 issue of *The New Republic* there appeared a controversial cartoon that depicted a charging army of ugly, ferocious seniors under the offensive headline "Greedy Geezers." Other headlines have included "The Coming Conflict As We Soak the Young to Enrich the Old," in the *Washington Post*; "Generational Fight Seen As Elderly Push for Benefits," in the *New York Times*; "Age Wars: The Coming Battle between Young and Old," in *The Futurist*; and "Today's Elderly vs. Tomorrow's," in the *San Francisco Chronicle*.

In his "Greedy Geezers" article, Henry Fairlie comments:

> Thirty percent of the annual federal budget now goes to expenditures on people over the age of 65. Forty years from now, if the present array of programs and benefits is maintained, almost two-thirds of the budget will go to supporting and cosseting the old. Something is wrong with a society that is willing to drain itself to foster such an unproductive section of its population, one that does not even promise (as children do) one day to be productive.

The group that has been at the center of the intergenerational debate, Americans for Generational Equity (AGE), was founded in 1985 specifically to carry the banner of the young in these struggles. The organization gets nearly 80 percent of its funding from large insurance companies and major employers with growing pension responsibilities. AGE's first pamphlet contained a picture of a young family that carried the caption "Indentured Servants" in bold letters; the text complained that the American family has been sold "into financial slavery." Philip Longman, AGE's first research director, commented: "Put bluntly, the old have come to insist that the young not only hold them blameless for their past profligacy, but sacrifice their own prosperity to pay for it." He has since put his arguments into a highly controversial book, *Born to Pay*. AGE president Paul Hewitt, 35, says that his movement represents "a growing uncomfortableness with the excesses of senior power."

Such representatives for the elderly as AARP and the Gray Panthers claim that AGE paints the elderly as uniformly affluent, stopping by the broker's on the way to the tennis club. Gray Panther founder Maggie Kuhn accuses AGE of "fallacious and antisocial assumptions" and of fomenting a "contrived conflict." She further claims that "AGE represents only a small segment of greedy, upper-middle-class yuppies who are idolatrous toward the bottom line and are trying to get out of paying their Social Security taxes. AGE represents the ultimate expression of ageism and gerontophobia in our society."

Cy Brickfield, former executive director of AARP, offers a less polarized analysis of the situation: "The number of poor children in America is a disgrace. But programs for the elderly aren't the cause. There's no link at all between the rising poverty rate among children and the decreasing rate for the elderly."

In many ways, these individuals and organizations simply voice the feelings of most Americans that it's time to revisit the assumptions of many of our intergenerational policies and programs. Most politicians do their best to avoid stirring this pot, and in any case, Band-Aids and minor amendments won't solve most of the demographically caused problems of today or tomorrow.

Or, perhaps the current roiling of the waters is symptomatic of the massive demographic restructurings that are now under way. The press has been keen to identify these conflicts as "age wars," battles between the generations that are based on intergenerational animosity and greed. However, I believe that they are more the signs and symptoms of massive "age quakes," which are rumbling below our cultural institutions and widening demographic fault lines, shifting intergenerational priorities, and creating new social landscapes. When the "walls" crack due to these tremors, is it because they are at odds with one another, or simply because the ground on which they have rested has shifted?

Perhaps the most illustrative example of an intergenerational conflict born out of shifting demographic plates is that of Social Security.

SOCIAL SECURITY: AN IDEA WHOSE TIME HAD COME

Social Security was perfectly matched to the times in which it was designed. This pay-as-you-go financial-transfer system between young workers and older retirees opened the possibility of a better, more financially secure life for older Americans, without excessively encumbering other generations in the process. When President Roosevelt and his advisors sat down to design the Social Security program, they had several demographic variables to work with. The nation was full of young working people who could contribute to an old-age pension; there was a small number of old people, and many of those were poor. And with life expectancy stabilizing at about 63, it was not expected that the few Americans who made it to 65 would live much longer.

When the Social Security Act became law in 1935, it provided small old-age benefits for a fraction of the retiring population in return for a small mandatory contribution, half taken out of the worker's paycheck and half paid directly by the employer. Over time, the system grew in many ways. First, the contributions mushroomed. As recently as 1951, the legal maximum contribution that either the employer or employee could pay was $30 per year. As the law now reads, by 1990 the amount each pays will stabilize at 7.65 percent of all income under $32,400. The combined tax (that is, for both employer and employee) for someone making that amount will come to nearly $5,000.

The number of people covered has also soared. At first designed solely for private-sector wage earners, the system was later expanded by Congress to cover spouses and children. Slowly, new groups of workers came into the system, including farm workers, the self-employed, some state and local government employees, many professionals, members of the armed forces, and, eventually, many federal employees. In 1956, Congress added new kinds of insurance for those who could not work because of a disability. And in 1965, when Medicare was formed, Congress made it part of the Social Security system. In 1972, Supplemental-Security Income (SSI) was added to provide welfare for the poor elderly, the blind, and the disabled.

Lobbied by the elderly over the years, Congress regularly raised Social Security benefits to keep pace with inflation In 1972, the system was officially "indexed" to inflation—that is, benefits were made to rise automatically through a cost-of-living adjustment (COLA) that was keyed to the inflation of the Consumer Price Index (CPI). This change allowed older Americans to feel confident that their income would keep pace with prices.

At this writing, some 37 million people depend on the old-age, survivors', and disability-insurance trust funds. In 1987, these funds accounted for an estimated $203 billion—more than one-fifth of the entire federal budget—with Medicare consuming another $78 billion and Medicaid a further $26 billion (with another $19 billion coming from state funds).

Old Assumptions, New Elderly

Today, the future solvency and appropriateness of Social Security is being seriously questioned. Perhaps the core difficulty is that Social Security may no longer fit the problem for which it was so well designed in the 1930s. In recent decades, the Age Wave has transformed the small group of old people receiving support from a large pool of young workers into a huge mass of long-lived retirees who are being supported by a steadily shrinking population of young workers. If you retired in 1935, there were more than 40 workers contributing to your pension; by 1950, there were 17. If you retire in 1990, the support ratio will have plummeted to 3.4 to 1. According to Richard Rahn, chief economist of the U.S. Chamber of Commerce, when the crest of the boomers reaches retirement in 2020, the support ratio will be a scant 1.78 to 1.

If the Social Security system continues as is, each working couple will, in addition to supporting themselves and their family, have to supply the entire Social Security income for one retired person throughout their working lives.

According to Rahn, this would mean a combined employer-and-employee payroll tax of 25 percent, nearly twice today's figure. The Social Security Administration's own experts estimate that if current trends continue, Social Security payroll taxes could rise to as high as 42 percent by the middle of the next century.

In addition, we may be taxing ourselves to provide benefits to "old" people—in a sense, to help fund the later, nonworking years of life—according to a somewhat anachronistic definition of what "old" really is. As we have seen, with the steady elevation of life expectancy from 63 to 75 years, 65 is no longer old. People who reach 65 have, on average, another 16.7 vital and productive years ahead of them.

Perhaps the greatest shift in the assumptions that drive Social Security has to do with the increasing financial power of the elderly. The media confronts us daily with images of older people as poverty stricken, wasting away in rented rooms. We cannot just dismiss this image entirely, of course, as there are a great many such people. But as a way to think about most older Americans today, such a stereotype is seriously out of date.

At one time, however, the popular perception of old age as a desolate and despairing time—with all elderly people in need of enormous government support—was closer to the truth. As recently as 1959, more than one in three Americans age 65 and over had incomes below the poverty line. But reforms in Social Security and private pensions rapidly changed this. By 1970, only one in four older Americans fell below the poverty line, and by 1985 only one in eight did so.

At the same time, the younger working generations have lost ground; their real income has actually declined as the economy has gone through several recessions. As a result, while the poverty rate for older Americans has fallen, that for other Americans has actually risen. In recent years the poverty rate for everyone under 65 has hovered around 14 percent, two percentage points higher than the poverty rate for people over 65. And reflecting an unsettling shift in our socioeconomic priorities, approximately 20 percent of America's children currently live in poverty.

If the nation were now to pick one age group for special economic treatment because it was so poor and had bleak prospects for the future, statistics show that this group would not be the old, but the young.

Of course, there are millions of poor and near-poor elderly people, and in the years ahead we will all share the responsibility of providing for them. The problem is especially acute for minorities: the 12 percent of white older Americans whose income falls below the federal government's poverty line compares with 22 percent of Hispanic elderly, 32 percent of Native American elderly, and 35 percent of black elderly.

In general, however, Americans over 65 are financially better off than other Americans in a number of ways. Not only do they have more spendable income and wealth than the rest

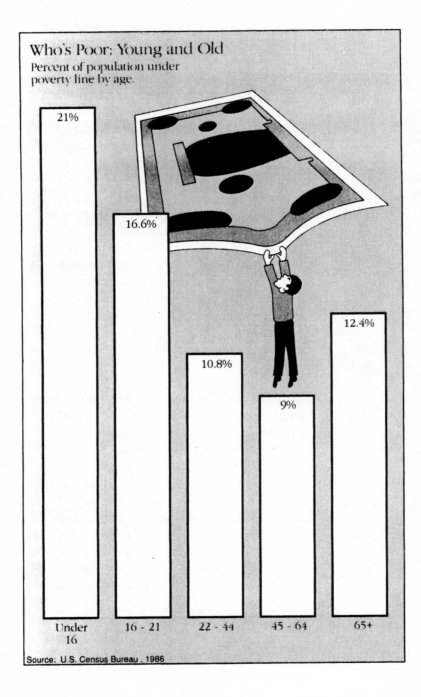

Who's Poor: Young and Old
Percent of population under poverty line by age.

21%   Under 16

16.6%   16 - 21

12.4%   65+

10.8%   22 - 44

9%   45 - 64

Source: U.S. Census Bureau , 1986

of the population, but they also get special tax breaks and benefits.

Income.   The contrast between the charts on pages 72 and 73 tells a fascinating tale. The first shows how much money people in a household make based on the age of the head of the house. As we might expect, it peaks between the ages of 45 and 54, when people are often at the top of their careers and few have retired. The second chart also shows income, but measured differently: *per capita* (the average of what each individual in the household makes) and *discretionary* (the money available for spending after paying for necessities). In other words, this chart shows how much money people can take down to the mall and spend. From the point of view of business, this is the most important measure of income. And on average, people over 65 have more discretionary income than any other age group.

Tax breaks.   Older Americans pay a smaller percentage of income in taxes than younger people do.

- Social Security and veteran's-pension benefits are largely excluded from taxable income.
- All taxpayers 65 and over enjoy a special extra tax deduction, indexed for inflation.
- A homeowner 55 or over selling his or her home has a one-time exclusion from capital-gains tax.
- Most older Americans pay no Social Security payroll tax, which takes a bigger and bigger bite out of younger people's wages.

If two people, one over 65 and one under 65, have the same before-tax income, the older person will end up with more money after the IRS has taken its bite.

Benefits.   Older Americans receive many more benefits than younger Americans, both proportionally and absolutely, from

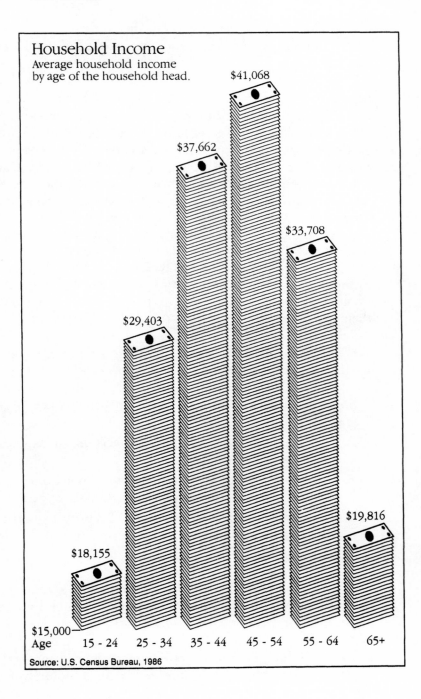

Household Income

Average household income
by age of the household head.

$41,068

$37,662

$33,708

$29,403

$19,816

$18,155

| Age | 15 - 24 | 25 - 34 | 35 - 44 | 45 - 54 | 55 - 64 | 65+ |

$15,000

Source: U.S. Census Bureau, 1986

Who's Got Money to Spend?
Discretionary income available
to individuals at various ages.

$5,633

$4,906

$3,701

$3,010

$2,833 $2,833

$2,000
Age 15 - 24   25 - 34   35 - 44   45 -54   55 -64   65+
Source: U.S. Census Bureau, 1984

government, corporations, churches, and community organizations.

Nearly every person 65 and over is covered by Medicare, which often has substantial value (an average of $2,450 per year per person). Besides the big programs like Medicare and Medicaid, dozens of federal programs—from subsidized housing to food stamps to energy-assistance programs—disproportionately benefit the elderly. In the 1986 federal budget, the total amount for the elderly came to $263.5 billion, or $9,088 for every older citizen. State and local governments add significantly to this total.

Wealth.   In our youth-oriented society, we are accustomed to measuring an individual's financial capabilities in terms of *income.* There are two problems with this. First, since most older people don't work, it's a given that many will have a lower active income than younger people still in the work force. However, long life has significant financial privileges and advantages, one of the most important of which is that older people are much more likely to have accumulated assets in the form of property and savings. Today, an estimated 500,000 to 600,000 millionaires receive Social Security payments. While these people are, of course, the exceptions, the point is that the majority of older Americans do have considerable assets.

The financial circumstances of the elderly will likely cause a complete redefinition of financial resources. A formula combining income, assets, benefits, and specific tax advantages may well become the new financial measurement. *Wealth,* not *income,* will be the standard.

All things considered, the image of Americans 65 and over as mass victims of grinding poverty is far from true. This group has an economic profile that is as varied as that of any other age group, with a small but significant number of wealthy people, a smaller-than-average group under the poverty line, and most spanning the vast middle. Many forward-thinking social analysts feel that we could be a great deal more effective at helping those who are truly needy if we didn't distribute so much money among men and women who could readily support themselves.

The Beginning of the End

Since the boomers will soon be migrating through their peak earning years, Social Security's annual operating surpluses are expected to continue to pile up until around 2020, when the surplus is projected to be approximately $10 trillion. But then, say the official figures, all that will change—and it will change quickly.

The first of the boomers will hit traditional retirement age around 2011. Within 15 years after that, Social Security could begin running huge annual deficits.

The amounts that will be needed for the boomers' retirement are projected to rise dizzily year after year, starting at $37 billion in that first year and reaching $1.1 trillion by 2038. That's a deficit for one year that would be five times as large as the entire federal deficit for 1986. And who will have to pay? The sparse generations coming behind the boomers. Although many social-policy experts assure us that the boomers' benefits will be there when they retire, no one is willing to comment on the availability of funds for members of today's youth generation—exactly the segment of our population that is most impoverished already—when they grow old. Is this fair?

But even these figures, grim as they are, are based on some very questionable assumptions about America's future. The Social Security Administration makes three sets of assumptions: an optimistic set (labeled "I"), an intermediate set ("II"), and a pessimistic set ("III"). These assumptions involve a wide range of variables, including unemployment rates, economic growth, population growth, and longevity.

Most government planning relies on the intermediate assumptions, which are described briefly in the following paragraphs:

Inflation.   Inflation is expected to average 4 percent in the coming years. According to the Department of Labor's Consumer Price Index Office, over the last 30 years—including the robust late fifties and early sixties—inflation (measured as the compound average of the annual rate of consumer-price change) has averaged 4.7 percent. In the more mature economy between 1977 and 1987, inflation averaged a staggering 6.5 percent per year.

Wages.   Real growth in wages is expected to be 1.5 percent yearly. Between 1978 and 1987, real wages actually dropped, by an average of 1.06 percent per year.

Recessions.   The intermediate projections show no economic boom-and-bust cycles for the next 60 to 75 years, with no recessions at all. By comparison, during the last 75 years America has experienced 16 recessions.

Unemployment.   This model assumes that after 1990, unemployment will average 6 percent. According to the Bureau of Labor Statistics, for the decade from 1978 to 1987, unemployment has averaged 7.4 percent.

Productivity.   An annual productivity growth of 2 percent is assumed. The average annual growth in American productivity has been dropping for three decades, going from an average of 2.7 percent between 1955 and 1964, to 1.9 percent in the decade after that, and then to 1.3 percent from 1975 to 1984. From 1984 to 1987, the average annual growth in productivity averaged less than 1.5 percent—hardly the growth rates the government is projecting.

Population growth.   The intermediate model assumes that the birthrate will reverse a decades-long trend and rise 11 percent, to 2.0, by the year 2010. In fact, the birthrate dropped from 3.5 in 1957 to an all-time low of 1.8 in 1986, and few demographers expect to see a reversal in this decline.

Longevity.   In the next 60 to 75 years, the Social Security Administration expects men to gain only another 3 years in life expectancy, on average, while women are expected to gain 4.4 years. In comparison, during the past 75 years, life expectancy has risen by 30 years.

Protection of funds.   By 2020, the Social Security Trust Funds are expected to have nearly $10 trillion in surplus, enough to cover the national debt. Between now and then, it's likely that various groups will campaign heavily to apply these savings to the problems at hand.

So, Social Security might barely be available for the first of the baby boomers, but only if over the next 60 to 75 years we have no recessions, continual economic growth, a rising birthrate, an increase in longevity of fewer than 5 years, and no dipping into the Social Security savings pot . . . all extremely unlikely phenomena. In fact, in a survey of 389 well-respected practicing actuaries outside of government, more than 70 percent thought the long-term inflation rate used by the Social Security actuaries was very unrealistic; 60 percent thought the same thing about the figures for long-term real growth in wages; and 63 percent thought that the long-term fertility-rate projections were at odds with every related trend that has taken place in decades. In general, these actuaries disagreed with almost every important assumption upon which the future of Social Security and our nation's intergenerational resource-sharing system rests.

Yet, even with these troubling ratios, Social Security spokespersons maintain that the retirement pension fund is secure. Henry Aaron, a senior fellow of the Brookings Institute, a prominent Washington think tank, recently stated,

"No one can be sure of the political climate of the future. But I firmly believe that it is adequately funded for the next 25 or 30 years, [and] probably even for the next 75 years." Robert M. Ball, the Commissioner of Social Security from 1962 to 1974, a member of the National Commission on Social Security Reform, and now a visiting scholar at the Center for the Study of Social Policy in Washington, D.C., has commented that "Social Security will be available for the baby boom generation, in the amounts promised. I don't know any knowledgeable person who would challenge these projections."

Despite these optimistic projections, I have a great deal of difficulty believing that the Social Security system will be solvent and in place in 2017—the year in which I am supposed to receive my first payment. When 40-year-old Dorcas Hardy, Commissioner of Social Security in the Reagan administration, was asked how she felt personally about the future of Social Security, she said, "I'll tell you, since I took this job I'm planning ahead a lot more. I'm saving as much as I can."

As more young Americans find themselves paying an increasing share of their limited incomes into a questionable Social Security system while they see growing numbers of elders doing well, there is likely to be a generational rebellion.

FUNDING HEALTH CARE: WHO PAYS? WHO LIVES?

Debates will also rage over the impact of the aged on the health-care system. Young people will see major increases in their health-care premiums as a result of the chronic, long-term illnesses of a growing elderly population, as well as of the intensive and expensive efforts that are made to extend the lives of the terminally ill.

Already, one-third of the $450 billion spent annually on health care goes to the 12 percent of the population over 65, and this group continues to lobby for even more funds.

But it is not the elderly per se who are the heavy users of health-care financing. It is the very sick and terminally ill, many of whom are also very old. In fact, analysis reveals that a very small percentage of the elderly are responsible for the very high Medicare bills. According to the Health Care Financing Administration (HCFA), in 1983 (the last year for which complete data are available), 2.3 percent of the 65+ Medicare beneficiaries accounted for 33.9 percent of program expenditures, and less than 10 percent of the beneficiaries accounted for more than 72 percent of the costs. A large portion of these expenditures is laid out for the terminally ill: 28 percent of the Medicare budget—approaching $25 billion —is spent on patients who are in the final year of life. These expenditures occur at a time when one-fifth of the children in America have not received a polio shot, one-third have never seen a dentist, and a large number of young families have no health insurance of any kind.

Perhaps it was this realization that in 1984 prompted then-Governor Richard Lamm of Colorado to offer the controversial comment that the terminally ill elderly had a "duty to die." While Lamm's comments were offensive to many, he is not alone in his concerns. Many people argue that instead of pouring billions of dollars into health care for the terminally ill elderly, we could be using this money to help young people live healthy, active lives. According to Dr. Paul Ellwood, chairman of the Minneapolis research firm Interstudy and a leading national health-care advisor, "With the amount of money we're spending for a small gain in life expectancy, I'm not sure we're buying very much. We're reaching the point where spending money on something else might be more worthwhile."

Daniel Callahan, Ph.D., is a medical ethicist who for the past 18 years has been head of the prestigious Hastings Center in Briarcliff, New York. In his book *Setting Limits,* published in 1987, Callahan argued that we should restrict the amount of health-care funds being set aside for the elderly.

> We have to begin to think about health care in a different way than [we did] in the past. We have given a lot of weight to the prolonging of life through acute care and high technology. We must shift our emphasis to providing the things that improve the quality of that life, such as long-term care and home care. We need to put the emphasis on quality of life over quantity of life.

Callahan believes that there are two major reasons why such a shift is necessary:

> In the first place, we aren't giving older people what they really need. They are themselves much more interested in an improved quality rather than quantity. Second, we can't afford to continue the present course. In the long run we will have to use age itself as a limit of some kind to health care. We have to ask how long a life we should try to support, at least with public funds. I don't think we can afford both more and more life-extending acute care and better long-term and home care. We're going to have to make a choice.

To this end, Callahan proposes that

- the medical profession should "give up its relentless drive to extend the life of the aged."
- Congress should restrict Medicare payments for such expensive, high-risk treatments as heart bypass operations, organ transplants, and kidney dialysis.
- states should give firm legal underpinnings to "living wills," which allow patients to stipulate that they not be kept alive by extraordinary means.
- respirators should not be used on the terminally ill.

- feeding tubes should be treated as "artificial intrusions" on the terminally ill.
- costly antibiotics should be withheld from the elderly terminally ill.

We may soon find ourselves being asked, at the ballot and in the field of public opinion, whether we should discriminate openly on the basis of age in health care, restricting the range of procedures and services available to the elderly terminally ill.

It seems unlikely; it seems so "un-American." But the British and many other "civilized" nations do it already: most kinds of major surgery and kidney dialysis are denied to patients over 70. Is this fair? Do such restrictions represent age wars, or are they instead the result of thoughtful and emotional debates on the appropriate distribution of national funds?

OTHER TREMORS

Although Social Security and Medicare are the largest and most obvious realms of potential intergenerational strife, the waking of the giant may cause strain in other areas of social interaction as well.

In the local arena, for instance, some seniors have begun to challenge the need to pay taxes for schools and have organized to defeat school-bond issues. Local budgets are becoming battlegrounds between such competing needs as childhood education and senior housing or child care and adult recreation.

In Arizona, Sun City West forced a rezoning of the outlying community in order to disengage itself from the Dysart School District, and Sun Lakes has attempted to pull out of the Chandler School District. The retirees argue that since they have no school-age children, they shouldn't have to be encumbered by school taxes. Angry opponents have argued that a convenient "amnesia" has allowed these elders to forget that for the great majority of them, their own education and that of their children and grandchildren was free and public, paid for by taxes.

In a curious twist on age discrimination, Amendment HR1158 to the Title A Civil Rights Act has recently passed in the U.S. House of Representatives and is currently working its way through the Senate. Under this amendment, age discrimination in housing will be illegal *except* in retirement communities. In these special environments, it will be legal to restrict purchase or rental of homes based on age. Young people and children can thus be kept out of such communities.

Is this fair? Does it make sense in a free nation for people to be excluded from living in the home or community of their dreams, simply because they're too young?

In the workplace, now that the mandatory retirement age has been struck down by Congress, younger people may find their careers thwarted because older people choose not to retire.

In contrast to earlier times, when most older workers peacefully stepped out of the work force to make room for the young, today's older workers are boldly exercising their right to keep working. As a result, increasing numbers of legal fights will erupt over age discrimination, retraining, seniority, and other workplace issues.

Between 1980 and 1986, complaints of age bias to the federal Equal Employment Opportunity Commission and state commissions more than doubled—from 11,000 to 27,000. Today, every 30 minutes, an older American worker files an age-discrimination complaint with the federal government. Almost 70 percent of these cases charge wrongful dismissal or involuntary retirement.

According to Landon Jones, editor of *Money* magazine and author of *Great Expectations:*

The working men and working women of the baby boom will find that, just as once there was not enough room for all of them to climb onto the occupational ladder, there later will not be enough room for them at the top. ... Millions of them [who are] crowded on the first steps of management will be forced to stay right there. A generation that had expected to be Chiefs will have to be Braves.

Is this fair?

Age-related conflicts may also arise as employers come to grips with the growing burden of retiree health-care costs—yet another manifestation of the waking giant. Until recently, companies could pretty much ignore such costs, since there were so few retirees and most of those didn't live very long. However, at American companies today, the average ratio of workers to retirees is only 3 to 1, which is even more extreme than the current Social Security ratio. In some older companies that used to offer generous retirement programs, the numbers are even more extreme. The Bethlehem Steel Corporation, for example, has 33,000 active employees and nearly 70,000 retirees and surviving spouses. The cost of helping to defray the health-care expenses of the growing retiree population will soon be enough to bankrupt many companies. These costs will ultimately be picked up by the consumers, the stockholders, or by the current workers, in the form of salary limitations.

Some companies have tried to bail out of their financial commitments to their retirees but have been stopped short by "retiree power." For instance, when the LTV Steel Corporation filed for Chapter 11 in 1986, it tried to cancel its retiree health and life-insurance benefits as a way to rid itself of paralyzing debts. The workers at one site immediately went on strike, and workers at all of the company's other locations threatened to do the same. All retiree benefits were quickly reinstated.

Conflicts will erupt in other areas as well. In recent years, a number of age-related discounts have been initiated in a wide range of businesses. Airlines offer reduced fares to older travelers. In 1988, AARP introduced a national credit union for its members, offering rates on savings and credit cards far better than most of those provided by banks. Movie theaters have senior-citizen discounts, and many hospitals now offer reductions in costs to older patients. Such discounts would never be allowed based on race or religion. Yet, our assumption of widespread elderly poverty has allowed them to flourish. Is this fair?

Many young people are beginning to grumble about being discriminated against in the marketplace, and some older people are also becoming concerned about the unfairness of any system based on age rather than need.

This concern was well stated by Joseph King in an essay in *Newsweek*:

> Not long ago, while waiting on line at our local movie theater, I tuned in to the conversations of the people around me. Ahead were two couples—in their late sixties, I think—chatting about their grandchildren, tax-free municipal bonds, and, at one point, the expensive Gucci bag one of the ladies was clutching. Behind me, several students talked about the horrendous cost of textbooks, the fare increase on the Bay Area Rapid Transit, and their inability to find a decent one-bedroom apartment for less than $500 a month. The ticket office opened. The two elderly couples—who, I gathered from my eavesdropping, lived in the luxury retirement community of Rossmoor in Walnut Creek—stepped up and paid $2.50 a ticket: half price. Having just turned 60, I qualified for the discount, too. The youngsters behind me paid the full $5.00. We seniors end up with the cash, the disposable income, while our progeny are taxed and shortchanged. . . . Would not more help be available for the real poor —old and young—if so many perks and exemptions did not go to the affluent?

In the years ahead, the discounts routinely given older Americans may be challenged as the image of seniors as automatically poverty-stricken disappears. For instance, in Dade County, Florida, Richard Grayson sued his bank for providing special discounts to seniors. He claimed it was discriminatory. He won the suit, but the state legislature changed the law to make such discounts legal. In time, all discounts based on age alone may come under challenge.

TOWARD INTERGENERATIONAL COOPERATION

So are the generations really at war with each other? Do they really dislike each other? Have they become enemies that will be battling over turf and dollars for decades to come? I don't think so.

Every national study that has been conducted on this theme reports that in general, young and old have great respect and affection for each other and want to do whatever is fair to assure health and financial security for all generations. For instance, a major national survey conducted by the Yankelovich Group in 1986 found that younger and older Americans are closer together in their attitudes, values, and opinions than many people suspect. According to Madelyn Hochstein, executive vice-president of the Yankelovich Group,

> Seventy-six percent of young adults say the government is "not doing enough" for persons age 65 and older. More than 90 percent of Americans favor the continuation of Medicare, with 75 percent supporting an expansion to include the costs of long-term care. Among young adults (ages 21 to 29), 74 percent favor high Social Security benefits for the elderly.

One of the great advantages of living in a free and democratic nation is that we have the charter to continually improve ourselves and our social policies based on trial and error. Through our successes (acknowledged by public support and confidence) and through our failures (identified through lively and often emotional protest and public dialogue), we can continue to update and upgrade our priorities and policies.

We are in the midst of that process now, spurred on by the Age Wave. To interpret these early social warning signals as representative of intergenerational animosity and age wars is wrong and undermining of the generous American spirit. And by focusing on the symptoms of the problem instead of addressing the underlying concerns and issues, we may not only fan the fires of unrest that have begun to spark, but we may also run the risk of being diverted from the chance to create a fair and equitable multigenerational national policy.

Without a doubt, there are unmistakable strains and serious fault lines emerging in our dated intergenerational social programs. With the waking of the giant and the shrinking of the younger population, glaring inequities can be seen in the ways in which resources are shared and distributed among the generations. Young as well as old have serious concerns about the future solvency and relevancy of Social Security and Medicare.

In a healthy, long-lived culture, many people will question the appropriateness of generous government support based on age, when there are so many people of all ages who are desperately needy.

And there is most definitely a growing discomfort among the young with the quickly rising power of the elderly.

And so there are really two problems here. The first is whether, and how, we will be able to maintain social programs that were designed for a different time and a significantly different demographic mix. The second, and perhaps more important, task is the critical social challenge of creating a fair and equitable national strategy whereby different generations—people who grew up during different periods of history, with different lifestyles and somewhat different expectations of themselves and government—can learn to cooperate so that we might all receive our fair share of the American pie.

In several later chapters we will explore a variety of innovative solutions to these age quakes, including portable private-pension programs, phased retirement, wellness and health promotion, care management, shared housing, age-specific marketing strategies, and the arrival of the "matrix" family.

CHAPTER

4

The Cyclic Life

The waking of the giant will affect more than just our institutions. The outer demographic changes that are rearranging our society are also touching our most personal inner thoughts, hopes, and plans. The gift of longevity and the added years it brings will cause us to rethink the pace and tempo of our lives as well as the relative purposes, goals, and challenges of its various stages. Under the influence of the Age Wave, the rigid ordering of the various activities of our lives is already coming apart at the seams.

Everywhere we turn, men and women are redefining the style and purpose of the later years of life.

With 28 extra years added to life expectancy during the past century, we now have a choice between growing old as we always have, with two to three decades of old age tagged on at the end, or of taking those precious extra years and cycling them throughout every part of life. Extended life will offer an elongation of, or even a revisit to, the periods of life we most enjoy—extra years of vibrant adolescence, an expanded period of youth, prolonged young adulthood, a slowed down middle age, a lengthened late adulthood, and a vigorous old age.

THE END OF THE LINEAR LIFE PLAN

Throughout all of human history, the average length of life was short. In a world where (if they survived the high infant mortality rates) most people did not expect to live longer than 40 or 50 years, it was essential, both for the biological continuation of our species and the maintenance of social order, that certain key personal and social tasks be accomplished by specific ages. Traditionally, important lifestyle activities such as "job preparation," "parenthood," and "retirement" were not only assigned to particular periods of life but were also supposed to occur only once in a lifetime.

Until now, the charting of our lives has been very neat and predictable. Stated simply: first you learned, then you worked (at family and career), and then you died.

Specifically, childhood and youth were the time for learning and play. By your late teens, you were supposed to know "what you wanted to be" for the rest of your life. If you were an unmarried woman over 30, you were on your way to spinsterhood. When you chose a mate, it was "till death do you part." The thirties and forties were the years for child-rearing; the fifties and sixties, if you lived that long, were for grandparenthood.

You were expected to pick a career in your late teens or early twenties, and to pursue it without respite throughout most of your adult life; in your job, you were supposed to learn, grow, and "climb the ladder." Once you reached "old age," you could expect the remaining years of life to be characterized by declining health, a gradual lessening of social and professional challenges, and a retirement from the work force prior to death. In general, the older you got, the less you were expected to try new things, meet new people, or experiment with new ways of living. You were definitely not supposed to go back to school, fall in love, begin a new career, or take up a social crusade.

Almost every event and decision of life, big or small—getting a graduate degree, marrying, adopting a child, learning a musical instrument, bicycling across the country, pursuing a new career—was thought to have a particular age at which it was appropriate, and lots of ages when it was not. It's as though the various activities of our lives had a plan against which they were measured. And the path from childhood to old age was linear: it moved in one direction, with little room for hesitations, detours, experimentation, or second chances.

This linear life plan was kept in place by the forces of tradition. If we didn't behave appropriately for our age, our parents, clergy, teachers, neighbors, and even children could be counted on to remind us of our proper roles. We still tell each other to act our ages, as if a commandment to "Act thy age" had been handed down on Sinai along with the other ten.

Just as you might produce shock and disapproval by doing what society considered the wrong things, you could also reap profound criticism by doing perfectly normal things at the wrong age. "Mom, do you really think you should be applying to college at your age?" . . . "Look at that silly old man trying to keep up with the young kids on the dance floor." . . . "What does that old woman think she's trying to prove by wearing a bikini to the beach?" . . . "Isn't it time you retired and made room for the young people?" . . . "Why in the world would that older couple want to adopt a child at their age?"

The linear life plan was also imposed by law. Government regulations and institutional rules have prescribed the ages at which we should go to school, begin and end work, adopt a child, or receive our pension.

And, most powerfully, the linear life plan has been perpetuated by our own assumptions. Almost all of us have said, at one time or another, "It's too late for me to try that" or "If I could only have one more chance to do it over again" or "If only I were younger, I would . . ."

In many ways, you were judged, and you often judged yourself, by how successful you were in following the linear plan. If you did things in a different order or didn't do some of them at all, your family and friends would undoubtedly have stories of others who had deviated from the path and ended up poor, childless, and socially ostracized.

The linear life plan was based directly on the biological and social requirements of the short length of life in earlier times. If you expected to be old at 50 and dead shortly thereafter, you didn't really have much time to deviate from the normal course of things. If you wanted to be able to have children and parent them until they grew up, you had to get married and start having babies when you were in your twenties. If you hoped to be able to support your family, you had to get started on building your career early, and you couldn't take any time off to reconsider or to change direction. Life's personal and occupational tasks were straightforward, clearly delineated, and heavily influenced by the brevity of life. Run like a 50-yard dash, the shorter life offered few second or third chances.

Underlying this approach to life were two basic assumptions:

1. The various activities of life were to be performed on time, and in sequence.
2. Most of life's periods of growth took place in the first half of life, while the second half was in general characterized by decline.

THE CYCLIC LIFE PLAN

Imagine that you knew you would live not to 50 or 60 but to 80, 90, or more, and that you could be vigorous and independent almost all of those years. If you could be assured of this longevity, would you be in such a hurry to get every-thing done early in life? Would you feel you had to select your career right out of school, in your early twenties, or would you take a bit of time to reflect on this important life choice and perhaps spend a few years trying different kinds of em-ployment? Would you assume that you would have only one career during your entire lifetime, or would you plan on having several? Would you be in such a rush to get married and start having children in your early twenties, or might you be inclined to slow your pace and wait a while? If you became divorced in your middle years, would you see this as the end of companionship, or rather as an opportunity to move on to your next loving involvement?

If your chosen career was no longer satisfying, might you consider going back to school to learn an entirely new profes-sional skill? If you knew you would live eight or nine decades, would you retire from all work in your fifties or early sixties, bunching all of your leisure time at the end of life, or would you instead take time off occasionally during your middle years? If there were special activities that you simply didn't have time for when you were younger—such as learning to play a musical instrument, becoming a gourmet cook, or run-ning in marathons—wouldn't you like to know that you could have a second chance at these activities later in life?

If any of these possibilities appeal to you, or if they affirm lifestyle directions you are already pursuing, you are not alone. The Age Wave is lifting the major components of adult life—family, education, work, leisure, and community service —free of their traditional moorings.

We are witnessing the dissolution of the traditional lin-ear life plan. In its place, a much more flexible arrange-ment, known as the "cyclic life plan," is emerging.

Family.   For example, when the average life expectancy was 45 to 55 years, we spent nearly every moment of our adult years raising our children. As a result, we have come to think of our family roles as being primarily that of parent. As recently as one century ago, by the time the last child was grown and ready to leave home, one or both of the parents had already passed away. With the coming of the Age Wave, most of us will have more years of adult life *after* the children have grown and have left home than we had when we were raising them. As a result, the role of parenting will fade in the overall architecture of family life, and the importance of mature friendship and companionship will rise as core elements of mid- and late-life marital relationships.

Education.   Whereas education has been primarily geared to preparing the young for their lifetime careers, we are now coming to think of learning as an ongoing, lifelong process. As the pace of discovery quickens and our appetite for learning increases, we will find ourselves being retrained and retooled many times throughout our lives. In addition, as our commitment and need for learning expands, our interest in non-vocation–oriented education will increase as well.

Work.   We have thought of work as the job we perform essentially nonstop from our early twenties until we either retire or die. We expect to expand and enlarge our abilities in the early years of our careers, reaching a peak in the late forties or early fifties, and then winding down to a halt during the remaining decades. We will soon find ourselves cycling in and out of several different careers throughout our lives, each interspersed with periods of rest, recreation, retraining, and personal reflection. And some older men and women will hit their career stride for the first time at an age when others are retiring.

Leisure.   We have thought of leisure as rest from work and as something we could enjoy for extended periods only during early childhood or old age. Now, we are beginning to envision leisure as an ongoing element of our adult years, with regular time taken away from work for recreation and personal growth.

Community service. Volunteerism and community service have long been the exclusive province of social crusaders, the rich, or older people with lots of spare time. Now, elevated life expectancy and the abundance of time it brings will allow all of us an expanded opportunity to invest our skills, knowledge, and accumulated resources in our communities and culture.

In the new social and economic atmosphere, family, education, work, leisure, and community service will blend into and influence one another, and even—as we shall see—masquerade as one another. Men and women will "retire," only to return to the work force a few years later, sometimes for pay, other times not. Our "families" will become an evolving blend of our true blood relatives and the revolving networks of friends who share our needs and interests at the various stages of our lives. We may devote our leisure time to play and recreation, or we may decide to enroll in a master's program in philosophy at the local college.

Longer life will eliminate the rigid correlations between age and the various activities and challenges of adult life.

Having the luxury of being able to choose how we arrange our various life tasks, long the prerogative of the "leisure class," will become commonplace—in a sense, democratized. Unhinged from the negative age-related expectations of the linear life plan, as we grow older we will be free to grow *more* expansive and diverse, not *less* so, as has been the case in the past.

According to Fred Best, Ph.D., a sociologist and futurist and the creator of the cyclic-life-plan idea,

> Changing patterns of learning [and] family life, as well as physiologically based trends in longevity and health, are creating lifetime scheduling options that were heretofore nonexistent. . . . In 1900, when the average life

expectancy at age 20 was 42 years, the notion of obtaining all of one's schooling in youth in preparation for adulthood was a sound idea. Today, life expectancy at age 20 is [another] 55 years, and the idea of recurrent education throughout longer life spans is both reasonable and increasingly common.

[Until] recent years, family responsibilities for dependents during mid-life required men to pursue continuous employment to fulfill a role as "breadwinner" and women to forgo or minimize job holding in order to care for children and elderly relatives. Today family units are generally separated from older relatives, couples are having fewer children, and women are seeking career involvements that embellish family incomes. As a result, husbands and wives are beginning to share housekeeping and income earning in ways that may allow more flexible life schedules.

Finally, increasing life expectancy and better health among the older population are altering the very definitions of "old age" and "retirement." . . . This suggests that failure to work in some fashion during the later stages of life may produce severe financial hardships over the increasing length of non-income-earning retirement years, and that growing numbers of older persons may both prefer and be able to work well beyond current retirement ages. All in all, there are notable indications that distinctions between the natural stages of life are blurring.

While there are as yet few role models for this emerging lifestyle, more people than ever have been opting out of the tight linear life plan and adopting elements of a cyclic life. For example:

- Increasing numbers of men and women are marrying later in life and choosing to delay parenting until after they have successfully launched their careers and settled into marriage. For women, the average age of first marriages has risen to its highest point (23) in the nation's history;

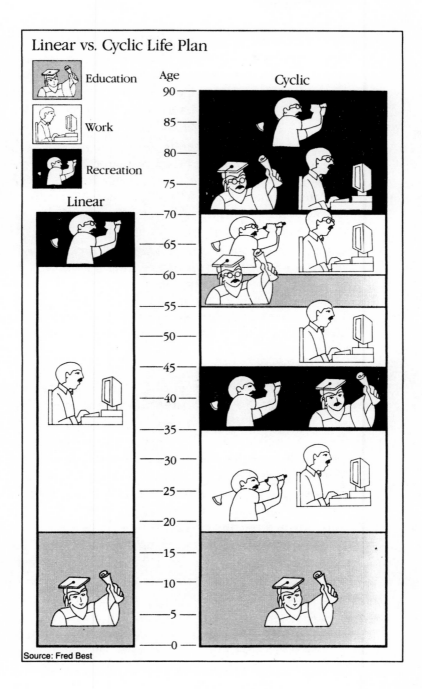

Source: Fred Best

for men, it has reached the highest point (26) since 1900. And more women in their thirties and forties are having children today than at any previous time in history. Between 1975 and 1985, there was a 71 percent increase in births to women 35 years and older in comparison to the preceding ten-year period.

- There are unmistakable trends toward increasing divorce and remarriage. Currently, more than 50 percent of all marriages end in divorce, a percentage that reflects a 43 percent increase since 1970. Eighty percent of divorced people remarry, making "serial monogamy" the norm rather than the exception in America.

- Learning is no longer exclusively the province of the young. In recent years, it has become increasingly common for middle-aged or older people to go back to school. In fact, in community colleges, which traditionally have been home to 18- and 19-year-olds fresh out of high school, the average age of evening students has soared to 38.

At the present time, 45 percent of all undergraduate and graduate students in the United States are over 25.

- Today, it's unlikely that the job you choose to pursue in your early twenties will be the one you'll be working at in your sixties. People of all ages take regular sabbaticals for education or leisure or start entirely new careers. The average American now changes jobs every three years, often with time off for regrouping between positions. And, in support of disengaging the traditional work/ leisure lockstep, it's estimated that nearly 14 percent of major American corporations now offer some form of paid sabbatical from work.

- Except for a few specified professions (such as airline pilot), mandatory retirement became illegal, by federal statute, in 1987. The results of a number of recent surveys agreed fairly closely that only about 27 percent of Americans want to stop working completely at retirement age, and more than 60 percent hope to keep working either full- or part-time. Changing attitudes and financial necessities will raise this percentage even higher.

- The percentage of out-of-work executives who start totally new careers rather than seeking new positions in the same industry has more than doubled in the last five years. According to a recent *Money Magazine* story about retirement, when ten retirees who had had a high degree of job success were asked, "What's the best thing about your retirement?" eight of them answered, "My new job!"

  And because of the incredible pace of technological and cultural change, the Rand Corporation, a futures-oriented think tank in Santa Monica, California, predicts that by the year 2020 the average worker will need to be retrained up to 13 times in his or her lifetime.

"ELDERHEROES"

What does a cyclic life actually look like? As with most important shifts in social behavior, some forward-thinking men and women have already broken away from the status quo and are setting the trend for more flexible and cyclic lifestyles. From the progressive attitudes and behaviors of these social pioneers, or "elderheroes," will emerge a new vision of the possibilities for us all.

Although we have heroes and models of success in most areas of our culture—for example, sports, entertainment, even business—our gerontophobia has left us with few positive examples of successful aging, especially of the "cyclic" kind.

We can all benefit from the example of individuals who have continued to evolve in their personal and professional relationships as they age, or who have pursued new dreams in their later years.

In my life, an assortment of men and women have emerged as my personal elderheroes. I am inspired by what they have done with their lives, and especially by the way they have continued to grow and evolve as they have aged. Some of these people were special all of their lives; some first caught their stride in their later years. None of them rested or backslid as they grew older. Instead, they all repeatedly attempted new personal and social challenges at ages when they could have simply resigned themselves to the modest later-life expectations of the linear plan. I have chosen to highlight these particular people not only because they are inspirations to me, but also because their personal struggles and breakthroughs represent some of the best of what the cyclic life may set free in all of us.

Mother Teresa

It is not yet six in the morning. In the small, bare chapel, a tiny old woman kneels on the floor and prays. She is wearing a worn white sari and blue sweater. The dawn light leaks in through the high windows, along with the clamor and stench of the fetid streets of Calcutta. The woman is 79. As she has aged, she has become the center of a remarkable global spiritual movement.

But although she has been a missionary nun for all of her adult life, she did not begin the work for which she is most revered until almost 40, a point at which people are supposed to have already settled into their life paths.

Born Agnes Gonxha Bojaxhiu of Albanian parents in 1910, Mother Teresa had an early passion for missionary work. She entered the convent while still a teenager, and was sent to India. She taught for more than 20 years in St. Mary's High School in Calcutta, a bastion of privilege under the raja. But out the windows every day as she taught, she could see the warrens of Moti Jheel, one of the most forsaken slums of Calcutta.

By the time she was 36, she had been made principal of St. Mary's. She was settled in her profession and respected in her order. She had found her place. If she had stayed there, no one would have said she had led any but the most exemplary religious life. At that early point in her life she was not yet a forceful leader or a great orator. She was a quiet woman. But her forays into Moti Jheel had awakened something in her soul that moved her toward an entirely new life path. One night, riding the dim and crowded night train to Darjeeling, she heard within her "a call within a call," she has said, to "leave the convent and help the poor while living among them."

The call changed her life. She exchanged her habit for a white sari and took to the streets of Calcutta, barefoot. She was 40 when she formally founded the Missionaries of Charity order, which has grown to include more than 3,000 sisters in 350 houses. At 49, Mother Teresa moved into the industrial slum in Calcutta where the lepers lived, sat down under a tree, and began to give out medicine and food. In time she founded a leprosy center there, the first of 119 such centers across India and around the world. At 58, she opened a house in Rome and founded the Coworkers of the Missionaries of Charity, a lay army that now numbers more than 3 million. At 60, she moved the order into London and, because of her advancing age, she considered retiring. But instead, she moved to New York and started the first North American mission in the ravaged and dangerous "Fort Apache" area of the South Bronx.

The Nobel Prize brought Mother Teresa worldwide acclaim at the age of 69. At that age she could have retreated without any reproach. Instead, this diminutive woman with a deep spiritual fire used the acclaim to bring a message to the world: when you touch the poor, the sick, and the dying, you touch the body of God.

As she approaches 80, she makes no claims to having a secret well of energy, and she is often visibly tired. As one of her followers commented, "She has a very bad heart condition—I know she has a lot of pain. But she makes no exemptions for herself. She's still the first for morning prayers, and she still moves like lightning."

People of all ages have flocked to follow her example. The Missionaries of Charity has expanded to 71 countries. Mother Teresa's army of followers runs 745 mobile medical clinics and 97 schools, along with countless hostels for AIDS victims, soup kitchens, and shelters for the homeless. It is estimated that at any one moment her order is teaching 14,000 children, feeding 126,000 families, and caring for 186,000 lepers and 22,000 dying homeless. As she has grown older, instead of "winding down," Mother Teresa has been continually "gearing up," seeking out the new challenge, the wider vision, the richer path.

Mahatma Gandhi

Mahatma Gandhi, one of the greatest spiritual and political leaders of our century, was not born wearing a *dhoti* and carrying a rice bowl. As a young and middle-aged man, he had no anticipation whatsoever that one day he would become a great spiritual leader. Born into a middle-class family, he rose to become a prominent Western-style lawyer, a role he pursued vigorously for decades. Then, at the age of 50, he experienced a kind of mid-life identity crisis and decided to become involved in national politics. But it was not until after his sixty-fifth birthday that he "found himself" in the deepest sense. After quitting the Indian National Congress as a relatively old man, he moved on to his next stage of development and proceeded to adopt the style of life and ideas for which we know him—living simply, wearing traditional rural Indian clothes, and relying on *satyagraha* (the power of truth) to bring about social change. It was in his old age—his sixties and seventies—that Gandhi became the living soul of the Indian nation through his moral power and grand vision.

Gandhi's life was cyclic, and his moral and political force grew rather than declined as he aged.

Just as a caterpillar gives no indication that it is to become a fantastic butterfly, the pre-50 Gandhi appeared to be a significantly different man than the one into which he evolved. Perhaps we all have aspects of ourselves hidden deep within, waiting to blossom in our later years.

Albert Schweitzer

The career of Albert Schweitzer represents yet another example of a classic cyclic life. Although most people assume that Schweitzer always wanted to be a physician and devote his life to helping the needy, he didn't get around to this role until he had had two other careers. He began his adult years as a renowned musician, an organist and interpreter of Bach. Then he switched tracks, becoming an acclaimed theologian, philosopher, and writer. But at 30, feeling that he still hadn't found the right niche for himself, he decided to backtrack and begin his professional life all over again, this time as a physician.

After returning to the life of a student and spending years in rigorous medical training, Schweitzer dropped out of "civilized" society and set out to help those who were less fortunate by becoming a jungle doctor. By the age of 38 he had established his hospital on the Ogowe River in Gabon, French West Africa. There he practiced humbly until he was interned as an enemy alien by the French during World War I. Upon his release, he faced a decision. His hospital was in ruins; everything he had worked so hard to build had collapsed from neglect. He was approaching 50, and no one would fault him if he returned to the comfortable life. He certainly had more than done his part.

But Schweitzer decided that it was not too late to start things up all over again. He went back to the jungle and rebuilt the hospital, which he ran until his death at 90. He drew life from giving life, and he never succumbed to the downward and confining pull of the linear life plan.

Claude Pepper

By 1950, Claude Pepper had been in the Senate for 14 years as a warrior for Franklin Roosevelt's New Deal. He had sponsored the bill that created the National Cancer Institute and the National Institutes of Health. He had been a prime mover in the creation of the resolution that led to the founding of the World Health Organization. He had done yeoman work in passing the nation's first minimum wage. He had invented the "Lend-Lease" idea that kept England alive during the Battle of Britain.

But in 1950 he fell victim to the smear-filled McCarthyite campaign. His opponent distributed a picture of him with Paul Robeson, a black opera star whom many people considered to be a Communist. A booklet called *The Red Record of Senator Claude Pepper* was churned out by the thousands. Labeled "Red Pepper," he was retired by the voters. Pepper, who was then 50 years old, chose to just wind down and go back to practicing some law. He had been a senator; that was certainly honor and involvement enough for most people's lives.

But in 1962, he decided that he still had time to attempt another round of his career. At an age when he was "supposed" to be retiring, Pepper ran for the House and won, becoming a 62-year-old freshman. From that moment on he became a force in Congress once again, a man to be reckoned with, serving first as Chairman of the House Select Committee on Aging and then as Chairman of the powerful Rules Committee.

At 88, with the aid of trifocals, twin hearing aids, a pacemaker, and an artificial heart valve, Pepper still keeps an exhausting schedule. He drives his own car, travels alone, and carries his own bags. He is a man of keen memory, and he is also a fluid and skilled orator. Even those who disagree with Pepper's politics respect him for his passion and his commitment to mature leadership.

Since his cyclic return to politics, Pepper has seemed to get stronger and tougher each year. The secret of Pepper's stamina is his boundless commitment to his beliefs and to his lifelong cause of helping others. To admirers who are concerned with his advancing years, he sometimes admits to retirement plans. "I've set the year," he says. "The year is 2000 —I'll be 100 years old then. But," he deadpans, "I reserve the right to change my mind."

Pepper's colorful career and positive attitude demonstrate the two key characteristics of the cyclic life: (1) second chances are always possible, and (2) with passion and commitment, inner strength and energy can grow with the passing years.

Maggie Kuhn

In 1970, the national office of the United Presbyterian Church forcibly retired a loyal and productive woman. The woman was 65-year-old "senior citizen" Maggie Kuhn, and by society's standards she had come to the end of her lifelong career. However, the insult of being forced to retire ignited something within her. Kuhn and five of her friends who were also furious about being thrown out of the work force banded together, forming a radical group geared to overturning society's ageist ways. Initially, they called themselves the "Consultation of Older and Younger Adults." But a New York television newsman saw in their radical pride a reflection of the Black Panthers and nicknamed them the "Gray Panthers." The name stuck.

For nearly two decades now, Maggie Kuhn's cyclic life has been running on its second wind. She has led the Gray Panthers in a striking variety of campaigns, all designed to eliminate ageism in America. Now 74,000 members strong, with chapters in 30 states, the Panthers have demonstrated at meetings of the American Medical Association and the National Gerontological Society; monitored municipal agencies, such as planning commissions and zoning boards, as well as courts, banks, and insurance companies; physically "liberated" men and women from unsafe nursing homes; and organized ongoing local and national "Media Watches" to eliminate all ageist programs and commercials from the air. Kuhn herself has engaged in a nearly nonstop program of public speaking, protesting, and testifying before Congress, state legislatures, and international bodies as the voice of elders for serious social change.

An outspoken example of a successful cyclic life, at 83 Maggie continues her role as one of the most radical leaders and social activists of our time, a role that she created for herself late in life—a role that, earlier in her life, she would never have guessed she would have.

Henri Matisse

As we have seen, for some people the cyclic life offers repeated opportunities for fresh starts and entirely new life paths. For others, extended years provide a special opportunity to go deeper and farther with their life's passions. Consider the unbounded creative force that poured forth from Henri Matisse despite the massive physical difficulties he encountered as he aged.

By the time he was in his sixties, Matisse was living in a large, well-lit studio in a hotel on the Riviera. Already, the great Postimpressionist painter had been a cultural revolutionary for 40 years. He had reached a time of life when he was expected to rest on his laurels and relax. Matisse temporarily succumbed to this stereotype and entered into a period of semiretirement.

However, he found the lack of challenge terribly unsettling. Old age, he felt, should be a time for "rebirth, not decline." At the age of 66, he set out anew to rediscover what he called "purity of means." For the next five years he pressed on, continually refining and evolving his craft.

Then in 1941, at the age of 71, he underwent an intestinal operation that left him bedridden much of the time for the rest of his life. This infirmity would have been a good excuse to quit working, if he had been looking for one. But Matisse had no intention of winding down—his ever-expanding creativity found new outlets regardless of his aging body's limits. He simply took his talents in new directions.

He invented ingenious ways to create art while bedridden. He had special easels made so that he could sit up in bed and work. When he could barely move, he used crayons and brushes tied to the ends of long bamboo poles to draw huge murals from his bed or wheelchair. Even with his limitations, Matisse's art climbed to new heights. His forms became purer, simpler, more daring. He made his colors brighter and bolder until, in the Mediterranean sunlight in which he painted, he had to wear tinted glasses as he worked to keep from getting headaches from the fantastic colors.

Between the ages of 75 and 80, he produced six major illustrated books that included hundreds of paintings. At the same time he produced his masterwork of graphic art, the book entitled *Jazz,* and designed the now-famous Chapelle du Rosaire—from the stained-glass windows and murals to the vestments and liturgical vessels.

Matisse worked almost until the day he died in 1954, at the age of 85. Critics rank the works of his last decade as some of the greatest expressions of human beauty and joy. Matisse's unbounded outpouring of creativity, far from diminishing with age, continued to rise from crescendo to crescendo as long as he was alive.

Mother Teresa, Mahatma Gandhi, Albert Schweitzer, Claude Pepper, Maggie Kuhn, and Henri Matisse are examples of true "elderheroes." All of these men and women did something unexpected: they grew, they changed directions, and they blossomed in their old age. They went farther in the later stages of their lives than they had ever gone before, often in directions that they had never anticipated during youth and middle age. Their remarkable examples make us all wonder who we, too, could become as we grow older.

ORDINARY PEOPLE

The individuals profiled above are not alone.

All around us, millions of ordinary aging Americans have begun to break free of the traditional expectations of age to shape new and rewarding cyclic lives for themselves.

Witness the case of Jacob Landers, interviewed by radio producer Connie Goldman for her "Late Bloomers" series. Now a public-interest lawyer in New York who gives voice and legal force to the elderly, Landers entered law school at 67, on a whim.

He had never thought of being a lawyer before, but the subject popped up one Thanksgiving in the chance comments of his daughter. The idea quickly became a challenge, the kind Landers had never been able to let pass by.

He had already had several careers. He had spent many years in education as a teacher, administrator, professor of education, and consultant on union educational funds. His career changes had been prompted by health problems: each time he "retired" for reasons of health, he would get restless and find something else to do.

On that particular Thanksgiving, Landers's daughter was talking about her struggles in law school. The emotion that arose in Landers was not pity but envy. "She was telling us about her experiences going to law school, about her classes and her friends. I said, 'I wish I could do that!' She said, 'Why don't you?'

"I said, 'How can I? Here I am—I'm already too old for that. Besides, what law school would want to accept an old man in his dotage?' I said the usual things one says when one doesn't want to do something.

"She was very direct. She said, 'Look, if you really want to do it, you can! If I can, you can!' "

By the end of the conversation, Jacob had promised that he would at least find out about it. The next Monday he called a registrar at New York University.

I asked her point-blank whether it was possible. She said, "Why not? You know there's an antidiscrimination law. We can't turn you down solely because you're too old. This Saturday we're going to give an exam. If you want to, you can be a walk-in candidate."

I hustled over to a bookstore to get some of the practice materials. I studied very hard. On Saturday I walked in and took the test. To my surprise, I did very well.

So I went to law school. I made friends among the people who were there. Most of them were very young. They were very kind. In the beginning they tried to baby me, as if to say, "Here's this elderly gentleman, and we have to be nice to him." But after a while they forgot about that. They accepted me. They treated me just the way they treated each other. I was subject to the same congratulations and derision. They argued with me and debated with me.

One of the proudest moments of my life was at graduation in Carnegie Hall. The dean had cautioned the audience not to applaud or do anything else that would disrupt the proceedings. And they didn't. But when my name was announced, *everybody* got up and applauded. I was so proud and so pleased for just that gesture. If I had won all the medals it would not have meant as much to me.

Like any new law graduate, Jacob Landers framed his diploma and prepared to search for a job. Then he received an offer from a foundation concerned with the legal issues of the aging. They had read about him in the newspaper. Landers took the job in order to advance the rights of the elderly.

According to Landers, "Most people have been brainwashed to believe that at a certain age they must turn up their toes and prepare to die. One day you might be in charge of a big organization. You're tremendously efficient and everybody kowtows to you. Everybody thinks you can do things. You retire, and the assumption is that the very next day you become a nonentity. You can't do anything. Society tends to place the elderly in a separate world. Society tends to feel that older people should just operate on the fringes, not in the center."

Today, Landers is a staff attorney at the Brookdale Center on Aging at Manhattan's Hunter College, lobbying for the elderly and taking on cases that involve retirement guidelines, Social Security, and Medicaid. He says of his job, "I feel I am able to do something. I feel a part of a larger society. Within my own sphere I have a certain amount of power."

And how about Detroit newlyweds Louis Gothelf and Reva Schwayder? He is 86, she 85. Both painters, they met and fell in love four years ago on a group painting tour of England. Each had been widowed in the early 1980s after more than 55 years of marriage. Of his first wife, Lou says, "After she died, I just sat in my apartment. When you're in your eighties and you sit alone day after day, it's so lonely. Oh, God, I felt alone."

Both assuming that romance would never touch them again, Reva and Lou were flabbergasted when they felt the pangs of "love at first sight" for each other. "This girl, she had a magnet," Lou proclaims. "As far as we were concerned," adds Reva, "there was no one else on that painting trip."

After experimenting with various live-in arrangements for several years, they finally decided to tie the knot last year, as much to quiet the neighbors as to legalize their affections. When asked how long they hope this new love will last, Lou philosophizes, "I live for today—you never know what's going to happen tomorrow. So I never, never buy green bananas."

Some lifestyle experimenters will use the opportunity of extended life to have a second chance at developing entirely different aspects of themselves. For instance, Bob Phelps, another of Goldman's "Latebloomers," worked as a conservative journalist for 40 years, cultivating the objectivity and detachment of a top metropolitan daily newspaperman, until he retired from the Boston *Globe* in his late fifties.

After retiring, Bob decided to become an actor. Not just a nights-and-weekends community-theater actor, but a pro— going to acting school, taking his résumé around to the agencies, getting small parts, doing commercials, dinner theater, summer stock—in short, making a career.

He explains:

> I had had absolutely no experience on the stage in any form. When I made the decision to retire, I remembered back as a young boy sitting on the porch of the house in which I was raised in Erie, Pennsylvania, thinking about what I was going to do after high school. At that point I had two choices in front of me: go to college, or go to the Pasadena Playhouse in California and become an actor. After due deliberation I decided that I was going to go to school. Now I thought, "Why don't I do the other thing now?"

Acting, for Phelps, is much more than a way to while away the hours of retirement. It's a complete personality change.

> As an editor, I held my feelings inside, and that was valuable. But in acting you have to follow the impulse. So to be an actor I've had to break down the training of over 40 years. And in doing that, I have learned that I hardly knew what an impulse was. I had submerged my freedom to do things, to say things, to raise an eyebrow. Now I'm trying to get that freedom back. I see things in people I never saw before, and I see them in myself. And

I wonder what would have happened in the rest of my life if I had not done this.

For Phelps, long life comes as a liberation: "Since we have only one life, why not live a number of its possibilities instead of just sticking to one?"

And then there's Sarah Conley. At the age of 104, she graduated from De Anza College in Cupertino, California. It took her ten years to complete her associate of arts degree in the college's Older Adult Services program, finishing her last courses while she was a resident of the Sunnyvale Convalescent Hospital. On graduation eve, as the other residents gathered around to celebrate her grand accomplishment, a local television reporter showed up to interview her.

"Are you proud to get a college degree?" he asked.

"Why, yes, wouldn't you be?" Conley answered with a smile.

It is not just older men and women who are taking on new challenges, careers, and relationships. Set free by the Age Wave, younger people are also breaking free of the traditional linear life pattern. Take Laurie Bagley, for instance. Laurie had worked her way through the University of California at Berkeley, obtaining an advanced degree in library science. After a decade in the field, including five years as my researcher on this book, she decided that it might be fun to try an entirely new career. After some reflection, she decided that she would like to become a veterinarian.

At 35, Laurie resigned from her position as director of research at Age Wave, Inc., and went back to the life of a student. "It will take me at least six years before I can hang out my shingle," she says. "I spent the first part of my twenties in the 'poor-student' mode. I had a wonderful decade as a successful professional, and now I'm going to spend my late thirties as a starving student again. But I feel that if I will probably live to be at least 80 and will in all likelihood be working most of my life, it's certainly not too late for me to embark on a new career and lifestyle."

Other people just want a break, and the cyclic lifestyle

easily accommodates this strategy. Jeri Flinn was director of public relations for Memorex, the Silicon Valley data-storage giant; her husband, John, had been a reporter for the San Francisco *Examiner* long enough to qualify for a sabbatical. When they had saved enough money, John took the sabbatical and combined it with accumulated vacation time, Jeri quit her job, and they headed off around the world. For a year they journeyed through the Pacific islands, Australia, Asia, and the Middle East. They celebrated John's thirtieth birthday in Katmandu, Jeri's in Edinburgh. When they returned, he got back the job guaranteed him by the Newspaper Guild contract, and she became the manager of financial public relations for Tandem Computer, another large Silicon Valley company. "We worked toward [the trip] for four years," Jeri says. "It was a fulfilling experience. I had never realized how much there was out there to see and experience."

BREAKING FREE

During my travels across America over the past 15 years, I have repeatedly been struck by how many stories I hear of men and women at all stages in their adult lives who have chosen to embark on a path or pursue a dream that was somewhat out of line with what most other people their age were doing, and even with what they themselves had been doing earlier in their lives. Although no one has yet conducted a study of the number of people who are shedding the confines of the linear life plan for the more diverse and flexible choices of the cyclic life plan, I am convinced that this is the wave of the future.

To date, medical science has done remarkably well at adding years to our lives. However, most of us haven't yet figured out the purpose or explored the opportunities of these extra years. And although a few years ago a 62-year-old Congressional freshman, an 83-year-old "wrinkled radical," a 67-year-old law-school student, a 35-year-old "retiree," a 104-year-old college graduate, or a 55-year-old aspiring actor may have seemed the odd circumstance, in the years to come such early lifestyle experimenters will come to be remembered as the true social pioneers—"elderheroes"—of the Age Wave.

Of course, not all of us will live in ways that are wildly at odds with the ways we have lived in the past. Most people will probably still choose to marry and start families in their twenties. For most, career peaks—at least for first careers—will still come between the ages of 30 and 50. Many people will continue to retire from work in their sixties.

What is different about the cyclic life plan is not that most people will choose to do things differently than they have in the past, but that they all have the option to do so.

The dead hand of tradition, the weight of regulations, and the power of our own expectations will no longer force us to do exactly what everyone else our age is doing. In a longer life, there are second and third chances—opportunities to go back and do some of the things we weren't able to do, for whatever reason, earlier in life.

In the next five chapters, we will take a more detailed look at the key elements of the new cyclic lifestyle. In chapters on "The New Leisure," "Wisdom in Action," "Reworking Work," "Love in the Second Half," and "Reinventing the Family," we will take a glimpse into the future to examine some of the unusual and colorful ways that the Age Wave will transform the core activities of our lives.

CHAPTER

5

The New Leisure

In picturing recreation for retired men and women in the years to come, we would be mistaken to picture a vast collection of shuffleboard and domino players.

As America's elders change, their definition of recreation will change with them, becoming progressively more active and adventurous, and physical as well as intellectual—in short, more intensely gratifying.

As long as man has struggled to survive, there has been endless work. We worked as soon as we could and for as long as we were able—from the simple chores of childhood, such as milking the cows, to the quiet tasks of old age, such as weaving and child care. It was work that fed the animals, built the homes, and harvested the wheat. Through every epoch of human history, work has dominated our waking hours. Since in almost every case men and women worked right up until they died, late-life ruminations about whether or not to keep

working (or about whether to take an adult-education program at the local community college or to spend the winter
in Miami) were nonissues.

THE DECLINING ROLE OF WORK

Due to the combined effect of the industrialization of work
and the elevation of life expectancy, the part that work plays
in our lives is diminishing significantly. According to the Metropolitan Life Insurance Company, in primitive times (that is,
before 4000 B.C.) people spent fully 33 percent of all the
hours of their lives working. In more recent traditional agrarian culture (4000 B.C.–1900 A.D.), the proportion of work
hours shrank, but only to 29 percent. By the year 1900, it had
shrunk, for American males, to 24 percent.

During the past century, the amount of time we spend
working has dropped by almost half. Today, the average
American works less than 14 percent of the hours that he or
she lives. During this period, the average work week dropped
from 70 hours to 37. For the first time, weekends and evenings became private property—time off. Vacations became
common, spread from one week to two or three, and became
paid time off. Holidays multiplied and attached themselves to
weekends. For a typical full-time worker, the year's 365 days
came to include 104 weekend days, 10 holidays, 10 sick days,
and 10 days of vacation, adding up to 135 days outside of
work. We now play, rest, and learn nearly as much as we
work. And for those who live long enough, work finally has
an end to it: most people now expect to experience not just
a few years, but decades of retirement. Leisure, once a rare
commodity, has become commonplace.

Our ancestors would certainly be perplexed to learn that
now that we have so much extra time, many people aren't
quite sure what to do with it. To date, we have responded to
the decreasing role of work and the increasing availability of
nonwork time by compressing the years we work more and
more into mid-life. We now commonly delay working until

after high school, college, or even graduate school. And although we are living longer and longer, we are increasingly retiring in our early sixties and even late fifties.

Much of the impetus for this widespread late-life leisure comes from three factors: increasing longevity, the pressure to replace older employees with younger workers, and an economic surplus capable of supporting pensions for a dependent elderly population.

According to a National Alliance for Business report entitled "Invest in Experience: New Directions for an Aging Work Force,"

> The last 25 years [have] seen a strong trend toward early retirement, resulting from various factors: the Social Security earnings test; the availability of pension and other retirement income; the ability of companies to deny accrual of pension after age 65; legislation that requires employers to provide private health care coverage for workers 65–69 if they provide such coverage for any workers; and the personal preferences and needs of the older workers themselves.

Perhaps the largest contributing influence in the current proliferation of retirement was the creation, during the past century, of old-age pensions. The first practical application of retirement pensions was created in 1875 by the American Express Company as a humanistic strategy to lessen the suffering experienced by displaced older workers as a result of industrialization. The idea of company-supported retirement pensions was slow to catch on, and by the mid-1920s only 4 million workers, mostly white-collar, were covered. By 1950 about 23 percent of all U.S. employees were covered by *private* pension plans. Today, 56 percent are covered.

The earliest *public* pension plans were initiated in Europe during the late 1880s. After decades of reluctance, the United States saw its first public old-age pension program when the state of Arizona enacted one in 1914. That plan was immediately declared unconstitutional by the U.S. Supreme Court, and it wasn't until the depression of the 1930s that the American people decided that the elderly needed government help to support themselves. In 1935, amid much controversy and widespread concern that it meant a turn toward communism, a national Social Security system was passed in Congress under President Franklin D. Roosevelt.

The effects of Social Security were direct and profound. The financial circumstances of the elderly improved, and they also began retiring from the work force in droves.

In 1870, about 80 percent of men 65 and older worked. By 1986 the figure had dropped to less than 15 percent, and the average age of retirement had plummeted to 60.6.

Today, as people live longer and retire earlier, we are experiencing something absolutely new to the human experience: a democratization of nonwork, a true mass leisure class.

The proportion of the years of his life that an average American male spent working declined from 67 percent in 1900 to 60 percent in 1970, and it is expected to drop to 56 percent in 1990, leaving a dramatic 44 percent of life to spend on other activities of choice.

As it was compressed, work time was also standardized into manageable chunks to accommodate lifestyle patterns in the modern industrial world. If you wanted to deviate—for instance, to work 22-hour weeks, or take a six-month sabbatical every five years, or alternate regularly between work and retirement—you would have found yourself with few options.

The reduction of the need to work by itself could have generated a wide variety of alternative lifestyles. For example, our national policymakers might have decided that work and nonwork time should be proportionately distributed throughout the life span. From this perspective, three-and-a-half-day work weeks, nine-month work years, or seven-year work decades might have become the standard. Within this kind of arrangement, work, leisure, and education would have been proportionately dispersed throughout the years of life instead of assigned to one period or another. Instead, we opted for a more rigid organization of work and retirement. Under this arrangement, after having worked nonstop for almost their entire adult lives, most people simply stop working and commit to a full-time life of leisure.

A New Concept of Leisure

We have struggled to create mass retirement, but we haven't completely figured out what to make of it.

Because the amount of nonworking time in our lives has expanded so dramatically, we are now challenged to develop a new point of view about leisure—the dominant national pastime for men and women over 60.

According to sociologist and futurist Max Kaplan, Ph.D., "Leisure functions fall into two primary categories: (1) those consistent with the Protestant work ethic, and (2) those associated with the classical interpretations of leisure."

To date, we have leaned toward the Protestant work-ethic orientation, in which leisure is defined as somewhat the opposite of work. In our hardworking culture, *work* has come to mean "that which is productive," while *leisure* means "that which is unproductive." The point of view that permeates our culture is that it is work, hard work, that has made it possible to survive and prosper as a nation.

In the Old Testament, we read of a God who labored for six days creating, ". . . and on the seventh day He rested." The Protestant work ethic sees leisure not as a worthwhile end unto itself but as something that serves the function of allowing the individual to rest "so that he or she could work harder and more efficiently," according to leisure expert Donald Mankin, Ph.D. Excessive leisure, from this perspective, is seen as lowly, a sign of laziness and ungodliness—"Idle hands are the devil's playground." Historically, too much leisure was branded "sloth" and was considered one of the seven deadly sins.

Although this traditional work-oriented point of view has served us satisfactorily over the years, it is now creating a perplexing problem, one most readily seen in the mixed messages we send to retirees. On the one hand, they're told to stop working and enjoy their leisure time; they've earned it. On the other hand, if they do this they are often cast aside and made to feel that they are unproductive and socially useless.

In contrast, the classical interpretation of leisure, having its roots in the traditions and philosophies of ancient Greece, viewed leisure not just as rest from work but as a desirable end in itself. In fact, in this view it was work that was lowly, a sign of slavery and nonproductivity. Leisure, on the other hand, represented a time for scholarship, contemplation, self-expression, and self-realization. The Greek word for leisure was *skhole,* from which we get words like *scholar* and *school.* Leisure was meant for fulfillment of one's higher potentialities. Work was only the necessary means of getting to leisure.

Work and leisure have always been the primary activities of adult life, and in our culture the balance has traditionally tipped heavily toward work. With the arrival of the Age Wave and the dissolution of the linear life plan, it is likely that America will move rapidly toward a new, "neoclassical" view of work and leisure.

In this new approach, instead of identifying leisure primarily as a means of promoting and enhancing work, we will increasingly view a more even blend of work and leisure as the optimal lifestyle arrangement. The true status symbol of the coming decades may not be a fancy car or an expensive home—as the young stockbroker challenged his greedy boss in the hit movie *Wall Street,* "How many boats can you ski behind?" Instead, the new American ideal will likely be a combination of successful work and free time, a sense of personal well-being, and the freedom and wisdom to fill one's life with productive, fulfilling, and expressive activities.

This redefinition will not only be expressed as a cultural dialogue but will also be felt as a shifting of gears within the psyche of everyone trying to figure out what to do with the later years of life. We have always come to think of these kinds of inner crises as being the province of young people making perplexing decisions regarding their entry into work and career. With extended life and the cyclic options it offers will come another round of self-reflective puzzling regarding whether to keep working, retire, or enter another career. The need for adult-centered vocational as well as avocational counseling will mushroom.

Many near-retirees are very concerned with the question of what to do next. Since we attach so much social value and worth to work and are, as a culture, uncertain of how we truly feel about leisure, people nearing retirement struggle with the fear of diminished purpose and activity. How telling that the suicide rate for American men is four times higher in retirement than in any other stage of life.

Regardless of retirement's uncertainties, the overwhelming majority of today's elders have chosen to answer the basic question, "To work or not to work?" by retiring and pursuing a life oriented toward leisure.

Today, more than 85 percent of America's men and women over 65 do not work.

In this and the following two chapters, we will explore many of the expanding patterns of a new approach to leisure in the expansion of four popular realms of adult activity: recreation, education, volunteerism, and work involving a more relaxed, flexible approach. In the synergy among these activities, we might find the seeds of a new vision of leisure, one that is appropriate to the personal and cultural needs of the Age Wave and the twenty-first century.

RECREATION

In the decades ahead, the range and scope of adult-focused recreational opportunities will blossom. Imagine all the new hobby-craft centers, mind-expanding amusement parks, longevity training centers, adult sports camps, sophisticated computer games, adventure and travel clubs, theme-focused retirement communities, worldwide time-share lifestyle complexes, and recreation counseling centers that will proliferate in the years ahead. These and other futuristic options will be the outgrowth of what today's retirees make of their newfound time off.

The first American leisure class of retirees has been responding to its respite from work in much the same joyous way that schoolchildren respond to the onset of summer vacation. After having toiled for decades without knowing whether they'd live long enough to enjoy some muchdeserved rest and recreation, most of today's retirees are taking the time to do the things that they particularly enjoyed doing, but didn't have enough time for, when they were younger—for example, sports, reading, socializing, and traveling.

If you were to fly over Levittown, Long Island, or any of the many other planned suburbs built to house the baby boom during the 1950s and 1960s, and then fly over Sun City, Arizona (or any of its siblings), the difference in the social focus between the two types of communities could not be more stark. From a height of a few thousand feet, you could see where the streets lead, where the roads radiate from, where the transportation is headed, and what the hub of community life is. In Levittown, life is oriented in two directions, toward school for the kids, and toward work for the parents. In Sun City, the focus is not on work and school but on the recreation center.

The enormous recreation centers at the heart of Sun City life, elaborate affairs nearly the size of shopping malls, with huge pools, golf courses, meeting halls, locker rooms, workout rooms, and auditoriums, are not empty symbols. Instead, they represent a great reality: recreation—travel, card playing, exercising, socializing, dancing, fishing, and so on—is central to the lives of many older Americans today.

As more Americans have been living longer and healthier lives, we have seen an explosion of country clubs, recreational vehicles, cruises, and senior centers—representing exactly the kinds of recreational activities that today's retirees enjoyed while they worked.

This growth shows up in one form of recreation after another:

- The YMCA and YWCA workout programs count over 1.2 million senior enrollees every year.
- There are currently more than 9,000 active senior centers and more than 1,300 AARP chapters across the country.
- The number of bowlers over 55 has climbed to more than a quarter million. The National Senior Leagues, founded in 1963, by 1987 counted 3,590 women's and mixed local leagues and 3,780 men's leagues, up by 200 from just a year before.
- Thousands of "mall-walker clubs" have sprung up, often cosponsored by the National Council on Aging and various local merchants and businesses. The malls open their doors early to allow seniors who want to exercise to take advantage of their enormous indoor spaces and controlled climates. A typical club is that at the Foothills Fashion Mall in Fort Collins, Colorado, which has 200 members; a program sponsored by Mother Frances Hospital in Tyler, Texas, boasts 500 daily mall-walkers.
- The nine-year-old, nonprofit National Senior Sports Association, which organizes trips to senior golf and tennis tournaments in such places as Scotland, Pebble Beach, Ocho Rios, Santo Domingo, and Hawaii, has grown to more than 12,000 members. Founder Lloyd Wright, a former communications expert for AARP, created this association so that groups of older men and women could fulfill their dreams of playing their favorite sports at some of the most extraordinary sites in the world, accompanied by others of similar age and interests, with the cost-effective tours led by a caring and supportive host.

- Sun City has more than 500 clubs, for everything from pinochle to yoga to motorcycles. The 600 members of the Sun City Players put on a play every month and a musical every year. There are dance bands—including Clancy Wolf's Music Majors, the Bob Hennis Combo, and Jed Lewis and the Sun City Swingers—plus a symphony orchestra and the Sun City Pom Poms cheerleader group.

- Not surprisingly, golf has become the quintessential retirement recreation for many. Currently, an estimated 3.2 million Americans over 60—nearly 10 percent—play golf, and many others are taking up the nonstrenuous game. In *Modern Maturity*, most ads for retirement communities show golf courses; all of the ads tout fitness and recreation facilities before almost anything else. From the air, Sun City and many other retirement communities look like islands of houses in seas of golf courses.

Fitness and the Active Lifestyle as a Way of Life

Living the active lifestyle has become a key ingredient in the world of retirement. Many older people, having the time and inclination to take care of their bodies, are getting serious about physical fitness. Everywhere you look these days, older people are flexing their muscles. Consider 72-year-old John Turner, muscular and bare-chested, holding a weight in each hand, staring out of the cover of Etta Clark's photo book, *Growing Old Is Not for Sissies.* Turner has been pumping iron for 25 years and looks it.

Or think about 85-year-old Eric De Reynier, who took up hang gliding at 72 and still sometimes stays up in the air for an hour at a time.

Imagine trying to keep up with 80-year-old Walt Stack, retired hod carrier and seaman, who describes a typical day this way: "Each day I ride my bike over to the Dolphins Club in San Francisco Bay. It takes about an hour. Then I take a little swim. Then I run across the Golden Gate Bridge to Sausalito and back, about 17 miles. Then [I take] another swim and bike back home. I do that five days a week. Saturdays and Sundays I take off and help clean up the house." Stack has even completed the grueling Iron Man Triathlon in Hawaii: a 2.4-mile ocean swim, followed by a 112-mile bike ride, followed by a 26-mile marathon. Although it took him more than 25 hours to complete the race, thousands came out to cheer him across the finish line.

Or go back a few years to visit Perris Valley, California, on December 15, 1985. On this particular day, the Perris Valley Sky Diving Society is sponsoring a rather complicated jump involving, among others, seven members of the Coors World-Champion Sky-Diving Team and the world's oldest father-son sky-diving team. The son is Jerry Smith, a businessman from Wichita. He's only 54; this is only his second jump. The father is H. T. Smith, known as "Smitty the Jumper," who was once described in *Sports Illustrated* as a "retired sign painter, ballroom-dancing teacher, and sex symbol." He's 87. This is his 216th jump.

Smitty sports flowing white locks, a long beard, and, today, a T-shirt with the legend SMITTY—WORLD'S OLDEST PARACHUTE JUMPER. What the T-shirt doesn't mention is that Smitty has already retired from parachute jumping. In fact, he's retired three times, the first time in 1937. He had been a professional daredevil jumper, but, at 39, he was getting too old for it. Besides, it was no occupation for a family man. When he turned 61 and the kids were out of the house, he took it up again. At 65, he retired again—too old. He took it up again at 73. At 76, he took a bad landing and shattered his left leg. He spent ten weeks in the hospital and retired for good—this time he was definitely and permanently too old. No question about it. Except . . . somebody came along and invented a tandem harness that allows two jumpers to use a single harness and parachute. It made the sport a lot safer for an old man, and he took it up again with gusto at the age of 86.

In 1984 Luella Tyra, 92, competed in five categories at the United States Swimming Nationals in Mission Viejo, California. Erna Neubauer, 73, teaches aerobics, swimming, and water exercise at a San Francisco senior center. Ada Thomas, who took up running at 65, ran her first marathon at 68 and is still competing in marathons at 72. Helen Zechmeister, at 84 the owner of eight national age-group power-lifting records, once competed in the men's 35-and-over category because no other women had come to compete. She beat the men.

The stories of people like these are remarkable in a way, but they are not unusual. There are, in fact, millions of people in their seventh, eighth, and even ninth decades who carry on with great vigor, agility, intensity, and physical courage.

More than 50,000 people participated in regional "Senior Olympics" in 50 cities across the country in 1987.

Here's Bob Richards, the man on the Wheaties box when we were kids, still competing in field events, his chest still the size of a boxcar. Here's muscular Henry Soudieres, a retired mailman from New York City, winning in the 65-and-over age bracket by power lifting a combined 870 pounds. Here is Marion Higgins, at 88 still competing in the swimming events.

Every sport, no matter how vigorous, is sprouting clubs for older athletes. For instance, Lloyd Lambert, 87, has been skiing since 1915. He found that most older people had to give up the sport not because they couldn't do it, but because they couldn't afford the rapidly rising cost of lift tickets on their fixed incomes. "I contacted some resorts about discounts," he says, "and they said we could ski for free. It grew from there. Now we ski all over the world. People like to see the old bags coming down the hill."

At last count, Lambert's 70+ Ski Club had 3,286 members, including one 97-year-old from Buffalo. "I have a waiting list now," Lambert says. "There are about 20 people on the list who will be eligible this year when they turn 70. Many of the new members are single women. It's become kind of a singles scene. We have a trip to Switzerland in March that's sold out. I already have 60 requests for spots on our trip to Argentina in August."

A typical member, 72-year-old John Gebhardt, skis two or three times a week all winter and enters two races each season. "I usually go up with a group of about six," he says. "I'm the youngest. I just got a letter from a fellow who wants to stay at our place while he goes skiing, but I'm not sure he'll make it. He's 92, and they won't let him on the plane without a doctor's certificate! One fellow I know didn't learn to ski until he was 70. His son recently told me, 'The old man's turned into a ski bum.' I know people skiing with metal hips and pacemakers. In Brody, Massachusetts, where we used to go, the club members would ski all morning at that high altitude. After lunch the band would start up, and you should see the dancing! When it gets dark everyone comes out. We ski all day and dance all night."

If you're too young for the 70+ Ski Club, you can join the Wild Bunch, for skiers over 60, or the Over-the-Hill Gang. As elder skier Paul Helm says, "Don't forget our motto: 'Once you're over the hill, you pick up speed.'"

Retired recreation seekers are even showing up in places traditionally geared to their grandchildren.

One hot afternoon I was on a long day's hike with friends up a rough uphill trail into California's Ventana Wilderness. We were 15 miles from the nearest road. As I broke through the brush onto a ridge from which I could finally see the Pacific, thousands of feet below and 20 miles away, I thought I was hallucinating. There stood a man in his sixties, offering me a daiquiri. In a proper daiquiri glass. Cooled with proper ice cubes. He had a pitcher full of daiquiris in the other hand. Behind him was a picnic table, covered with a linen table cloth, linen napkins in napkin rings, silverware, wine bottles, wine glasses, stoneware plates, and a stoneware soup tureen. As I sipped the daiquiri, he explained, in response to my questions, that he and his three friends—all over 60—once a year carried 80-pound packs all the way up that trail from the

Pacific just to have this one magnificent meal with this magnificent view, "in," he said, "this magnificent company." All four wore T-shirts with the bold legend THE OLD GUYS.

Another time, I was invited to Alaska to speak at the governor's conference on aging, held at a beautiful convention center in Denali National Park near Mount McKinley. That evening, my wife and I saw a notice for a midnight-sun white-water rafting expedition on the swift Susitna River nearby. It would run until 1 A.M., far past our bedtime. We were too bushed even to consider it. But the river ran right under our window. At 1 A.M., we were awakened by the whooping and hollering of the rafters clambering ashore. There they were in the dusk of Alaska's wee hours—soaked to the skin, bursting with adrenaline, laughing, having the time of their lives. When we stepped outside our room to catch a glimpse of the young athletes who had the nerve and the energy to attempt such a challenging trip, we were shocked to find that the rafters weren't kids at all—they were the "senior citizens" I had addressed earlier that day.

Travel to Faraway Places

The business of travel, more than many fields, will go through enormous changes as the population ages.

Leisure travel is already a booming enterprise, accounting for $181.1 billion a year, according to the *Wall Street Journal*. And leisure is one sector of the American economy that responds to the marketplace with remarkable plasticity. So it is not surprising that these industries, more quickly than most, have already begun to reflect the changing shape of the American population and the value changes that come with it.

Older Americans are major customers both for luxury travel and for budget excursions. They are the main consumers of round-the-world luxury cruises and other pricey tours. At the same time, low-cost motor-coach tour operators rely on the older market as a mainstay of their business. Older Americans buy nearly a third of all bus charter trips in the country.

Because they have the flexibility to schedule their time as they wish, older travelers are able to plan vacations during off-peak periods. Increasingly, they are being wooed by special off-season discounts and other promotions aimed at filling seats on buses and planes and rooms in hotels that would otherwise stay empty. All Disney installations have off-peak senior discounts. TWA, Eastern, American, and United airlines all have programs offering seniors a pass for unlimited domestic travel (except on weekends and holidays) for a flat fee.

All major bus lines offer discounts for seniors, and car-rental agencies are also cutting prices for older customers. In fact, the off-peak discount for older travelers has become the industry standard. And many tourist destinations are going all out for the older traveler. For example, the state of Tennessee has a yearly statewide promotion known as "Senior Class" during the usually slow month of September. More than 500 hotels, restaurants, sightseeing attractions, and merchants organize special events for older visitors and offer discounts. Greyhound Bus Lines and Ozark Airlines cooperate by offering reduced fares. In 1986 the state chalked up nearly 21,000 requests for the senior-citizen discount book. Other state and city tourism departments, inspired by Tennessee's example, have begun similar promotions. Williamsburg, the restored colonial town in Virginia, mails out 30,000 brochures a year for its September "Senior Time." The federal government now offers "Golden Age Passports" to all Americans over 62 for free entry to all national parks and recreation areas.

But there is much, much more that travel companies could be doing to draw the older traveler in. Consider the car-rental business, for instance. Most transportation companies think that a cheaper price is the only thing that counts. While this may be true for the younger market, it's not so when you're targeting the older renter. For older men and women, dragging their bags to a rental van, traveling from the airport to the rental-car agency, and dragging the bags to the car is a lot of work—maybe enough to make them not want to rent the car. Why not create a "premier" rental club?

Members would get special tags for their bags, which would be picked up by a representative from the car-rental agency when they reached the airport. The older travelers could go get a cup of coffee and refresh themselves—fifteen minutes later the car would be in a special holding area, with the bags in the trunk and everything ready to go. They'd be renting the same car, but the added convenience would create an entirely different traveling "experience."

Today, 80 percent of the *luxury* travel in America is purchased by people over 55. For them convenience and access, not cost, may be the main issue.

Other variations on the traditional themes of travel are beginning to pop up with regularity. For those seniors who would like to travel but are uncomfortable doing so alone, Nightingale Travel Attendants provides screened, trained travel companions who can watch out for medical needs, help with bags, and run interference with officials at airlines and customs.

In the future, a significant number of older travelers will be looking for travel that is more individualized, intimate, unusual, stimulating, informative, and challenging. Already, the American Youth Hostels are finding that an increasing number of their guests, who sleep dormitory style and help make the meals, are not youths at all but seniors.

In the sixties, free-spirited young travelers began showing up everywhere from Nepal to the jungles of the Yucatán, toting backpacks. By the mid- and late seventies, a new business had crystallized: adventure travel. For the right fee, a guide would take you climbing in the Andes, white-water rafting down the Rogue, or fishing off the Arctic ice pack.

It was only a matter of time before it occurred to forward-thinking travel planners that with a few minor adjustments, such adventures could be made available to the senior market, which had the most money and time for travel. As the *Wall Street Journal* quoted one travel expert: "Many older customers have done the 'if-it's-Tuesday-it-must-be-Belgium' tour and are now seeking less conventional tours."

Mountain Travel of Albany, California, one of the oldest adventure-travel agencies in the nation, estimates that at least 30 percent of its clients are 55 or over, while some are in their seventies and even eighties. One 68-year-old group leader recently took a group through the mountain passes of Tibet by Jeep. One couple in their seventies just returned from their fifth trip to the base camp at Everest.

Another company, Society Expeditions, offers trips to such off-the-beaten-track destinations as Antarctica, the Amazon, Krakatoa, the Galápagos Islands, and Tibet. The company estimates that more than half of its clients are over 50 because, according to a company representative, "the cost and the length of our itineraries make it necessary to have both the time and the money." In fact, the company reports that it has clients over 80 years old on almost all of its trips. Customers are typically "curious, active, well-traveled people who have done everything and are looking for more."

As leisure becomes more fully integrated into our lives, we will be seeing a wave of travelers who are more interested in exotic travel and in cultural information, and who are more willing to trek, to backpack, to get wet—in short, to do whatever is necessary to have that exotic experience.

"Rides" of the Mind

Recreation in the future will, of course, include theme and amusement parks. But will they be the same as the amusement parks we loved and enjoyed when we were young? This question was answered for me in an unusual way this past year.

Several times each year, Age Wave, Inc., holds a three-day planning retreat for the board of directors. My board members are a very bright, imaginative, and hardworking group whose ages range from the mid-thirties to the mid-sixties. We held our last retreat in a beautiful conference setting on the dunes near Santa Cruz, California. One evening after dinner, one of the people said, "Isn't there an amusement park not far from here, and wouldn't it be fun to go play on the rides?" Everyone thought this was a great idea, so we stopped working, gathered up our spouses, and charged off for an evening of recreation.

The amusement park in Santa Cruz is a glorious collection of old carnival booths, roller coasters, and twisting, turning rides, all set along the beachfront boardwalk. Our group of ten immediately started playing at the carnival booths trying to knock bottles down with softballs, toss rings around candles, and shoot the clown's nose. We were all laughing and having a terrific time.

After the booths, we found ourselves behind a long line at the entrance to a fantastic roller coaster. This was, I thought, a ride that was going to separate the men from the boys. My wife and I got in line, where we were quickly joined by other brave members of my team. We were strapped in our seats in the small cars, and before we knew what had hit us, the crazy ride began. Up, down, charging wildly left and right, dashing through pitch-black tunnels, then emerging and being thrown over the heads of the observers below, we screamingly endured the breathtaking ride. During this hectic, stomach-turning experience, I was so involved in keeping my wits that it never occurred to me to turn around to see which of our party had come along and which had stayed behind.

When we stumbled off the ride, heads spinning, I noticed that the older half of my board members and their spouses had not taken the ride and were waiting below for us. I asked several of my over-45 board members why they hadn't joined us. Were they frightened of the roller coaster? No, they had always loved the thrill of amusement-park rides like this one, but they feared the risk of having a heart attack on the ride.

It struck me that so much of what we have designed as "amusing" rides are geared primarily to challenging the body's limits of comfort. By having our bodies violently shaken, rattled, and tossed around, we have fun. For people with concerns about vascular trauma, osteoporosis, or inner-ear imbalance, these rides are completely off-limits. Perhaps older people would enjoy an amusement park that deemphasized "rides of the body" and offered, instead, equally exciting "rides of the mind."

The first adult theme parks, geared to an older, more educated audience have already begun to emerge.

The prototypes of the new parks are several: recent world's fairs in Knoxville and Vancouver, which were essentially enormous temporary educational institutions; the trend toward cruises centered around a strong educational element; such hugely successful new hands-on informational experiences as the Smithsonian's Air and Space Museum; the original "science rides" at Disneyland; and the high-tech information onslaught of Walt Disney's popular Epcot Center.

Epcot Center, in fact, twinned as it is with Disney World, provides an interesting test of generational differences: the median age of the people coming through the turnstile at the center is 35, seven years higher than the median at Disney World. On many days, the feeling is more one of being at an AARP convention than at a multigenerational theme park. And the rides reflect the older visitors, with glimpses of foreign architecture, tastes of international cuisine, demonstrations of hydroponic gardening and controlled fish farming, views of undersea vegetation, and the experience of holographic cinema.

My favorite intellectual amusement park, the Exploratorium, is located at the Palace of Fine Arts in San Francisco. Housed in this environment are thousands of scientific experiments you can interact with. Paint a picture with electricity, try to see through optical illusions, experience a simulation of weightlessness, compose a song on primitive instruments, hear yourself speak backwards, or test your wits against a computer gameplayer. Any self-respecting fan of the 1950s' Mr. Wizard would give a week's salary to have a weekend to play in the Exploratorium.

Play and Recreation— Morning, Noon, and Night

Some older men and women are so taken by recreation that they choose to build their entire lives around it. For them, recreation-centered retirement communities are a dream come true. Here, they have the chance to play, learn, and socialize every day—morning, noon, and night.

The growth of retirement communities is unmistakable. Before World War II, age-segregated "retirement villages" didn't exist. By 1984 some 2,300 had been built, the majority of them in California, Arizona, and Florida. Today, more than a million people live in such complexes.

Sun City and Sun City West, near Phoenix, together comprise one of the oldest (1960) and largest (about 75,000 people) experiments in recreation-focused retirement living. During my years of professional involvement there, I have often been struck by the gap between the popular image of such places and the reality. At the mention of Leisure World, Sun City, and other retirement communities, people often make comments about the creak of rocking chairs and the click of canes, about wheelchair traffic jams and lost dentures. The image is of a vast convalescent home in the desert, of mental vacancy and physical decrepitude.

The reality is that in Sun City it's hard to find time to talk to people; they're too active and busy. I've seen college campuses where the young students appear more worn out and less active than the residents of these adult communities.

At one lapidary center, monitor Herb Molenveld, 77,

from Detroit, said over the sound of the grinding wheels and sanding belts, "Sometimes I think I'm more active here than when I was working at General Motors." Lifelong dance instructor Rose Lorenz, now 85, teaches nine aerobic exercise classes a week, and every one of them is packed. She says, "I thank God every morning that I live in Sun City. This is the life I always dreamed of living. It is absolutely perfect."

Several major factors bring people to a place like Sun City:

A safe, controlled environment. Sun City is secure. Its crime rate is one of the lowest in the nation. Shrubbery is kept low, fences between yards are few, and neighbors are vigilant. A young person walking alone will be visited rather quickly by a "posse" squad car and will be cordially asked his business and destination. An older person can take a walk at night without fear of being mugged.

More than that, a resident may stroll the streets without fear of surprise, of unpleasantness, of unsightliness. The streets are kept uncommonly clean. The sidewalks are swept, the fallen branches are picked up, and even the fruit is picked from the trees by a volunteer group called "the Prides." Sun City is a leisure oasis that exists without demonstrations, beggars, vandals, vagrants, public drunks, or visible poor people.

Friends, and plenty of activities to share with them. As one resident points out, "I don't know where I could go that I could get so involved in the community." It's easy to make friends here. A woman in her late eighties who doesn't drive says, "I never lack for people to take me places. We could have a party in five minutes."

Not only does Sun City have every imaginable facility, but it also has partners and participants for every activity. There are hundreds of clubs, dances, bands, lectures, concerts, plays, movies, workshops, and volunteer groups. There are libraries, swimming pools, golf courses, recreation centers, jogging tracks, woodworking shops, sculpture studios, lapidary workshops, pool halls, weight-lifting rooms, and horseshoe courts.

And there are always other people available to join you. If you need a foursome for bridge or golf, an audience for a poetry reading, a quorum for a club, a group to go jogging, you will have no trouble finding it. One new resident in his mid-sixties said, "I have a pretty strong tennis game, and I play a lot. When I bought a house here, I thought that I would probably be going in to the clubs in Phoenix to find partners who were good enough. I've been here three months, and I haven't had to leave yet. Everything and everyone I need to have a great time is right here."

A supportive atmosphere. It never snows in Sun City. Traffic moves gently and rarely stacks up. No one is in a hurry, and many of the stresses and strains common among young working people are conspicuously absent. Every service is nearby. The houses are designed for low maintenance. Most of the yards sport cactus gardens instead of lawns. A lot of people drive golf carts instead of cars, which contributes to the mood of a year-round vacation setting.

In addition, many couples are drawn to Sun City and other similar retirement communities because of their concern for the future. In particular, some feel that if one of them should pass away, at least the surviving spouse will be assured of a complete social and support network. They may not have any other close family. According to Sun City resident James Nordstrom, 73,

> I love my wife more than anything else in my life. I always have. I've read the statistics; I know that I'll probably die before she does. When that happens, I intend to leave this life knowing that during her remaining years she will never feel isolated and helpless and without supportive and available friends. The way I figure, if she was stuck all alone in an apartment in the city or a house in the suburbs, she'd never have the opportunity she has

here to take a walk, go to the movies, or attend a lecture
with groups of like-minded people. Buying a home in
this community was as much a commitment to my wife's
safety and security in the years ahead as it was an investment in our pleasure now.

Recently, recreation-oriented retirement housing has
begun to blossom in several new directions. One approach is
to create specialized "lifestyle towns," each appealing to a
specific market niche. For instance:

- Worman's Mill, near Frederick, Maryland, is modeling its
  entire community along the lines of an old-style farming
  village, where residents can raise their own animals or
  convert their ground floors, which face the town square,
  into shops.
- Heritage Village, a former convent on 32 acres of land in
  Grand Rapids, Michigan, is to be a "living museum"
  focusing on the history and culture of Michigan and
  staffed by 350 elder residents.
- Williams Hill, in Providence, Rhode Island, is planning to
  reproduce a complete New England village of the mid-
  eighteenth century.
- Byron Park, a 186-unit "congregate living" house (in
  which residents have separate quarters but share dining
  facilities and other amenities) in Walnut Creek, California, is planning to reproduce an eighteenth-century
  English country inn, down to such details as a horseshoe-
  shaped courtyard with a pen for peacocks.

According to George Wolfson of the Byron Group of
Menlo Park, California, which came up with the idea for
Byron Park, "Developments like this reflect the lifestyles that
some of today's older people relate [with] simpler and safer
times." David Wolfe, who helped plan all of the above developments and who is former president of the National Association of Senior Living Industries, says, "These projects attempt

to get away from the prevailing messages given older people by most retirement centers—a message aimed at their vulnerabilities and limitations. They focus, instead, on traditional themes and basic values. And today's seniors like that."

Retirement Living Plus
24-Hour Health Care = Lifecare

Many older people worry about what would happen to them if they fell seriously ill, or if they died, what would happen to their spouses. Today, the most common option is temporary respite in one of America's 23,000 skilled nursing facilities. But many older men and women abhor the thought of having to move into a nursing home, however temporary the arrangement. And in any case, there are nowhere near enough available nursing-home beds in America to meet the needs of our aging population. In fact, it's estimated that between now and the year 2000, a new, 220-bed nursing home would have to be opened every day just to keep up with the demand.

Churches, universities, and private companies have moved quickly in recent years to provide an innovative type of housing that meets these fears directly. Such housing is marketed under a variety of names, including continuing-care retirement center (CRC), lifetime care, and—the most common—lifecare. Lifecare developments typically provide an array of individual homes and apartments, group dining, and a broad spectrum of recreation activities, as well as fully staffed medical and long-term care facilities, all on one campus.

With full-service lifecare, everything from recreation to bypass surgery is paid for in one package, guaranteed. New residents usually pay an entrance fee to purchase the home or apartment they'll be living in, plus a monthly maintenance charge that includes everything from complimentary transportation around town to regular maid service, home maintenance and repair, recreation, 24-hour security, and intensive care or a nursing home, if needed. If a wife finds that it has gotten too difficult for her to care for her failing husband, she can ask for help—at no additional charge. Staff and volunteers are available to help people get up and dress and do other tasks that have become difficult.

The entrance fees at Royal Oaks in Sun City, Arizona, are in the range of $40,000–$120,000, plus an average monthly maintenance fee of around $800; at the more luxurious Villa Marin in San Rafael, California, entrance fees range from $150,000 to $500,000, with monthly dues of $734–$1,934. Most developers offer a 90 or 100 percent refund on the entrance/purchase fees if a resident decides to move out.

By having housing, lifestyle, and medical services merged in this fashion, residents never have to worry about outliving their means or seeing their life savings consumed by a catastrophic illness or a stay in a convalescent home.

So far, lifecare developments have tended to attract a population that is more educated than average, somewhat better off financially, less connected to family and children, and somewhat older and more concerned about serious illness than are the more typical retirement-community residents. The idea is being very well received, and the number of lifecare facilities is rising rapidly. In 1979, there were only about 100 lifecare centers in America; by 1988, there were more than 800. Across the country, most lifecare residences report high occupancy rates and long waiting lists. Developers such as the Marriott Corporation and the Forum Development Group are scrambling to build fast enough to meet the growing marketplace needs.

According to Tom Curren, vice-president of strategic development for the Marriott Corporation,

> When we step back and look at the demographics of the age wave, we can see that lifecare and elder housing represent growing markets. We're very excited by our activities in the lifecare arena. There are opportunities for a variety of products and different price levels.

A company that comes from a background of hospitality, such as Marriott, has a lot to offer America's older men and women. I believe, for instance, that 30 percent of the people in nursing homes would rather be living in comfortable and attractive assisted-living situations, which would cost them much less. We hope to meet this need, and we expect that our new lifecare division will bring Marriott a billion dollars per year in sales by the mid-1990s—and I expect double-digit growth for several decades after that.

According to Jim Sherman, a partner in Laventhol & Horwath, an accounting and consulting firm that specializes in the lifecare industry, "Lifecare will experience an explosion in the next few years. We estimate that there is a nationwide market for about 150 new projects per year for the next 15 years." Sherman sees most of the growth coming in developments aimed at the average pocketbook. "In the past, we have addressed the top 15 percent and the bottom 15 percent. But that's not where the largest market is. Most of the new growth will come from the middle class."

Over the next decade, the retirement housing market, now worth $3 billion per year, is expected to experience phenomenal growth, rising to more than $35 billion per year.

But Sun City, Villa Marin, and their siblings are clearly not for everybody, and many social observers are disturbed by the trend toward age segregation that the growth of such communities represents. For all that such places have flourished, only 4 percent of Americans over 60 live in "retirement villages" of any sort. Although there are elements of this kind of living arrangement—such as the apparent isolation from and absence of other levels of society, namely young people and minorities—that are controversial and disturbing, the advantages are worth noting.

Stephen Golant of the University of Florida has studied the living situations of older Americans for 15 years. In a paper published in the journal *Aging,* titled "In Defense of Age-Segregated Housing," Golant articulates the many benefits of living in an "adults only" retirement community:

> Living in an age-segregated setting gives elderly people the option of reducing their involvement with a society that seems overly preoccupied with the desirability of youth, the rewards of employment, and the joys of child-raising—a society that offers pitifully few clear guidelines as to how individuals are expected to conduct their lives when they retire. Old people in age-segregated settings can literally create their own subcultures, surrounding themselves with other elderly people who value their worth, understand their contributions, similarly interpret the meanings of their lives and environment, and offer satisfying role models. . . . It is easy to demonstrate the many positive social, economic, and psychological consequences of planned residential concentrations of the elderly.

Merging Retirement Housing with Travel: Mobile Towns

Another fascinating manifestation of an individualized approach to recreation-oriented retirement living is a curious blend of two enjoyable pastimes: retirement living and travel.

When you cross housing with travel, what you get is a Winnebago or an Airstream trailer: a "mobile" home. According to a recent census, some 800,000 older households were set up in mobile homes. In 1984, 45 percent of all manufactured homes were owned by people over 50, up 4 percent from just two years before.

And when you put enough of these moving residences together, you get a peculiarly American phenomenon, the mobile town.

One such "town," near the Salton Sea in California's Imperial County, is called simply "the slabs," for the stretch of desert in which it's located. Here, thousands of "snowbirds," mostly seniors from small towns in the north, find a sense of community every winter. Every evening a snowbird known as "Good Sam" clicks on a CB radio and calls roll. If anyone fails to answer, someone goes out to check on that person.

There are scores of these movable towns in California and Arizona, through the wide reaches of the desert and up the banks of the Colorado. There is no "snowbird central," no data bank on snowbirds, no registration book. That's not the nature of the movable town. Imperial County's Sheriff Oren Fox, who counts snowbirds from the air, estimates that the mobile population of his county reaches 15,000 in the winter, fully 3,000 of them out on the federal land in the "slabs." He guesses that most of the snowbirds are between 60 and 75 years old. Yuma, Arizona, in summer a town of some 45,000, is home in winter to as many as 25,000 more. The city organizes special events, auctions, and dances for the snowbirds. In Yuma, Imperial County, and elsewhere, entrepreneurs have seen opportunities in the snowbird invasion, building golf courses and RV parks and providing needed services.

Nationally, there may be as many as several hundred thousand people living on the road.

RETIREMENT LIVING:
A GLIMPSE INTO THE FUTURE

Tomorrow's seniors might prefer a different spectrum of offerings beyond lifecare, old-fashioned villages, and mobile towns. To anticipate the future needs of retirement living, the best place to look is in the lifestyle preferences of today's middle-aged men and women. According to Kevin

McCarthy of the Rand Corporation: "If you want to know where the elderly will be moving by the year 2000, it's a mistake to focus on the elderly now. It's the nonelderly you want to watch."

Studies conducted by the Center for Social Research in Aging and the Rand Corporation, supported by the National Institute on Aging, show that retirees in middle and late adulthood increasingly flock to the exact places and do the exact kinds of things they enjoyed on vacation during their working years. According to retirement-housing expert Charles Longino, "Take any place that you develop a substantial vacation market or tourist industry today, give it a 20-year lag, and you'll have retirement migration. People want to go where they had fun while they were working." This is the reason why, in the absence of perfect Sun Belt weather, areas such as Ashland, Oregon; Green Bay and Rice Lake, Wisconsin; the Ozarks; Alpena and Huron counties in Michigan; Cape Cod; and the New Jersey shoreline—places today's retirees enjoyed when they were younger—have become booming retirement regions.

The wise residential real-estate developer of tomorrow will keep a close watch on the desirable vacation spots and preferred hobbies, sports, and social activities of today.

If there is truth to these lessons, tomorrow's retirement communities might include the following:

- An "Olympic village" for older men and women who love sports and athletics. This would be similar to a year-round "Club Med," complete with indoor and outdoor swimming pools, running tracks, tennis, racquetball and basketball courts, and a cadre of available sports coaches. Residents could thus satisfy their desire for nonstop sports amid a community of like-minded enthusiasts.

- A "longevity complex," built around a physiology-and-fitness research institute, where all the restaurants would serve only health food, every apartment would come equipped with the latest high-tech exercise equipment, and every resident would receive regular massages, facials, acupuncture, and wellness counseling from his or her own medically trained "longevity coach."

- "Mandala village," a residential, Esalen-type community geared to spiritual self-development. This setting might offer meditation rooms, Zen gardens, regular sensitivity-training sessions, and affiliation with a local graduate program in psychology so that residents could earn academic credits for the interests they are pursuing. On this campus, instead of a resident golf pro there might be an assortment of religious leaders, psychotherapists, and philosophers.

- "Eden village," a horticultural-oriented retirement community with acres of flower and vegetable gardens. Each resident would receive ongoing instruction in gardening and would be given ample land and supplies with which to experiment.

- "Tron Center," a high-tech wonderland complete with interactive home-video consoles, computer workstations in every neighborhood, "smart" homes, air-suspended underground-transportation tubes, and holographic community theaters.

- "Lifestyles Unlimited," a time-share style, roving-retirement program. Instead of committing to spending the rest of your life in one place, you could spend two years at Eden village, then a year at the Longevity complex, and then move to the Olympic village the following year.

We will explore a variety of other innovative 50+ living arrangements in the following chapter, "Wisdom in Action," and in chapter 9, "Reinventing the Family."

When you think of retirement housing in your future, count on the fact that all of the lifestyle, social, and design preferences of your generation will be translated into the retirement communities of tomorrow.

With the coming of the Age Wave we are challenged to create a new blend of life's various activities and involvements. Today, more and more adult Americans are discarding a traditional, work-centered way of life and are pursuing a more well-balanced lifestyle. As we have seen here, key to this shift is an increased emphasis on leisure not just as a means of rest and occasional play, but as an opportunity for lifelong learning, continued personal growth, and the expansion of oneself through service to others.

CHAPTER

6

Wisdom in Action

Although a later life filled with play and recreation is the dream of many a current worker, for many retirees, recreation alone may not be enough to make a life. Instead, reflecting the approach to leisure described in the previous chapter, many older men and women wish to spend their later years learning, growing, and doing things for others. As a result, networks of lifelong education and volunteer services are blossoming throughout America.

When Harry Gabel was in his mid-sixties, he had open-heart surgery, and his doctors told him he could never work again. Gabel spent a lot of time looking out the window of his Manhattan apartment, until suddenly it struck him that what he was looking at was Fordham University, four blocks away. Gabel had never had more than a junior-high-school education. He had spent his life working in a factory in the garment district, making women's clothes, scrimping and saving to put his kids through college and graduate school. Now, he says, "I wanted to keep up to their level."

So Gabel signed up at Fordham for a program called "College at 60," in which each semester more than 200 people (the oldest of whom to date has been 94) take part in regular, credit-bearing academic seminars with their peers. "At first," says Gabel, "going back to school was very difficult. Every day I wanted to quit. Not having even gone to high school, there was a big void. But it worked out. I graduated cum laude." In fact, Gabel had earned a bachelor's degree by his third year, a master's by his fifth, and a doctorate by his seventh. He did his dissertation on the hospice movement, and has since done work for the New York Department of Aging.

Harry Gabel is unusual in his persistence, and in his interest in the traditional academic environment. But his love of learning is shared by millions of older adults in this country and around the world.

In the future, education will not be just a preparation for the practical aspects of life or for job advancement but will be used to make life richer, especially in the second half. Lifted by the coming Age Wave, a new leisure lifestyle focused on a flexible balance of recreation, play, and continued intellectual growth and learning will emerge.

Many of today's older Americans—and many more of tomorrow's—will treat the search for new awareness, knowledge, and insights as a way of life. Studies have shown that the more educated a person is, the more likely it is that he or she will seek further education. The age groups that follow today's elders have progressively higher and higher levels of education. Continuing that education will become a major part of the lifestyle of tomorrow's older Americans.

BACK TO SCHOOL

Harry Gabel's program at Fordham is only one of many college programs nationwide that are responding to this quest for lifelong learning. If we want to search the horizon for the pioneering men and women pursuing the new leisure, we need look no farther than the local college campus. Take, for example, California's huge state college and university system, the largest such system in the nation. According to traditional expectations, college freshmen are 17 or 18 years old. However, the average age of all freshmen at California community colleges is not 17 but 22, and the average age of the part-time freshmen is 31. At Cal State Dominguez Hills, the average age of all seniors is 29; at Cal State Bakersfield, the graduate students average 37 years old. City University of New York today counts more than 2,000 over-65 students, double the number in 1980.

Harvard's Institute for Learning in Retirement has older Americans both as professors and as students. Each term, some 400 students, some as old as 95, pay the $140 fee to go to Harvard (a good deal, considering the $10,000+ typical yearly tuition paid by Harvard undergraduate and graduate students).

The University of North Carolina is in the process of opening what it considers to be the nation's most comprehensive higher-education program aimed at older Americans. The plans call for, among other things, a health-promotion program, workshops on elderly issues, and a council of older experts to provide consulting for small businesses.

At Eckerd College's Academy of Senior Professionals in St. Petersburg, Florida, more than 120 retirees serve as advisors, career counselors, and mentors to the 1,200 young liberal-arts students there. Eventually, Eckerd plans to house the retired professionals right on campus, creating a complete living/learning/teaching community.

Nationwide, more than a thousand colleges now actively encourage people over 65 to take classes for credit, and more than 120 schools have adopted special programs just for the older learner.

Returning to school at 30, 53, or 67 for more education is no longer an oddity but a common practice.

All of this is part of a nationwide trend toward older students. In 1970, only 22 percent of the college population was over 25; by 1985, the proportion was over 45 percent. Clearly, the old expectations no longer hold. One of the reasons for the keen interest of colleges in the older student is, of course, that the number of available younger students is shrinking. Between 1980 and 1990, as the baby boomers grow older, there will be a greater than 20 percent decline in the number of 18-to-25-year-old students. In the years to come, many of the services, materials, and skills of education will be revamped to focus on the needs, styles, and preferences of an increasingly older student population.

- College-level instructors will need to be retrained in how to be most effective with older learners, who are motivated more by group interaction and peer learning than by the traditional, authoritarian teacher/student model.
- Learning materials will need to be modified to match the skills and experiences of adult students. In addition, many older men and women would prefer to learn from nonwritten instructional materials, such as cassettes and videotapes.
- Course scheduling will need to conform to the lifestyles of older men and women, who often have children, jobs, and other commitments to balance. The tendency will be toward seminar formats in evening and weekend programs, conveniently located (for example, at the worksite or local community center).
- Facilities will need to be designed to meet the physical-comfort needs of older students.

CLASSROOMS WITHOUT WALLS

An increasing amount of this lifelong learning is taking place outside the traditional academic environment. As the Age Wave gains momentum, a vast array of special programs aimed at older citizens is springing up not only at colleges but also at worksites, churches and synagogues, Y's, people's homes, community centers, and adult-education centers. This makes good sense. When we're young, not yet working, and still living in our parents' homes, we gather in schools. It's a good idea for early education to occur in this dedicated and isolated environment. But when we're older, there is a great deal more diversity in the ways we spend our time. In response, the form and function of education will need to conform to the more adult lifestyle.

A wonderful example of this trend is being pioneered by Elderhostel, a self-supporting, nonprofit program based in Boston that has been combining leisure, learning, and travel for older Americans since 1975. Every year thousands of Americans over 60 travel to a college campus, retreat, or other site during the off-season and take courses. They live in dormitory rooms and eat together in dining halls. The environment is safe, the rooms and meals are inexpensive, and the social interaction is exhilarating. Whereas young people can't wait to leave school for their vacations, Elderhostel students can't wait to attend school for theirs.

Since its founding, Elderhostel has grown enormously in popularity.

In 1975, its first year of operation, Elderhostel had 220 course enrollments at 5 sites. By 1988 it counted over 170,000 course enrollments at 1,000 sites in 37 countries, and it was growing at the rate of 20,000–30,000 students per year.

Elderhostel students range in age from 60 to 93. In this relaxed atmosphere of intellectual stimulation, elder students find not only new ideas but also new friends. Debates begun in the classroom carry over into the dining hall and the dorm rooms. Skills learned in long careers are brought to bear on new facts and new ideas. The instructors love the liveliness of the classes. Professors accustomed to classes of passive 20-year-olds sleepily taking notes are confronted with people who debate important points, ask penetrating questions, and even bring in new perspectives from their own expertise.

One veteran Elderhostel couple recounted the variety of their experiences with the organization over the years:

> We've carved linoleum; found a beaver dam; climbed around mountains, temples in India, a Roman bath in Wales, and over the remains of an amphitheater in England; sailed on Loch Lowan in Scotland; ridden in an ancient outrigger canoe in a bay out of a palm-shaded lagoon near Kuna, Hawaii; and found giant pinecones at 7,000 feet in Idlewild, Colorado. Ed played jazz piano with fellow students at two Elderhostels at Chapel Hill, North Carolina, and in shows on Friday nights at many other Elderhostels. We've enjoyed cookouts at programs in Amherst, Massachusetts, and Lyndon, Vermont, and a luau in Hawaii. We've sat on the lawn drinking coffee at Cambridge University, danced English dances and sung Welsh songs, drunk Scottish scotch, and become hula experts. We learned how to wear a sari and eat with our fingers in India. There they venerate older people, so when we become old we'll visit India again.

Note the phrase "when we become old" . . . learning freshens the mind.

Another innovative example of new trends in education combines learning and travel. Society Expeditions, a 12-year-old company in Seattle, takes more than 2,500 people on exotic journeys each year. When we asked the company to list the attractions of its trips, the list was preceded by these two paragraphs:

> ——An atmosphere of learning: on every Society Expeditions program, you are encouraged to participate. That's why distinguished anthropologists, ornithologists, historians, and naturalists are along—to lead informal presentations on the places visited, to deepen your understanding of the world, its people, and its ecology.

——You share the excitement of discovery. We've created a "Laboratory at Sea" for the prestigious Hubbs–Sea World research institute of San Diego. On the *Society Explorer*, you will work with the scholars who conduct important research on marine and bird life, and share in their joy of discovery.

The Society expects that "an atmosphere of learning" will attract older customers, who are likely to have more time, resources, and interest in these kinds of extended learning adventures than do younger people. The majority of the passengers jumping into the rubber Zodiac boats to examine the plant life on some obscure atoll or to learn about the ecology of a river on these vigorous expeditions are over 50. According to the company's Aaltje E. van Zoelen, "The passengers are very active participants. They want to experience firsthand what they hear in the lectures."

The University of Pittsburgh's floating campus, the SS *Universe,* run by its Institute of Shipboard Education, is seeing an increasing number of people in their sixties and seventies. These students are taking such accredited college courses as international business, communications, economics, fine arts, and theater. Robert Powell and his wife went on a cruise to India and the Middle East with 367 "college kids" and 56 other "adults." The 71-year-old retired engineer already had a degree, so he thought he wouldn't get too involved. But when he sat in on the lectures in Middle Eastern diplomacy and politics, he found that "the classes were so fascinating that I started taking notes. The result is that I'm buying a computer. I'm learning to type. I'm compiling my notes, and I'm going to write a book on the subject."

Regular cruise lines, too, are beginning to stress strong educational components, including lectures and workshops on everything from natural history to money management. A typical agenda on Royal Cruise Lines includes lectures on the history of each port, as well as computer workshops, dance classes, writers' workshops, sessions with financial advisors, and retirement planning forums. Even Club Med is now peppering its "escape from civilization" vacations with child care and seminars on computer programming, personal finance management, and leadership skills to more completely meet the needs of its older (the median age is now over 37) guests.

Driven by this powerful hunger for new experience and understanding, more than one market niche will spring from the examples of Elderhostel and Society Expeditions. We can imagine:

- Upscale versions of Elderhostel, in more luxurious surroundings, with more privacy than a typical college dorm and with better food than the typical college fare. Perhaps the best current example of this model are the "universities" put on throughout the world by the Young Presidents' Organization (YPO) for its members. Dozens of times each year, hundreds of corporate leaders and their families check in to four-star hotels and get set to learn. At each of the YPO universities, top-notch faculties are assembled to provide instruction on timely and relevant subjects. Faculty and topics have included Henry Kissinger on "World Affairs," Walter Cronkite on "Media Relations," Lee Iacocca on "Turning Your Company Around," Joyce Brothers on "Dealing with Difficult Children," and John Naisbitt on "Anticipating the Future." Between learning sessions and informal gatherings with faculty—or "resources," as they are called—members find time to play golf, visit with old friends, sightsee, and, yes, even make a few business deals.

- Complete self-study programs in thousands of subjects. For those adult learners who are unable to attend formal classes or who are uncomfortable doing so, a massive home-learning industry will emerge. Whether people are interested in receiving an MBA degree, polishing up interpersonal communication skills, or learning more about home repair, they will be able to pursue their educational desires with the support of self-paced audio, video, and workbook learning programs.

- Lifestyle expeditions in which students take part in actual lifestyles they may have found intriguing. They might share the building tasks on a Quaker commune, travel with a working dance band, help cook for a team of threshers in the Midwest, take a turn at the wheel of an Alaskan salmon boat, or tune the instruments for a rock band. Structured apprenticeships will become a leisure industry of the future.

- Longer and more adventurous learning holidays, in which students take part in actual scientific expeditions or project development in remote locales. For a period of several weeks to a year or more, students might wish to enroll for an internship at a South American astronomical observatory or a fancy San Francisco restaurant, a research assistantship with an established author, a stint as an assistant on a seagoing research vessel or at a local radio station, or an internship with the United States Forest Service, helping to reforest a wildlife refuge that has been damaged by fire.

One program of the last type already in existence is Earthwatch, a Massachusetts organization that since 1971 has matched more than 15,000 amateur volunteers with scientific expeditions around the world. Along with the National Geographic Society and the World Wildlife Fund, Earthwatch ranks as one of the world's largest private sponsors of field-research expeditions. Volunteers not only pay their way to and from the site, but they also split the costs of the expeditions among themselves, contributing an average of $1,250 each. According to the organization, 39 percent of the volunteers are over 50.

Jennie Mae Tucker, a 77-year-old retired banker from Jackson, Mississippi, has gone on a number of Earthwatch expeditions. She recalls with particular fondness a 1982 whale study: "It's very exciting to find a whale three times the size of your boat right next to you. When I'm on vacation, I want to be doing something as different as I can from my everyday life, and Earthwatch is about as far away as you can get." Other Earthwatchers have unearthed Egyptian temples, hiked into live volcanoes, and worked on dolphin-communication projects.

RETIREMENT CAMPUSES

The learning lifestyle has begun to cause another fascinating new trend: college towns are becoming choice retirement spots for the education-minded elder. Instead of Sun City and Leisure World, towns such as Eugene, Oregon; Madison, Wisconsin; Austin, Texas; Ann Arbor, Michigan; Williamstown, Massachusetts; Ithaca, New York; Burlington, Vermont; Annapolis, Maryland; Charlottesville, Virginia; Hanover, New Hampshire; and Chapel Hill and Winston-Salem, North Carolina are beginning to see a significant growth in the number of older immigrants who want to be in the middle of, not removed from, the action.

When the American Association of Retired Persons (AARP) ran an item on academic retirement villages in its newsletter recently, it was deluged with hundreds of letters asking for information. According to AARP researcher Leah Dobkin, "A lot of older people don't want to play bingo and shuffleboard. They want more compelling activities. These centers associated with higher education not only offer the academic environment, [but] many [also] offer the possibility of a job on campus, as well as training opportunities for a new career."

For instance, when asked why he moved to Chapel Hill, retired insurance executive John Kittredge commented, "We wanted a temperate climate with fewer people than the New York area, but we also wanted to avoid the golf and tennis communities that are basically for retired people. But what we especially wanted was a place that offered a wide choice of cultural events as well as good shops and restaurants, and a college town was perfect." Dr. Henry Veatch, formerly a philosophy professor at Georgetown University, moved back to Bloomington, Indiana, because "the move to a small, welcoming college town made sense to us. I use the [Indiana University] library all the time, and we attend the opera, theater, and concerts." Hester Phreaner, whose husband, Edgar, had attended Amherst College in Amherst, Massachusetts, said, "Amherst is a pleasant, busy environment, and we think the mix of students at the five colleges here with golden oldies like us is perfect."

Just as some elders are building homes or renting apartments in college towns, colleges and universities around the country are now responding to the Age Wave by building their own specialized adult communities with a focus on lifelong learning.

For example, the Marriott Corporation and the University of Virginia have built a community called the Colonnades in Charlottesville, Virginia. The Sisters of St. Joseph of Nazareth College in Kalamazoo, Michigan, has built senior housing, as have Syracuse University, Indiana University at Bloomington, and College Harbor at Eckerd College in St. Petersburg, Florida. Even The George School, a Quaker boarding school in New Town, Pennsylvania, has built a place for elders called Pennswood Village. And Friday Mountain, a new, 1,500-unit development in Austin, Texas, is planned as a corporate continuing-education conference center that will be staffed by its elder residents.

THE HELPING HAND

One of the most pervasive misperceptions that the Age Wave will wash away is the idea that older people have nothing more to contribute to society. National studies have repeatedly shown that as people grow older, they have a marked tendency to become more interested in what they give to others than in what they get. Our elders are a vital national resource, with many wishing to give, not take.

Volunteering for every manner of helping enterprise—in the community, for political and social causes, for charities—is increasingly becoming a way of life for millions of older Americans.

According to Clem Bezold, the head of the Institute for Alternative Futures near Washington, D.C., "A key aspect of successful aging is having a meaningful self-definition. As the continued rise of expert systems and automation bring us more unemployment in the future, we will have to figure out how to distribute wealth and well-being apart from paid work. For the elderly, this will mean finding meaningful roles that are not necessarily monetary." In other words, volunteer work will grow rapidly as a way for older people to make meaningful use of their lives.

Several years ago, I was invited to present a lecture on "New Images of Aging" to a community group in Dallas. The audience of around a thousand was made up of students, social workers, physicians, and clergy from the area. As I began my lecture, I couldn't help noticing a smartly dressed, attractive older couple seated in the first row, directly in front of me. They appeared to be in their seventies or so. Throughout my talk they held hands, smiled up at me, and occasionally leaned over to plant a kiss on the other's cheek. This was a happy and energetic pair of older Americans.

As soon as my lecture ended, they rushed up to the stage to talk with me. First, they told me how much they had enjoyed my presentation and said they felt that they themselves were living examples of a new image of aging. We continued to exchange pleasantries for a few minutes, until I asked them where they lived.

"Nowhere," they said, and then turned to each other and giggled. When they saw the look of disbelief on my face, they explained further.

"Right now we don't live anywhere in particular. Until

last year we lived in Los Angeles where we owned and ran a restaurant. We've worked hard throughout our lives, and we've raised three wonderful children who now have families of their own. However, last year we decided to sell the business and retire from working forever."

"So what are you doing here in Dallas?" I asked.

The wife turned to me and with all seriousness said, "When we retired we decided that we wanted to devote the rest of our lives to serving others. Now, we are driving around America to find the best place to stay and give."

They were in the process of transforming themselves into self-directed missionaries.

Like this special couple, for many older Americans the decision to retire from the traditional work life does not lead in the direction of self-satisfying recreation. Instead, the dream of such people has always been to help others, to serve where their skills and compassion are needed. The termination of work sets them free to fulfill this dream. In the years to come, perhaps "serving" will join "playing" as one of the primary components of the new leisure lifestyle.

Gray Panther founder Maggie Kuhn once told me, "It's such as shame to live long enough to learn so many answers, when no one bothers any more to ask you the questions." In addition to gaining new knowledge and insight in their later years, increasing numbers of older men and women will find ways to give back to society the many lessons they have learned and the abundant resources they have accumulated. For many men and women who are hoping to give back some of what they have learned in life, becoming teachers and volunteers will be the focus of the learning lifestyle.

Volunteerism is not new. Americans have always used a good part of their free time helping others. As we get more free time, we will spend an even greater proportion of it in service to others. According to an AARP-sponsored survey, more than 30 percent of Americans over 55 do volunteer work. They do it to meet people, to keep active, or to fulfill a sense of duty, but mostly, they report, they volunteer because it gives them a great deal of personal satisfaction. AARP itself has an army of more than 350,000 volunteers, working at everything from tax counseling to community-service work.

A national study by the research organization Public Agenda found that as people grow older, their desire to work is often independent of the need to earn money.

Senior Companions, part of the federal ACTION program, was founded in 1974. A year later it had 1,000 volunteers, and by 1987 it had more than 7,000. ACTION's Foster Grandparents, founded in 1965, grew to 18,000 by 1984, and to more than 23,400 by 1987. Its Retired Senior Volunteer Program could count 250,000 volunteers within six years of its 1971 founding and more than 365,000 by 1987, with 750 offices nationwide.

The Peace Corps, which requires a serious commitment of 10 weeks of intensive training, followed by two years in the field, is actively seeking older volunteers. According to spokesperson Sandy Sinclair, "The older person is accorded greater respect than the younger person in a village in a developing nation." In 1987 there were 563 Peace Corps volunteers over 50, and 23 of them were over 70. Many of these volunteers are people of a practical bent—for example, retired mechanics and engineers. One volunteer, says Sinclair, is an "86-year-old retired AT&T lineman. The day after he retired over 20 years ago he joined the Peace Corps. He's been building roads and bridges ever since."

The huge retirement community at Sun City, Arizona, gives a good example of the many forms that volunteerism can take. Volunteers do most of the work needed to run the community—from pruning the bushes to patrolling the streets to producing the audiovisual materials at the hospital. Every volunteer "job" is broken up into 4-hour chunks. Volunteers can take on as little or as much as they want, from 4 hours a week to 40 or more. With this kind of flexible commitment, volunteering can become much like adventure travel—an opportunity to try on completely new styles of life and ways of relating to others.

Captain Bert Brosius of the Sun City Posse illuminates what is perhaps the most interesting point: volunteering is a quick way to cast yourself in a new real-life role overnight.

Captain Brosius puts in more than 60 hours a week running a force of 250 deputies, who help to insure that Sun City continues to have what Brosius claims is the lowest crime rate in the country. The lot outside his office sparkles with a dozen brand-new squad cars. The communications room down the hall squawks and hisses with radio calls.

Brosius wears a sheriff's uniform, complete with a gun, bullet belt, star, and epaulets with bars. But he is not a professional cop; he's a retired Bell Systems executive. He's a volunteer ("I work almost twice as many hours as I did before I retired, only now I don't get paid," he says), and so is everyone who works for him. All have been deputized to the Maricopa County Sheriff's Department. Asked about his decision to volunteer, Brosius says, "I didn't need money. I needed something to do—I've been active all my life."

Others do their volunteer work outside Sun City. Some work as volunteer teachers at the Indian school in nearby Peoria, helping Mexican children learn English. Ken Crawford, 75, former head of training at the paper company Blake, Moffit & Towne, lectures on sales and marketing at Northern Arizona University and also speaks for the Make-a-Wish Foundation, which grants the last wishes of dying children. Crawford feels that volunteering helps keep him young. "Age," he says, "isn't something on the calendar. It's just two things—your health and your attitude."

A terrific example of the range of assistance that skilled, mature volunteers can provide can be seen at nearby Boswell Memorial Hospital. Boswell's 2,000+ volunteers—the largest hospital-based volunteer corps in America—offer doormen who park patients' cars, retired accountants who help people fill out Medicare forms, retired doctors who offer free blood-pressure screenings, retired disc jockeys who run the hospital radio station, retired corporate-training directors who contribute to the hospital's health-education program, retired gym teachers who teach the exercise classes, retired secretaries who help out in the offices when the work load is heavy, and retired librarians who manage the hospital's First Edition Health and Lifestyle Library.

Volunteerism is hard to differentiate from work—in the intensity of involvement, in the central place it can take in the life of the volunteer, and in the many intangible ways in which the volunteer is "paid."

Knowledge, Energy, and Resources to Give

The growing numbers of older Americans represent a vast, untapped potential, as shown by research published by Dr. William H. Perry in the *Journal of Gerontological Social Work*. He asked: How many older citizens who do not now volunteer would like to, if the setting and the time were right? Of the nonvolunteers Dr. Perry studied, 59 percent said they would like to volunteer, if the right circumstances could be found. As Dr. Perry writes, "The results of this investigation indicate that the challenge does not lie in finding older persons willing to volunteer . . . but rather in creating volunteer roles in which these elder persons can be channeled."

The coming years will see a proliferation of ways to bring out the power of volunteerism.

For example, I strongly believe that we should create an organized national Elder Corps. Like the Peace Corps, this organization could be a channel for the great untapped reservoir of time, energy, love, and experience represented by America's older citizens. At local, state, and federal commissions on aging, at legislative hearings, and at the conventions of AARP and other organizations, we hear how much is being done for the older citizen. But at the same time, we need to hear more about what older people can do for young people, for their communities, and for one another. This is a call to which many older Americans would respond with enthusiasm. It's necessary to feel cared for, but it's equally necessary to feel useful. It's exciting to learn: it can be exhilarating to teach. America's older people have an abundance of knowledge, energy, and resources to give.

Knowledge.   78-year-old Anne Eaton had worked as a credit manager for a fashion chain, as a commercial artist, and as director of social work in a nursing home. She already had a degree, but at age 69 she went back to school because, she said, if she was going to be an "old person" the rest of her life, she wanted to know something about it. She earned a master's degree in sociology with a specialty in gerontology from Georgia State University.

When she was done, she felt prepared to take on larger things. In Atlanta, she founded Life Enrichment Services (LES), a nonprofit group that helps older people help one another. With no government money but with some 40,000 volunteer hours each year, the venture bloomed. LES now provides older people in Atlanta with an extraordinary array of useful services, including the following:

- "Adventures In Learning," which every year brings together some 400 volunteer lecturers and 2,000 to 2,500 enrolled students for courses on everything from macrame and clogging to investment strategies and world affairs.

- A widowed-persons service, which arranges for peer counseling to help new widows and widowers cope with surviving.

- The local Meals on Wheels program, through which older volunteers deliver thousands of nutritious lunches and dinners to homebound older people each week.

- Inexpensive home services, provided through 15 semi-volunteer older handymen.

- An exchange program with seniors in Hanover, Germany.
- Seminars on aging with prominent gerontologists and activists.
- Training courses for people who might like to start a clone of LES.

Already, at least four spinoffs of LES dot DeKalb County, Georgia. Eaton, who is still active in helping to oversee the program, in arranging seminars, and in lecturing at councils on aging in this country and Europe, has been a great benefactor to her fellow seniors, and she finds the work more satisfying than anything else she has done in her life. LES is part of an emerging pattern of self-help community senior organizations around the country that use the skills and energy of seniors to help other seniors.

Energy. We might even see the day when elders will be able to receive and exchange "volunteer credits" for the useful contributions they make. Edgar Cahn, a law professor and senior research fellow at the Southeast Florida Center on Aging at Florida International University, Miami, has made a simple yet radical proposal that has excited a great deal of interest. Called the "volunteer service credit program," it is a modern, formal, computerized version of something that has existed at the village level for thousands of years: help others, and they will help you. It works like this: every hour you spend helping other older Americans—volunteering at the hospital, for instance, or helping someone paint shutters —is logged in a computer. Then, when you yourself need help—whether a ride to a movie next week or round-the-clock care when you are ill—you can draw on the "credits" in the computer and have volunteers sent to help you.

Florida and Missouri have already set up pilot programs based on Cahn's idea, and the Internal Revenue Service has already ruled that the credits will be tax free.

The idea is appealing precisely because in the later parts of our lives we often have more time than income. Yet when we need someone else's time, we usually have to spend our income to pay for it. In many cases it would be much easier to exchange some of our time for the time and services of others.

Related ideas are spreading into both public and private sectors. Eastern Airlines, for instance, is working out the details of a plan in which its retirees would provide technical advice to younger mechanics and service personnel, in return for access to discount travel packages.

Possible extensions of this idea include:

- Retired journeymen teaching younger people the carpentry skills needed to make houses safe and accident-proof, in exchange for having their own or a friend's house worked on.
- Older members of a congregation earning volunteer credits by helping out in the church's after-school education programs. These credits could be exchanged for home-care services so that these people wouldn't have to go into a nursing home if their health failed temporarily.
- Older men and women helping out at day-care centers and tutoring schoolchildren in return for barter services from the children's parents.
- Older community tour guides who would receive special discounts from local merchants in exchange for the community service they perform.

Resources. Some older people will be able to directly give back some of the success, opportunity, and financial resources they derived during their lives.

For example, when 100-year-old Rhea Stambaugh decided that the 2,000 people of Plymouth, Ohio, needed a real library to replace the old house full of books that it had, she built one. She not only paid for it but also found the land, hired the architect, and turned down his first four designs. She saw it through construction and delivered a speech at the dedication. Afterward, she commented, "Next to my marriage, it's the best thing I ever did."

Eugene Lang is a self-made millionaire with an unusual and powerful mission. When Lang was waiting on tables as a 14-year-old, he happened to serve Swarthmore College trustee George Jackson, who was so impressed with Lang that he arranged for him to attend Swarthmore on a scholarship. Once out of college, Lang built a fortune through his Refac Technology Development Corporation, which invests in new high-tech ventures.

In 1981, at the age of 62, Lang was invited back to his grade-school alma mater, P.S. 121 in Harlem, to give a commencement speech to a class of 61 sixth-graders from low-income families. What he said surprised them, but it surprised him, too. In a district in which only one of every four students makes it through high school, he made the sixth-graders a promise: if they studied hard and stayed in school, he would personally send them all to college. Over the next years he backed up his promise with encouragement, field trips, study groups and seminars, guest speakers, after-school jobs, and sometimes just a sympathetic ear. Fifty of the 61 graduated and took him up on his offer. Through a foundation he named "I Have a Dream," Lang has spread his idea to Dallas, Cleveland, Los Angeles, Boston, Baltimore, Chicago, Jersey City, Washington, Detroit, and twelve other cities. In each city, he finds a philanthropist to personally "adopt" one class of kids, see them all through high school, and help them in college.

I recently attended the opening of the first "Aging Resource Center," a complete health-and-lifestyle library available free of charge to the public, in Tulsa, Oklahoma. Managed by Hillcrest Hospital, the Aging Resource Center was made possible by a generous donation from one of the community's successful businessmen, John Babbitt. During the dinner honoring Mr. Babbitt for his caring contribution, he was invited to say a few words to the several hundred community leaders who had gathered on his behalf. His remarks were simple, to the point, and, I think, reflective of a future trend. He said, "I have lived a good life here in Tulsa. I have been fortunate

enough to have raised a healthy and loving family here. My
business grew and prospered in this community. Nearly everything I have came from my fruitful life here. It's about time
I gave some of it back."

Stambaugh's, Lang's, and Babbitt's increasing involvement in their own chosen causes illustrates an important reality: the satisfactions of giving can be an older person's greatest
gift to the community as well as to himself. I believe that in
the years ahead, increasing numbers of older men and women
will donate their money and property, in addition to their
skills and resources, to activities, programs, and services they
care about and believe in, whether or not a formal contribution program has been established by the government or by
a charitable organization.

Corporate-Sponsored Volunteer Corps

All three of these forms of volunteerism—knowledge, energy, and resources—come together in the proliferation of
corporate-sponsored volunteer corps.

**Some companies recognize volunteerism as a vital and
fulfilling part of their retirees' lives, as well as good com-
mon-sense public relations for the company.**

Wells Fargo, for instance, runs a statewide "Volunteer
Network" in California that recruits retirees to help local
nonprofit agencies. Levi Strauss, headquartered in San Francisco, has 25 part-time retiree coordinators whose sole job is
to orchestrate the volunteer work of the company's retirees.
Frances Henson Brune, the regional coordinator of the program in the East, talks about the power of volunteerism in the
lives of the volunteers:

> People would still come to work, even after they had
> retired, and sit at my desk and talk. They didn't know
> what to do with themselves. A lot of people got sick

because they had nothing to do. People have actually
gotten well when they became active in the volunteer
program. . . . We're like one big family. We care for one
another. If someone lives alone we call them every day.
If someone is ill we shop for them. We save money on
hospitalization by staying active.

And while staying active helps the volunteers, their activities
help the community around them. A Levi Strauss group in
Warsaw, Virginia, works with abused children; one in El Paso
sews flannel gowns for the disadvantaged; and another in
Knoxville has adopted a dance school. All of these groups can
ask for funds from the Levi Strauss Foundation.

One of the best examples of this corporate approach
emerged when Blue Cross/Blue Shield of Indiana realized
that many older subscribers were confused about their insurance policies and needed someone to explain the confusing
interaction between Medicare and their private insurance
policies. Some of these people were bedridden; others
couldn't drive. Blue Cross/Blue Shield figured that hiring
representatives to personally meet with and counsel all of its
older consumers would not be financially feasible.

Through a series of focus groups, the company arrived
at an ingenious solution, creating the Blue Cross/Blue Shield
Ambassador Corps. The trained "ambassadors" are older
men and women who usually have some background in insurance, accounting, or teaching. Each week, these volunteers
drive to consumers' homes, sip coffee, and carefully explain
the ins and outs of the insurance program. Other than reimbursement for gas and out-of-pocket costs, the ambassadors
work essentially for free. The volunteer ambassadors love the
work because it keeps them busy in a very useful way, and
they enjoy the respect, appreciation, and satisfaction that
comes from helping others.

The consumers, for their part, love the ambassador program because they get helpful personal attention from their
insurance company, along with financial savings through
wiser management of their accounts. And, as might be ex-

pected, Blue Cross/Blue Shield also loves the program, because it now has a service corps that incurs no real overhead, it receives a great deal of good public relations, and its consumers are happy.

This kind of volunteer service could easily be applied to other areas in which older people might offer their skills and abilities. For example:

- Bookstore-sponsored *reading-club and bookstore counselors and "recommenders"* (terrific for former English teachers or librarians), who could help buyers select books.

- Grocery-manufacturer–sponsored *food purchasing and preparation advisors,* who could be available at local supermarkets to assist older consumers find foods that are healthy and appropriate to their special needs. In regularly offered educational programs, these volunteers could demonstrate ways to easily prepare nutritious meals at home.

- Hospital- or HMO-sponsored *health-care advocates* (perfect for retired doctors, nurses, and allied health professionals), who could be available in doctors' offices and hospital admitting rooms to help patients fill out forms and to answer their questions about Medicare, patients' rights, outreach services, and so on.

- *Tourist guides and day companions* for out-of-town guests (perfect for retired taxi and bus drivers), sponsored by chambers of commerce. These volunteers could escort tourists to the best sights and experiences in the area.

- *Volunteer drivers*, sponsored by shopping malls or local merchants. Many older people are unable to drive themselves to a friend's, to the store, or to the beauty parlor. Assistance in getting around would be a terrific aid for them.

- Merchant-sponsored *shopping assistants* (perfect for retired salespeople) could go to supermarkets and department stores and make purchases on behalf of those who are unable to do so themselves.

- *Banking assistants*, sponsored by retail banks. One of the biggest responsibilities that family caregivers usually have to assume, even if they live miles away, is helping their loved ones with basic banking responsibilities, such as paying the bills and balancing the checkbook. A personal banking assistant (an ideal volunteer role for retired bank employees, bookkeepers, or accountants) would be greatly appreciated.

- *Home-safety and energy-conservation consultants* (perfect for former utilities employees and handymen), sponsored by utility companies. These people could help make homes energy-wise and safe.

- *Community-crisis mediators* (perfect for older ministers or community leaders), sponsored by chambers of commerce or local merchants, could help settle neighborhood difficulties.

- Neighborhood-sponsored *landscape consultants* (ideal for people who love to garden), who could help keep parks and recreation areas attractive.

- Merchant- or community-sponsored *recreation directors* (perfect for retired gym teachers) to work at schools and community recreation centers.

- Corporation- or church-sponsored *child-rearing support*, to assist working mothers and single parents in learning the essential ingredients in child care, and to offer respite if needed.

LEARNING AS A LIFESTYLE

If living longer meant only spending more years in declining old age, most of us would not choose it. But today we face a different choice. What the late twentieth century has begun to give us is the prospect of many more years before the arrival of old age. The effects of this great gift will ripple through our lives in many unexpected ways. With more leisure time in our lives, we will tend to seek out deeper experiences, experiences that are more exotic, that teach us more about the world and ourselves, that satisfy more of our own needs, and that make us more useful in satisfying the needs of others.

With the coming of the Age Wave, we will learn to see our retirees as a vast and untapped resource, not as a drain.

As we plan for a more cyclic lifestyle, we might even find ourselves taking a cue from those older men and women whose departure from work has afforded them the special personal rewards that come from helping others. For just as it might make sense to experience periods of reflective leisure throughout our lives instead of saving it all for old age, it would be wonderful if we didn't wait until retirement to dedicate some time, energy, and compassion to help those less fortunate than ourselves.

CHAPTER

7

Reworking Work

Are we approaching—or perhaps well beyond—the point of
diminishing returns regarding the compression of work into
the middle of life? Is it necessary or practical to have all of
one's schooling during youth, and most of one's leisure years
in old age? Does the long life offer more opportunity for
second or third chances?

What if tomorrow's older workers prefer to work less
and play more and are willing to sacrifice some salary for extra
recreation time? What if they would rather enjoy chunks of
their retirement along the way instead of saving it all until the
last years of life? What if tomorrow's older workers prefer
time to develop many facets of themselves in a Renaissance
fashion, instead of putting all their energy into one job? What
if tomorrow's elders see the doorway between work and retirement as revolving instead of one-way?

**Challenged by the swelling Age Wave, the youth-ori-
ented work policies of American business, which offer**

employees the black-and-white choice of working or not working, are beginning to dissolve. As people's social, financial, and lifestyle needs change to reflect a more longevous, cyclic perspective, the way we work will change, too.

To Work or Not to Work?

As we have seen in previous chapters, although there are a growing number of cyclic lifestyle pioneers, most people still stop working in their later years. Research suggests that there are several key reasons why so many people retire as early as they can.

First, they are tired of doing what they do and see no other worthwhile alternatives. Expecting to have only one career during their lifetimes, many of today's older Americans don't think they can start a whole new career late in life. And age discrimination, although illegal, can make the barriers to reentering the work force extremely difficult to overcome.

Second, work schedules today are usually all or nothing: you work full-time, or you don't work at all. Most surveys of the needs and desires of the elderly suggest that most don't want to stop working altogether; they just don't want to work as much or as hard. If their employers were more flexible and offered more accommodating part-time, flextime, or consulting work, many would love to continue some work activity, for both psychological and financial reasons.

Third, the more physically demanding and the less intellectually stimulating the work, the more likely it is that the worker will retire as soon as he or she can afford to. Judges, politicians, college professors, musicians and composers, architects, reporters and editors, religious workers, entrepreneurs, and many other professionals tend to stay in their careers as long as they can. More than three times as many doctors as other health-service people keep working past 65. A lawyer or judge is seven times as likely to keep working as the laborer, and the college professor is four times as likely as the cafeteria employee to continue working.

However, in recent years, growing numbers of people have begun to question not only when to retire, but whether retirement as it now exists makes sense at all. They see retirement as an uncertainty, or even as a problem—something that will separate them from the kinds of productive lives they are capable of living well into their seventies and eighties.

With the coming of the Age Wave, several social forces are converging that will allow many people to continue working, albeit with reduced work loads or more flexible work schedules, throughout the later years of their lives.

More older Americans want to work. Now that mandatory retirement has ended, older workers have much more flexibility in choosing when, and whether, to retire. Many people are discovering that the traditional nonworking retirement can be emotionally unsatisfying. Recent polls sponsored by AARP and the National Council on Aging found that the closer workers get to retirement age, the more they want to keep working, and that 40 percent of retired people would rather be working.

According to Gray Panther leader Maggie Kuhn, "People should have a lifelong opportunity to work. Businesses have found that, with mandatory retirement, they have thrown away many irreplaceable skills. But the answer is in the workplace. If you humanize the workplace, restructure it around flextime, around mentoring, people will be less eager to retire. Personally, I want to die in an airport, briefcase in hand, mission accomplished."

In a national poll conducted by the research firm Public Agenda, the majority of people responded that not only did they want to work in one way or another after 65, but they would also continue to work even if they had enough money to be comfortable for the rest of their lives. The reason chosen by 94 percent of those polled was simple: "I like working." At Boston's Towle Silver Company, the head of the mailroom is 70-year-old Barbara Byrnes. She's been running the mailroom for 50 years, and at last notice she had no intention of quitting. Byrnes says, "I have my health. I love people. And I love that mailroom."

Retirement expert Elwood Chapman, author of such books as *Comfort Zones* and *The Unfinished Business of Living*, says, "Very few men, especially, can make the life of pure leisure work. I have traced the lives of dozens of men; almost all of them find they have to go find something in the way of work."

In fact, most older people do not want to stop working. They just want to have a better blend of work and leisure than they did in their earlier years.

Older Americans are getting healthier, and work is becoming less physically demanding.   The health of older workers will continue to improve. Changes in diet and lifestyle, increased awareness of the importance of exercise, and other habits of wellness will lead to a continuing increase in the vitality, strength, and endurance of older Americans. Even though we tend to think of older workers as being ill more often than their younger counterparts, it is actually the younger workers who consistently have more sick days per year.

At the same time, as the postindustrial economy matures, more and more jobs are based on knowledge, experience, and judgment, and fewer on gross physical capabilities. These decreased physical demands mean not only that more older Americans are able to continue working but that more desire to do so.

Samuel Ehrenhalt, the regional commissioner of the Bureau of Labor Statistics for New York, says, "At the same time that people are living longer, in better health, with their faculties more intact than we ever dreamed, you have all these productive people leaving the labor force. Is that a sensible way to use the country's resources?"

One day, in addition to blue- and white-collar workers, every company might have a fleet of "wisdom workers": mature men and women who will be retained and whose compensation will be based not on the number of hours they work but on their experience, contacts, and wisdom.

My two most valuable and effective resources at Age Wave, Inc., don't work in the office. They don't contribute 40 hours a week, and they don't even live in California, where our offices are based. Instead, 50-year-old Fred Rubenstein and 49-year-old Dr. James Bernstein live in New York and Washington, D.C., respectively. Fred is a marketing and business-development genius, and Jim, although initially trained at Harvard and Cornell Medical School to be a surgeon and biomedical researcher, has since become an expert on managing entrepreneurial firms.

I have retained these experienced men not for the number of hours they work but for the amount of knowledge and insight they have. They contribute what they have learned from a lifetime of trial and error, and they love the challenge. The experience and guidance they share are largely responsible for our firm's rapid growth and success. I am convinced that many corporate blunders and well-intentioned misdirections could be avoided if there were a better blend of the energy and ambition of youth and the vision and seasoned experience of age.

Older people will need to work.   Whether full-time or part-time, seasonally or year-round, self-employed or as employees, tomorrow's elders will work as long as they are physically able. They will work partly because they want to, because work gives them fulfillment, control over their own lives, and a useful place in society.

And they will continue working because they will have to. As we saw in the chapter, "The Giant Wakes Up," increased longevity and shifts in the worker-to-retiree ratio will in all likelihood lead to changes in Social Security, including a rise in the age of eligibility, the taxing of benefits, a reduction in protection from inflation, and the elimination of some benefits to the financially secure. As Social Security becomes an even more narrow financial base for later life, older people will find it increasingly difficult to maintain a reasonable standard of living without work of some kind. Commenting on the proliferation of nonworking retirees, U.S. Commissioner on Aging Carol Fraser Fisk stated flatly, "Many of these people would be far better off if they remained in the work force."

Last year I was invited to Colorado Springs, Colorado, to conduct a seminar on retirement for a group of several hundred benefits directors from large corporations throughout the United States. When I was met at the airport by the hotel's limousine, I couldn't help noticing that my driver, although fit and vigorous, was very much an older man. During the half-hour ride to the hotel, I asked him how old he was. "Seventy-two," he answered proudly. I then asked him if he had been a limousine driver very long. "Seven years," he said.

He told me that he had begun driving 20 hours a week after retiring. (I am always fascinated by people who are obviously working, but who for some reason refer to themselves as "retired.") When I asked him what he had done before this, he told me about the 23 years he had worked for the postal service as a mail carrier in Baltimore. But becoming a mailman, he said, was only something he had decided to do after retiring from his earlier job.

Wondering if I was working my way into a never-ending Dr. Seuss–style fable, I inquired what kind of work he had done two retirements ago. "Well," he said, "before I retired and began this job, and before my earlier retirement from the postal service, I was in the navy . . . a career man. In fact, I served in the navy for 22 years and then retired with a very pleasant pension. Of course, I also receive another pension from the postal service. But, with the cost of living today and with my third wife having three kids in college, I figure I need to keep working some hours each week just to keep the extra spending money coming!"

In the years to come, many "retirees" will need to continue working to keep "the spending money coming." And, perhaps, we'll soon realize that this kind of retirement isn't really retiring at all. According to *Webster's Ninth New Collegiate Dictionary,* to "retire" means "to withdraw, especially for privacy; to fall back, recede." Because an increasing number of today's retirees are definitely not retiring in the true sense of the word, perhaps we'd be better off using such terms as "first retirement," "second retirement" (just as we now are comfortable with the concept of "first and second marriage"), or "final retirement" to describe these professional punctuation points.

Donald Underwood, director of retirement programs at Merrill Lynch, refers to the process of making the transition from work to retirement and back to work again as "career veering." With millions of people regularly moving in and out of the work force, we might instead use the terms "disengagement" and "reengagement" to refer to our cyclic involvements.

Mid-life career changes, as well as regular exits from and reentries to the workplace, are becoming more commonplace. Structural changes in the economy and the rise of new automated technologies are loosening the lifetime relationships many older workers thought they had with their job and their company, shifting them at least temporarily out of the work force, and demanding that many of them retire or change their careers. Precision welders find their niche filled by robots; television assemblers find their jobs shifted overseas. What becomes of these individuals? Do they simply stop working? Will progress halt to keep today's workers comfortable in their jobs? Increasingly, with each wave of professional obsolescence, millions of men and women at varying stages of life will find themselves going back to school in order to begin the sometimes frustrating, sometimes exhilarating process of beginning entirely new careers.

In fact, it's not just welders and mechanics who will need to get used to an ongoing process of skills enhancement. In past centuries it might have taken a lifetime for a particular skill or craft to become obsolete. Now, the short life cycle of most skills and professions has made regular retraining necessary for nearly everyone from secretaries to brain surgeons. This process of lifetime learning, in contrast to the once-a-life learning process of the linear life plan, is popping up everywhere. Architectural draftsmen find they need to learn the intricacies of computer-assisted design; hospital executives immerse themselves in everything from the insurance industry to real estate development. Even 20 years ago it would not have occurred to most 50-year-olds to go back to school to learn new skills for their jobs. Now, such retraining is often essential.

Older workers are becoming more desirable and necessary.   The invention of retirement was in part a response to a need to remove older people from the work force so that younger workers could find jobs. As a result of the birth dearth that began in 1964, increasing shortages of qualified and available workers will make it easier for older Americans to start new careers if they want to, and for those in mid-life to take some time off and feel secure that they can find a job when they return.

As more older people continue to work, business leaders will increasingly recognize the value of older workers. More and more, the overemphasis on the perceived strength and eagerness of young workers will be balanced by an appreciation for the sound judgment, personal skills, accumulated experience, low absenteeism, and ready availability of older workers.

Warren Buffett, who is chairman of Berkshire Hathaway and whose portfolio includes significant ownership of such companies as the Washington Post Co. and Capital Cities/ABC, was recently asked how he felt about the fact that Rose Blumkin, the chairman of one of his companies, Furniture Mart, had just turned 94. Said Buffett, "She is clearly gathering speed and may well reach her full potential in another five or ten years. Therefore, I've persuaded the board to scrap our mandatory-retirement-at-100 policy. . . . It's about time. With every passing year, this policy has seemed sillier to me. . . . My God, good managers are so scarce I can't afford the luxury of letting them go just because they've added a year to their age!"

The first active call for older workers is already showing up on the lower and upper ends of the wage scale. Although every politician has been taking credit for the dramatic drop in unemployment—joblessness in the United States is now at its lowest level since 1974—the main cause of the labor shortage is the baby bust. As the last of the boomers migrate past the entry-level jobs, gaping holes are left in the employment landscape. Just as grade schools, high schools, and colleges have each been forced in turn to scale down operations and diversify, so businesses that depend upon inexpensive entry-level employees have begun to experience labor shortages.

Economist Jon Sargent comments, "With fewer teenagers out there, industries that rely heavily on younger workers will have to find new groups if they are to avoid shortages of labor."

According to Cyril Brickfield, who recently retired after a long tenure as executive director of AARP,

> The census figures don't lie. They project that there will be 5 million fewer 18-to-24-year-olds in 1995 than there are today. During that same period, according to the U.S. Department of Labor, the economy is expected to generate 16 million new jobs. Three of every four of these new jobs will require some education or technical training beyond high school. Based on these and similar projections, Labor Secretary William Brock has predicted a major skills shortage in this country before the end of the century. But that need not happen. Surveys show that fully one-third of all retirees age 65 and older would prefer to be working. By 1995, that will represent a potential pool of some 35 million experienced, willing workers. Surely, that's more than enough to prevent any national shortage of skills or loss of productivity.

These trends are causing reactions among corporations such as Marriott and McDonald's. Tom Curren, Marriott's vice-president of strategic development, says, "The biggest challenge that the aging of America presents at Marriott is the change in composition of our labor force. Teenagers, on whom we depend for our employee base, are a dying breed. We already employ one out of every 500 Americans between the ages of 14 and 24. As we continue to grow, we are going to have to look to the elderly for our new recruits."

McDonald's has already made a significant corporate commitment to rounding out their work force with older employees. They advertise and send recruiters around to senior citizens' clubs, as McDonald's spokesman Terry Capatosto put it, "to find out who wants to work." And they pamper them once they find them: McDonald's offers its older recruits their choice of days, hours, and jobs and puts them through a special "McMasters" training program. According to a 1986 Department of Commerce report, with McDonald's taking the lead, fast-food restaurants are becoming major employers of what it terms "gold-collar workers."

In the years to come, we will see increasing numbers of older people working in a variety of other service positions —for example, as security guards, hotel clerks, receptionists, limousine drivers, baby-sitters and nannies, small-company consultants, airline reservation agents, exercise instructors, lay family therapists, media advisors, insurance-claims adjusters, travel consultants and tour directors, adventure guides and travel companions, political lobbyists, editors, researchers, free-lance writers, ad hoc religious ministers, lay health advisors, adult-education teachers, landscape artists, handymen, hobby advisors, and interior decorators, to name only a few.

Businesses that are considering whether to recruit older workers have much to learn from the positive experiences of a number of firms that have never had any mandatory retirement policies in the first place, such as Macy's in New York and Tektronix in Oregon. Hastings, the University of California's College of Law in San Francisco, has never had a mandatory retirement age and has long had a tradition of hiring older faculty who are retired from other institutions. A quarter of the faculty at Hastings is over 65.

At the high end of the wage scale, many older men and women are being courted back into the work force as corporate chairmen and directors. According to *Fortune* magazine, the average age of the board members in the 900 largest corporations in America is 62. Although it may seem that young people are zooming about in their efforts to run America, if you look more closely you'll notice that older people are often pulling the strings.

Retirement as we now know it will soon disappear.

For all of the reasons discussed above, retirement will probably not remain as it has been for much longer. And since most older people would enjoy a chance to continue working but in a more flexible, less pressured fashion, the key to redefining retirement will lie in a restructuring of the way we work and the ease with which we are allowed to interweave work and nonwork throughout our adult years. As America matures, its values and priorities will shift in favor of a more cyclic life arrangement. The past trend toward early final retirement will slow and finally reverse itself, at first in a few professional and managerial fields and eventually across the whole work force.

NEW WAYS TO WORK

On hearing a description of the cyclic life, many people respond, "I wish my job allowed that kind of flexibility." Many near-retirees wonder, "Aren't I supposed to stop working when I'm older? What if I don't like being retired? Will the door back to work be forever closed to me?"

The problem has been that most of America's employers haven't yet taken notice of their adult workers' desire for a more flexible life arrangement. Older workers don't want to punch the clock, would like a better blend of work and play, usually want to collaborate with intergenerational teams, and want to be more appreciated for their unique skills and experience.

In the years and decades to come, tens of millions of outspoken, long-lived men and women will force a redefinition of the purpose and arrangement of work in our lives.

Already, numerous changes are being introduced in the workplace, including hour banks, retirement rehearsals, flextime, flexiyear contracts, sabbaticals, job retraining, part-time work, project-oriented work, job sharing, casual employment, and telecommuting. Such changes are beginning to make a lifetime blend of work and leisure a real possibility.

A data base put together by the Institute of Gerontology at the University of Michigan turned up 369 distinct variations of such ideas in practice in American business today. We will review some of the more exciting and practical of these new strategies in this chapter.

What most of the new options for work have in common is that they offer employees more control over their lives and they accommodate a more even blend of work and leisure—key to the cyclic lifestyle. Some of these ideas require only small shifts in policy or an added line in the budget to provide for a new program. Others can change the face of the corporation that adopts them. The firms that will be mentioned more than once in this chapter are among the most forward-thinking major American corporations, far more ready than most to realize the consequences of rapid demographic change. Some of the options described no longer seem like news, since they have already become familiar at most progressive corporations. But because their connection to the longer life span has not yet been widely recognized, few American corporate managers are aware of how strongly woven a part of the fabric of American life these options are quickly becoming. In the years to come, many businesses will find it necessary to construct benefits packages that offer such options in order to compete for the best employees.

Try to imagine how each of the options described could affect your life. Which of them would you choose for yourself? How might they allow you to redesign your life in a more comfortable and functional manner?

Retraining

One of the main reasons people stop working is that the skills they developed in their youth are no longer appropriate to tomorrow's needs. This obstacle is easily removed through retraining. The pace of change in today's economy is so quick that in many fields employees have to have at least some retraining every two or three years.

And older workers will increasingly fight for the right to be retrained. Many companies still effectively limit retraining programs to younger workers, undermining the job status of older employees. "It's a foolish policy," says Alan Pifer, president emeritus of the Carnegie Corporation. "Companies are quite willing to invest in the retraining of a younger worker, and yet in all probability that younger worker won't stay with them as long as the older one. So the investment is sort of wasted.

"Consequently," he suggests, "employers should look seriously at the question of retraining employees aged 50 and over. They should do so with the thought that these people might be with them another 10 to 15 years and they would get back more than their investment."

The fastest-growing type of education in America is corporate-sponsored training.

According to a recent Carnegie Foundation report, American corporations now spend some $60 billion per year on training. Bell Labs, to take one high-tech example, offers some 500 workshops and courses each year, making it competitive with many colleges and universities in terms of the range and breadth of instructional offerings. Managers at IBM are required to take at least 40 hours of training per year, regardless of age.

As Janet Norwood, commissioner of the U.S. Bureau of Labor Statistics, puts it, "The changes in our economic structure will require more skill, not less—and more education, not less."

Ed Shugrue of IBM agrees: "Every generation of products, every shift in marketing and development, involves retraining and schooling for our employees. It's a fact of life at IBM. We recognize this. Our employees recognize this. Every potential employee is notified of the fact that they will have to retrain at least once, maybe a number of times. They have to go along with this kind of thinking to work at IBM."

But at IBM and elsewhere, retraining is beginning to go beyond learning how to do the same job better. Shugrue points out that people within the electronics giant often retrain for entirely new career paths: "We have assemblers who have become administrators, secretaries who have become programmers, and engineers who have become executives—not to mention executives who have become engineers." In fact, the subject that is most in demand in adult education by men today throughout the United States is not pottery, poetry, or gardening. It's engineering.

Control Data, Grumman, and a number of other companies have training programs specifically designed to help employees advance or even switch careers within the company. The "staleness" sometimes associated with older workers is often not the staleness of age, but the staleness of working for decades in the same job.

Some firms not only train their employees for new positions and careers but also teach them how to deal with life changes themselves. Companies such as IBM and Ford have introduced *life-span career planning* to help employees manage the inevitability of career change. This planning may encompass such themes as multiple career paths, on-the-job development, career planning, individual career counseling, and mentor-protégé relationships.

Control Data, for instance, has put 1,800 of its over-45 employees and their spouses through a comprehensive two- to five-day workshop called "LifePath." Designed to enhance the employees' middle years, the workshop is modeled on research from the University of Southern California's Andrus Gerontology Center and covers the following seven key areas: health and wellness, life transitions, relationships, time utilization, housing and lifestyle, finances, and work.

After going through the workshop and an individual computer-based lifestyle analysis, the employee uses a manual to go through "action planning," marking specific actions that need to be done. Follow-up surveys show that most em- ployees are eager to put their new skills and ideas into action, and most do carry out the changes that they plan.

Some companies offer retraining even beyond the em- ployee's time with the company. To help their former em- ployees reengage after first retirement, IBM, Pitney Bowes, Levi Strauss, and other companies even provide funds for retirees to take courses, some of which might lead to new careers.

At IBM, in 1985 alone, 9,000 employees took advantage of the company's Retiree Education Assistance Program (REAP), which provides up to $5,000 in tuition aid to em- ployees and their spouses during the three years before and two years following retirement. People use the money to study everything from real estate to bridge, from painting to carpentry.

A number of government and nonprofit programs also offer retraining to older Americans, usually to those at a lower income level. For instance:

- In Long Island, New York, more than 2,500 people have been attracted to each of seven "Ability Is Ageless" job fairs, attending seminars on such topics as résumé writ- ing, the reentry of women to the work force, and job search for the Spanish-speaking. In addition, private- sector companies interested in hiring older workers are exhibitors at the job fairs.

- In Wichita, Kansas, the Junior League of Wichita, the Kansas Elks, and Senior Services, Inc., have established a Senior Employment Training Program to match the skills of older workers with the needs of business and industry. Several hundred older Kansans have found full- or part-time work through its job club.

- In Oklahoma, former state representative Hannah Atkins works with the state's Department of Human Services running the New Vistas Program, which offers everything from the "McMasters" curriculum (training older people to work at McDonald's), to a course on caring for "latchkey" children and one on "Auto Mechanics for Older Women." (Atkins says, "They just put on jeans and gloves and get into those engines!").

Under Oklahoma's New Vistas umbrella, budding older entrepreneurs of every economic level can now find training and help. The program offers training in such practical skills as repairing small engines on chain saws, lawn mowers, and outboard motors. According to Jim Hicks, an employment and training coordinator for the Eastern Oklahoma Development District, "This kind of work allows people to bring in outside income at their own pace. It is a form of entrepreneurship." Instructor Steve Choate says, "These are first-class older Americans. They're here because they want to be. They want to learn. They're always on time. They are always prepared for class. They may be economically deprived, but there are no failures in this class."

At a higher economic and professional level, California's innovative New Career Opportunities, Inc. (NCO), provides older people with hands-on professional training to help them get started in their own businesses. NCO is partially supported by grants from Grumman, Rockwell, and other high-tech aviation and computer companies. Many of the student entrepreneurs get their first contracts from their former employers. This arrangement allows a company to use the talents of its former employees on a more flexible basis, at competitive, market-rate prices, while allowing the employee to be his or her own boss.

To meet the challenges of the future, workers will need to retrain, either in specific new skills for the jobs they now have or in the abilities required for entirely new careers. Retraining allows people to start fresh, to meet new challenges, and in effect to put the cyclic life plan into practice in the work place. And better-educated, more experienced employees are greater assets on the job.

Unless employers offer continuing professional education to their employees, the best, brightest, and most ambitious will leave.

Sabbaticals

Formal sabbaticals—periods of leisure, with a job guaranteed upon return—represent a very attractive option for a long-lived work force and could represent the next round of innovative employee benefits. Although new to the general work force, sabbaticals have been in popular use in academic environments for more than a century. According to futurist Fred Best:

> The idea of breaking from the routine of work existed primarily within religious writings and rare utopian proposals until the late nineteenth century, when the academic sabbatical was first established within scholarly communities. Harvard became the first university to instigate a sabbatical with pay for its faculty in 1880. By 1910, some ten major campuses had sabbaticals; in 1922, some 58 out of 590 institutions had such programs. By 1932, the idea had been adopted by 300 of the existing 575 colleges and universities.

Today, academic sabbaticals are offered at nearly all American colleges and universities. The new trend is the growing acceptance of scheduled extended breaks from work in nonacademic work environments. Some companies already offer *educational sabbaticals* that allow employees to pursue training in their areas of expertise—for example, in an MBA or other advanced-certification program. In response, college programs throughout the country, such as Pepperdine College's "Key Executive" MBA program, offer most of their classes on weekends or during intensive four- or six-week programs to accommodate the schedules of older professional students.

Similarly, Stanford and Harvard universities both run a series of high-power, high-priced business skills training programs in weekly blocks during the summer months. (Since the employer usually pays, there is less price sensitivity than would be the case if the student were responsible for payment.) The student can thus intersperse short, intense blocks of learning within an active career. For the more ambitious and self-motivated adult student, the Union Graduate School in Cincinnati, Ohio, offers fully accredited, complete doctoral curricula in such diverse fields as psychology, marketing, and urban studies through an interactive field-study program tailored to the unique lifestyle characteristics of each adult learner.

Some companies allow employees to take *personal sabbaticals* to pursue their own interests. This kind of leisure-oriented leave epitomizes the dream of the cyclic approach to work. At many companies, such as the San Francisco newspapers that contract with the Newspaper Guild, the sabbaticals are long—up to six months—but unpaid. At other companies, the sabbatical is shorter—eight weeks at McDonald's and Intel, six weeks at Tandem Computer—but fully paid. Said one Intel vice-president, "You get it every seven years. Most people combine it with vacation, so it's really more like three months. I've never known anyone not to take it. When you do come back, it's like coming back to a new job."

Tandem Computer executive Patricia Becker states:

> It's the most popular benefit we have. . . . Like most
> high-tech companies, Tandem is very fast-paced. After

working here four years, our employees often need to step back from their work and look at the personal side of their lives. They can do anything they want with their sabbatical. . . . Most of them travel, but some do amazing things. One enrolled in the Cordon Bleu cooking school, and another built an airplane. The benefits that the company gets back are tremendous. People return to work renewed. It's wonderful what time to reflect and think can do for a person." Jeri Flynn, manager of financial public relations at Tandem, says that "the sabbatical policy is definitely one of the reasons I came to Tandem."

After working at Wells Fargo for ten years, employees may take a fully paid, three-month personal growth sabbatical to pursue a personal activity or interest. In one recent year, paid sabbaticals were granted to an assistant vice-president/department manager to take a semester of formal fine-arts training; to another assistant vice-president to prepare for and participate in the Master's World Swimming Championship in Australia; and to an operations officer to learn the art of rug weaving that is traditional in her Navajo family.

Several years ago, Stanley Marcus, driving spirit of the Neiman-Marcus department store empire, decided he needed a break from his work. He took a sabbatical and enrolled in clown school!

Some companies, such as Xerox and Wells Fargo, offer employees paid *community-involvement sabbaticals,* during which they work with nonprofit agencies. At Xerox, employees can take up to a year at full pay and benefits; at Wells Fargo, they can take up to six months. Recently, a senior systems analyst at Wells Fargo took six months off to organize and promote recreational programs for disabled people; a project manager helped a child-abuse prevention program develop drop-in centers; and an assistant vice-president developed a countywide organ-donor awareness program.

Already, 14 percent of American firms incorporate regular sabbatical programs into their personnel structures.

The corporate philosophy behind these programs is straightforward. The sabbaticals help build the character of the individual involved, while improving public relations for the sponsoring organization by clearly showing its concern for the good of its community.

In the future, you may choose to take a significant amount of time from work—two months to a year or more—to pursue other leisure interests. Whether for public service, recreation, or continued education, sabbaticals will be a key element in relaxing the lifelong grip of work and in contributing to the flexible, cyclic life that more and more of us seek to live. Employers and personnel directors will find themselves having to grant sabbaticals as an alternative to losing restless employees, and as a way to enrich and expand the skills and capabilities of the employee base.

Phased Retirements and Retirement "Rehearsals"

Perhaps you are at the age when you are thinking of retiring, but you aren't sure whether you will like it. At some firms, such as Tektronix, Varian Associates, and Polaroid, you can try retirement—and then, if you find you don't like it, you can return to work, often with a more flexible work arrangement.

Last year I had the honor of being invited to deliver the keynote address on "The Aging of America: Implications for American Business" to the CEOs of 100 of the largest corporations in America at the Institutional Investor CEO Roundtable. Because my presentation was pertinent to the personal as well as business concerns of the participants, the conference planners asked if I would offer a special workshop the next day for the wives of these high-powered CEOs entitled "Your Husband's Successful Retirement: Fact or Fantasy?"

I accepted, thinking that it would be fun to see what I could learn from the spouses of some of America's most powerful leaders. I began the session by asking all of the participants to break up into small groups and to discuss both their biggest hopes and their biggest fears concerning their spouses' retirement. For the next few minutes the room buzzed with activity.

Then I asked if any of them would like to share their biggest hopes. One attractive woman, who looked to be in her late fifties, stood up and said, "My biggest hope is that retirement will give me more time with my husband." Many of the other women burst into laughter. When I asked why, they answered, "More time with our husbands was our biggest *fear*!" Like these wives, for many Americans retirement is filled with more uncertainty than anything else. Why not have some time to try it out before you make such an important decision?

The Polaroid Company in Cambridge, Massachusetts, calls its leaves of absence before retirement "retirement rehearsals." If you fail to make a comfortable transition to retirement, the job is there when the rehearsal is over. About half the Polaroid employees who rehearse retirement take their jobs back afterward. At Polaroid, you can also rehearse by reducing the number of hours per day, or days per week, that you work. Maybe you'd like to try a three-month summer vacation, for example, or one of a number of other time-reduction plans, for as long as five years before actual retirement. According to Joseph Perkins, Polaroid's corporate retirement manager, "No one wants to admit that they're dispensable, but we've had managers and vice-presidents take advantage of these programs, tapering off their hours and trying out retirement."

The Aerospace Corporation in Southern California offers its employees a list of options for "rehearsals": reduced work loads (20–40 hours per week), part-time work (fewer than 20 hours), and unpaid leaves. At Varian Associates in Palo Alto, California, soon-to-retire employees can work a four-day week for one year and then a three-day week for another year before finally leaving.

Phased retirements, which are a well-established practice among European companies, blur the lines between work

and leisure, and can take the stress out of the change in life stages.

Phased retirement gives employees a chance to sample retired life and to build up the activities and associations that will enhance their new lives. This practice and its educational sister, preretirement planning, will undoubtedly become more commonplace in the years ahead. The International Society of Pre-Retirement Planners (ISPRP), founded in 1976, had only 150 members in 1985. By 1988 it boasted more than 800 members, employed by major corporations to assist older workers with their retirement-related concerns.

Some companies have even begun hiring gerontologists to handle the special needs of older employees. Denise Jessup, for instance, recently came on board at The Aerospace Corporation as retiree relations administrator. Only 27 herself but armed with a master's in industrial gerontology from USC's Andrus Gerontology Center, Jessup has had her hands full answering the retiree hotline, giving preretirement counseling, managing part-time employment under a retirement transition program, and running special programs of interest to retirees, such as the AARP's Caregivers Fair for "sandwich generation" retirees and employees.

Part-Time Work, Part-Time Retirement

Many older men and women wish they could work occasionally, on a part-time basis. The major obstacle to the spread of this practice is the traditional view that part-timers are less useful than full-timers, with the subsequent treatment of part-timers as second-class employees.

Benefit packages, for instance, are typically unavailable to part-time employees. Employers who would like to take advantage of the flexibility inherent in employing many skilled, seasoned older workers on a part-time basis would do well to look into prorating benefit programs, bonuses, and incentive arrangements, as well as providing such employees with the opportunity to participate in educational and social functions. At Toro, a Minneapolis-area lawn- and snow-products company, everything from medical, dental, and disability insurance to profit sharing, holiday pay, and vacations is prorated for part-time employees.

When considering whether to return to work part-time at a new job or to reenlist with their former employer, many older people prefer to return to the more familiar environment. The employer thus has access to a valuable pool of potential employees who are familiar with the company and eager to keep a hand in. Using retirees this way enables the company to alter the size of the staff as needed. For example, retired employees can be extremely useful during seasonal demand peaks, at inventory time, or whenever the work load in any department gets too heavy. At the same time, such stints make it possible for these employees to enjoy many of the financial and psychological benefits of both work and leisure. Retired employees of Kentucky Fried Chicken can come back as part-time managers on an ongoing or occasional basis, working 20 to 30 hours a week, with full benefits.

The Aerospace Corporation brings back close to 100 former employees per year for what it refers to as *casual employment.* Under the corporation's pension rules, an employee can work up to 1,000 hours a year (about half-time) without losing pension benefits. According to officials at the company, interest in such work has grown steadily in recent years. Out of each year's retiring "class" of 100 or so workers, 20 or 30 people are interested in coming back part-time, and most start immediately. The hours vary tremendously: one person may work the full 1,000 hours, while another may just fill in for a full-time employee who is on vacation.

A typical Aerospace retiree "casual," 66-year-old Robert E. Malcho of Corona del Mar, California, was recently dividing his time among sailing, designing a computer system for a local dentist's office, and keeping his hand in at Aerospace. He says, "Last year, after I retired, I worked pretty much full-time. I didn't want to uproot too quickly. This year, every two months I go to Minneapolis to meet with clients, and when I return I write a report. I don't even have to go to the plant anymore. I'm technically oriented, and things are changing so fast these days that if I didn't keep my hand in it I'd soon be obsolete."

One of the less obvious benefits of this kind of program, according to Aerospace officials, is that it not only allows the company to use the talents of its retirees but also denies those talents to competitors. According to Robert Rubenstein, a personnel director at the firm, "For people with highly marketable skills, it would be possible for them to leave our company, take our retirement benefits, and then go to work for somebody else. That wouldn't make any sense. So why not give them the opportunity to work here?"

At the Travelers insurance companies in Hartford, Connecticut, such casual employment is handled by a *job bank*. Employees determine the number of hours they will work each year, arranging their schedules with their job supervisors. For example, Travelers allows retirees to work 960 hours per year (nearly half-time) without any diminution of pension or health benefits.

Travelers recruits these part-time workers from its own retiree pool. Sylvia Corvo, one of the job bank's coordinators, describes the company's unusual recruitment process: "When someone retires, there is usually a retirement party. Well, we decided to put on a party for 'unretirement.' We didn't know what to expect, but 700 people showed up on a snowy November afternoon. Of those, 300 'unretired' and signed up for our job-bank program."

The company's job bank of retired casual workers now includes hundreds of people. On an average day, some 80 or more work at Travelers as everything from secretaries to systems analysts, from clerks to underwriters. Barbara Greenberg, administrator of Travelers' Older Americans Program, sums up the reaction of permanent employees to the "unretired" workers as "totally positive. We get more supervisors' requests for them than we can handle."

Another unusual approach to part-time work, *job sharing*, was initially created to assist single parents who wanted to work but couldn't work full-time. Most large corporations now have a few examples of job sharing. This practice, which is well known in the personnel field, is expected to become increasingly common. At Pittsburgh's Mellon Bank, for instance, two people share the $30,000 position of "corporate identity coordinator," working two and a half days each. The Travelers had, at last count, 38 people sharing jobs throughout the company, including the coordinators of its job bank, 77-year-old Sylvia Corvo and 69-year-old Evelyn Smith. In the company's Office of Consumer Information, which is charged with answering thousands of customers' questions every year over the phone, four jobs are shared by 16 people.

Over 44 percent of employers now use part-time help of all kinds; three-quarters of those started the practice only in the last eight years.

Some companies have come to depend very heavily on older part-timers. The Intertek Company in California has more than 12,000 employees, over 9,000 of whom are retirees working part-time as independent contractors. Sterile Design of Clearwater, Florida, is a medical and hospital supply firm located in an area that has a lot of retirees. Of the firm's 300 employees, 180 are senior citizens who work four-hour "minishifts" to supplement their Social Security income.

Some older people prefer to work on a temporary, *project-oriented* basis with a different employer than the one they had before retiring. In response, temporary agencies such as Kelly Services, which were once used solely as a source of clerical help and unskilled labor, are increasingly handling older men and women who are "retired" engineers, computer programmers and consultants, marketing specialists, accountants, and paralegals.

According to Caroline Bird, who has written extensively on the future shape of work, these semiretired older professionals who migrate from one temporary job to another, constantly giving themselves the option of whether to work or not, are "pioneers of the project-oriented future work."

Under this arrangement, as specific projects arise, employers assemble teams of individuals whose personal skills are appropriate to the job at hand. By working for a period of time on a project in this fashion, the older, semiretired worker can share in the excitement and action that teamwork offers, without having to make the full-time, long-term commitment normally required for such participation.

Flexplace

Flexplace, which allows employees to work at home or at a recreation hideaway at least part of the time, is another corporate strategy that is gaining in popularity.

Flexplace opens up work opportunities for the parents of young children; for people whose health makes it difficult for them to commute or to work long hours without a break; or for busy older people who would like to work if they could fit it in around their other activities.

A 1986 survey of 100 top personnel directors conducted by the employment firm Challenger, Gray & Christmas found that more than half of those surveyed believed that more and more white-collar workers would be working from their home computer terminals for at least part of the time instead of commuting. Pacific Bell now uses such *telecommuting* to accommodate some employees. This type of arrangement can involve establishing small satellite offices in areas where many employees live; employees can do their work in these offices by computer rather than commuting long distances to a large, centrally located office. Working at home is becoming increasingly common among employees of the Mellon Bank, as well as of the Mutual Life Insurance Company of New York, where 3 percent of employees take advantage of a "variable work site" program.

It is projected that by the year 2000, over 20 percent of the work force will go to work without leaving home.

Flextime

According to the Bureau of Labor Statistics, among men receiving Social Security benefits, 68 percent of those self-employed were still working, compared to only 32 percent of wage and salary workers. According to the bureau's Phillip L. Rones, one of the main reasons for the difference is that the self-employed "can adjust their hours and working conditions more easily to meet their health needs or desire for increased leisure." Flextime, or sliding work hours, offers a means to increase the positive sense of independence and self-determination commonly associated with self-employment.

If you are a little older and have fewer responsibilities at home, you might want to work unusual hours. You might like to sleep late and work into the evenings. You might prefer to work on weekends, so that you can use public recreation facilities when everyone else is at work. You might be willing to work long hours for a few days so that you can take regular three-day weekends. Or perhaps you'd like to begin work very early in the morning so that you can have your afternoons free.

With flexible work scheduling, companies allow employees a choice in their work schedules. This strategy, which a number of companies first experimented with as a solution to rush-hour traffic jams, has turned out to be a very satisfying work arrangement for many employees, especially those with unusual scheduling needs.

Mutual Life Insurance Company of New York, for instance, allows its managers to start work any time between 7 and 9 A.M. Corning Glass Works allows employees in its research and development division to design their own schedules, within certain guidelines and subject to the approval of supervisors. General Motors allows some employees, including managers, to work a 32-hour compressed workweek it calls "flexible service." Employees at Mutual Life can earn a three-day weekend whenever they choose by squeezing ten days' work into nine.

As recently as 1985, only 12 percent of American companies offered flextime. By 1987 that figure had more than doubled, to 26 percent. A 1987 survey found that only 60 percent of American companies still stick to the traditional 9-to-5, 40-hour week.

There already exists a more expanded version of flextime that could turn out to be just what the older worker ordered. Called the *hour bank,* it is an idea that has been advocated by a number of specialists in work and leisure, including Dr. Max Kaplan, director of the Center for Leisure Studies at the University of South Florida. According to this concept, you would first identify the number of total hours you would need to work over a period of time, such as a month, a year, or even a decade. Then, as you work, you save these hours in an "hour bank," becoming entitled to withdraw hours of leisure as work hours accumulate.

This arrangement is pretty much the same as the one we now unconsciously follow: we work for approximately forty years in a row, with the ongoing hope that one day we'll be able to cash in all of that effort for fifteen to twenty years of nonworking leisure. But this hopeful approach could be brought a great deal more under our control. Given a choice, most of us would probably prefer to enjoy blocks of well-earned leisure throughout our lives rather than storing it all up for our later years.

For example, under a yearly job-bank arrangement, you might negotiate a contract that allows you 10 days of leisure for every 20 days of work. (Our existing 5-day workweek plus vacations is comparable.) If you wished, under this arrangement you could work 20 days in a row and then have a 10-day holiday. Or, you might work every other weekend for 6 years and then enjoy a fully paid 6-month "leisure holiday." Similarly, the yearly job-bank concept could be easily stretched to accommodate a decade-long, or even lifetime, arrangement. You might, for example, wish to "retire" for a year at the end of each decade.

In Germany, these kinds of flex-year contracts are gaining in popularity. Some employees want to work as many hours as the company will let them, while others prefer to work the absolute least amount of hours that is acceptable. Some choose to work three-quarter time the year through, while others prefer to accumulate ongoing vacation time for extended holidays. The alternatives are not unlimited, but the firms using this sort of individual negotiation find that it not only makes the employees happier but also allows the company extra flexibility in planning its work force.

Flexible, Portable Pensions

As our work schedules shift to accommodate our more flexible and cyclic lifestyles, benefits and pension programs will change as well. The day may soon come when Social Security and other employee pension programs will be transformed into several entirely new systems more appropriate to our changing times.

For years, Nobel Prize–winning economist Milton Friedman has led a vigorous attack on Social Security. If he had his way, he would change Social Security dramatically. As he told us:

> Social Security has helped the wealthy much more than the poor. On the one hand, the relatively well-to-do have a longer life expectancy. On the other hand, they tend to enter the work force later and contribute to the fund for a shorter time. My children, for instance, entered the work force after college in their twenties. A kid from a working-class family, if he's lucky enough to get a job, will enter the force at 15 or 16. This bias greatly overweighs the payout formulae that are weighted toward the poor.

Friedman and others believe that the current Social Security program should be dismantled into two separate programs. One would be a tax-supported, means-based program for the indigent. "We should help people because they're indigent—not because they're old," he says. Friedman's view is shared by others from seemingly diverse camps. Richard Lamm, controversial former governor of Colorado, argues, "If you're a retired doctor living in Florida driving your boat around when you've got $100,000 in retirement income before Social Security, why the hell are we taxing the poor black worker in Denver and transferring his money to you, and on top of it not even taxing you? That's immoral." Gray Panther radical Maggie Kuhn says, "With increased longevity factors and the growing gap between the rich and the poor, we need to take another look at the whole Social Security system; and means testing may be one of the ways to make it work." The first gingerly step toward means testing for Social Security has already been taken. The old tax law treated everyone the same as long as they were old, regardless of whether they were rich or poor. Under the new law introduced in 1984, half of Social Security benefits are taxable for individuals who make over $25,000 per year in other income and for couples who make over $32,000.

Under Friedman's plan, part of Social Security would become essentially a targeted welfare program for a smaller number of people than Social Security now serves. The non-poor majority of Americans would be assisted through the other half of Friedman's plan, which calls for a fully vested, self-supporting insurance program—a portable pension plan. "This not only will be necessary, it will be a highly desirable alternative to what we have now," says Friedman.

Currently, many Americans depend on the government for financial security in their later years; some blame the government if they run into periods of financial uncertainty. At the same time, most men and women are somewhat irresponsible in their own financial planning for later life. As an illustration of this pattern, among the 40 wealthiest countries in the world today, the average American's income is number two, just below the Swiss. But the American personal savings rate is at the very bottom of the list. Because of distressing statistics such as these, many policy analysts have begun to argue that if we did a better job of saving and planning for our later years, many Americans might not be so dependent on the government.

In the years ahead, instead of the government managing our retirement savings accounts through Social Security, it might instead provide IRA-like tax incentives for the creation of personal, portable pension plans that we would ultimately manage ourselves.

To date, pensions have been a relatively hit-or-miss system. Until recently, employees were not legally entitled to pensions unless they had worked for the same employer for 10 years. Now the legal minimum is five years, and many employers require longer periods. Because of this and the high level of job turnover throughout work life, the majority of American workers have no pension plan at all. Across the country, less than 60 percent of all workers work for companies that offer pensions, and only 24 percent are entitled to any future benefits.

In place of the existing Social Security system and these spotty pension programs, a nationwide Portable Pension Program (PPP) might be established. Under such a plan, you would start accumulating benefits, and have rights to them, the day you started work. If you stopped working, the value of your pension would be deposited into your federal PPP account, which might be managed by the government or perhaps by private companies set up for this purpose, much as IRAs are handled now. For periods when you were out of the work force, or if your employer did not provide a pension program, you could contribute a certain tax-deductible amount of your savings or salary to the account. If you switched jobs, you would have the choice of transferring your account into your new company's pension plan or leaving it in your own account. For those unable to work because of illness, inability, or burdensome family responsibilities, the government might make a contribution to the fund out of general revenues.

Portable pensions are not new. The Civil Service Retirement System, with nearly 3 million members, already provides portability throughout the civilian federal government. Major companies have portability between their many divisions, as do the 11 companies that once formed the Bell System. Some industries, such as car dealers and savings institutions, have industrywide portable pension plans. The Teacher's Insurance and Annuity Association–College Retirement Equities Fund covers more than 400,000 active employees in over 80 percent of the nation's educational institutions.

Aside from the enhanced lifestyle flexibility and greater control over one's own account that this type of system provides, it also holds the promise of offering a better payback than the existing Social Security system. For example, suppose you took the same money that you and your employer now put into Social Security and put it, instead, in an IRA invested in some broadly based, fairly safe instrument such as a market-index mutual fund. Would the money you end up with be more or less than you would get from Social Security?

A study funded by the National Chamber Foundation, a think tank associated with the United States Chamber of Commerce, suggests that it would be as much as six times more.

According to this study, based on the Social Security Administration's intermediate "Alternative IIB" projections, for young workers now entering the work force "the real rate of return paid by Social Security will be less than 1 to 1.5 percent, with returns for many workers virtually zero or even below zero." Peter Ferrara, former Reagan White House policy aide and the study's principal author, reports that, based on the average rate of return on the stock market over the last 60 years, if the same money were invested in stock index funds:

> . . . most workers would be able to receive from such investments 3 to 6 times the retirement benefits offered by Social Security, while still matching the pre–age 65 survivors and disability benefits promised by the program. A two-earner couple . . . would reach retirement

age under such a private investment program with a total accumulated fund of $1.3 million in today's dollars, which could pay them about six times the retirement benefits offered by Social Security.

This type of alternative to Social Security has already been tried in several other countries.

For example, Chile began a national experiment in 1980 that parallels many of the conclusions of the Ferrara plan. For the previous half century, Chileans had a system much like social security systems elsewhere: workers contributed to a general pool, out of which they received benefits beginning at age 65. When the system began to fail because of many of the same demographic and bureaucratic problems that our program is currently facing, Chile tried a daring social experiment. Beginning in November 1980, Chilean citizens had a choice. They could opt out of the government social security system for an alternative plan, under which they were required to set aside 10 percent of their gross income in an IRA-like account in any financial institution they chose. They could deduct the money from their income for tax purposes. When they turned 65 (or 60 for women), they would have another choice: either withdraw the money a little at a time, or roll the entire amount over into an annuity contract that would provide a set income for life.

The Chilean plans are managed by private companies set up specifically for this purpose. They compete in the marketplace, much the way various financial institutions compete for IRAs in the United States. As a result, it costs the central government little to administer the plan. Low-income workers are also provided for: if a worker's fund is not large enough at retirement age to buy an annuity of a certain minimum size, the government makes up the difference out of general revenue.

This innovative alternative proved immediately popular. Within the first year, out of a pool of some 2 million eligible workers, 1.5 million—75 percent—moved to the new plan.

By 1986, 90 percent of the eligible workers had switched. Over the first four years of the plan, workers' funds averaged an impressive 10 percent annual real rate of return.

When the British government tried a similar experiment with its supplementary pensions, it had the same experience: more than 90 percent of eligible workers preferred the private alternative. Perhaps such a system, where more control and responsibility is shifted from the government to the individual, would find fertile ground in the United States.

This kind of system offers several attractions:

- It separates the issue of providing government support to the truly needy from retirement planning for the majority of the population, a distinction that Social Security does not make very effectively.
- By allowing people to withdraw from their pension account at various times throughout their lives if they choose, as well as in their later years, it could accommodate the needs of an aging work force interested in more flexible life scheduling.
- It would give people greater control and more personal responsibility for their lifetime retirement accounts. It wouldn't be quite as easy to blame the government in those situations when it was the individual's mismanagement of savings that caused financial problems.
- Because it would place less of a drain on general government revenues and would require minimal government bureaucracy to manage, it could conceivably free up more tax dollars to pay for special social attention to the truly needy.

Perhaps the time is arriving when we will not only redefine work and its role in the cyclic life but will also envision a new lifetime finance management system that is fair, that helps those who need it the most, and that gives us tax incentives to act more responsibly in planning for our later years.

A NEW ARRANGEMENT OF
LIFE'S PARTS

We are witnessing the end of yesterday's retirement, with Grandpa asleep on the porch, the gold watch the company gave him ticking in his vest pocket, and his friends coming over later to go fishing or play cards or checkers.

This picture is giving way to a more involved mixture of work and leisure that will soon become standard, typified by the homemaker who has finally made it back to the university for her master's in social work; the retired handyman who has just started an alarm-and-lock company; the retired bookkeeper who now works a flexible schedule as an office temp; the former construction worker who puts in 20 hours a week in a McDonald's management-training program; or the engineer who has gone from full-time work to part-time consulting.

Later life is rapidly becoming a time when you do not stop working completely, but instead shift gears to part-time, seasonal, or occasional work, mixed with productive and involved leisure activities.

Recent studies have shown that members of the baby boom generation are much more inclined than either their parents or grandparents were to trade work time for unpaid leisure. And members of this generation have already demonstrated their cyclic work style by changing jobs an average of every three years, usually taking some time to rest and reflect between obligations. (In a way, these between-job breaks represent a kind of cyclic retirement program, frequently underwritten by the government as unemployment.)

If these generational styles continue, innovative work/leisure strategies such as phased retirement, sabbaticals, part-time work, hour banks, flexplace, flextime, and portable pension accounts will not only be a godsend for today's older men and women but may also establish an entirely new approach to the lifetime distribution of work and leisure, one that will reverberate backward through the generations.

When this happens, the cyclic life plan will be set free to emerge as a more balanced blend of work, leisure, education, and community service throughout every decade of our lives.

CHAPTER

8

Love in the Second Half

If we had to name what makes life worth living, most of us would say the people we love—wives, husbands, children, friends.

Intimate relationships make a profound difference in the quality of life at any age. Yet, in the later years of life, the making and keeping of relationships can become more difficult. Parents who find themselves in an "empty nest" may become disoriented and depressed because there is no longer a need for their child-rearing skills. Many older people have been cut off from the life of the workplace, which is a breeding ground for many friendships and romances. Long-standing friends of the same age retire and move away. And retirement from work can create a host of interpersonal tensions, as couples find themselves having to relate to each other around the clock. Finally, there are few experiences more devastating than the death of a spouse or close friend.

Between now and the turn of the century, we are going to experience great changes in all our relationships.

The new longer life is accelerating the trend away from the lifetime marriage to that of having several mates over a lifetime ("serial monogamy"). And the shortage of older men will give rise to an unusual mix of later-life social arrangements. Beyond the changing boundaries of primary relationships, the "nuclear," or child-centered, family is being transformed into an adult-centered "matrix" family composed of blood relations and voluntary friendship networks. This chapter and the one that follows ("Reinventing the Family") will explore several of the key interpersonal elements in the search for love, friendship, and family in the second half of life.

"Until Death Do Us Part"

Last year my wife and I attended a special anniversary party for my Aunt Sylvia and Uncle Martin, held in their home in Union, New Jersey. It was their *seventieth* anniversary. Like two mature, twisted garden trees, they had grown through all of those years together. Since nearly all of our personal friends and associates have been married and divorced at least once in their lives, our minds reeled in an attempt to comprehend the depth, range, and fullness that such a longevous union offered.

Although there is an unmistakable trend toward serial monogamy, those who do go the distance in one marriage will experience something relatively new to human history—five-, six-, and even seven-decade-long marriages.

According to the U.S. Census Bureau Office of Marriage and Family, of the men and women who were married in 1910, 18 percent lived to celebrate their fiftieth wedding anniversary. Of those married in 1930, a remarkable 26 percent were still together after 50 years!

For those deeply in love, long life offers more time to play, more years to hold each other, more experiences to share, and more of life's secrets to discover together. As gerontologist Robert Atchley, Ph.D., reflects in his book *The Social Forces in Later Life*, "For the happily married older couple, marriage is a blessing. It is a source of great comfort and support as well as the focal point of everyday life, and happily married couples often experience an increasing closeness as the years go by."

Research into the characteristics of today's successful golden marriages suggests that the key ingredients are sharing, accommodation, and companionship. As one older woman commented in a survey conducted by the Consumers Union:

> Now that the children are grown, we are delighted to be a "single couple" once again, and have been on a honeymoon ever since we have been alone. We find that our shared experiences have made us closer, wiser, and funnier. Our little understandings, communicated by a lifted eyebrow during some cocktail party; the little words that are a private joke within the family; and the ability to sit down and talk about feelings have all come with age. We like being able to make love in the afternoon, if we wish, or to wait a few days longer if one or the other of us is not in the mood. It is a LOVELY time of life.

Many older couples report that their relationships have become more romantic, even more sexually satisfying, as they have aged. In a major national study conducted by Drs. Bernard Starr and Marcella Weiner, 75 percent of the older respondents reported that "sex is the same or better now compared to when they were younger." And 36 percent of the sample reported that sex had gotten better with age (41 percent of the females and 27 percent of the males). Some of the respondents offered comments on how their sexual lives had changed with aging:

"I now have less inhibitions and a feeling of accomplishment in giving pleasure."

"Sex has gotten better, I have more understanding and awareness. Plus I'm a lot less uptight than I was when I was younger."

"Sexual relations are much more fun now because we are both more tolerant and understanding."

"Sex was always hurried and worrisome in my youth. And I was always frightened of becoming pregnant. Now it is much more enjoyable."

"It's no longer a catch-as-catch-can experience, but one to be thoroughly enjoyed."

After interviewing hundreds of older men and women about their sexual experiences, Starr and Weiner concluded that with increasing maturity, "it is the quality of the lovemaking experiences, not the frequency, which is the measure of satisfaction . . . and far from sitting on the sidelines or giving up their sexual selves, many older adults have achieved higher levels of sexual satisfaction."

In the years to come, as we study the special nature of successful longevous relationships, we may find that there is no other human activity or association more loving, intimate, or sacred than the bond of a marriage that has had decades to take root, grow, and blossom.

SERIAL MONOGAMY

Although successful, long-term marriages provide an unequaled opportunity for love and intimacy, with today's rising divorce rate, less than 3 percent of all married couples will live to celebrate their fiftieth wedding anniversary. Lifetime monogamy is becoming the rare exception. For the other 97 percent, the cyclic life serves up a curious blend of new options and new ways of viewing the purpose of marriage.

In the months before she died, author and anthropologist Margaret Mead was interviewed about her long and fascinating life. When the reporter probed about her "failed" marriages, Mead quickly reacted by saying, "I didn't have any failed marriages. I've been married three times—and each marriage was successful."

She went on to explain that in her long life, she had gone through several distinct adult stages. During each stage she had become, in essence, a different person, with a new and different assortment of likes, dislikes, and lifestyle preferences. And at each stage she had discovered that she had an entirely different set of needs and priorities for a mate.

When she was young, she sought out a husband who could share her vigor and enthusiasm. She found such a person and for a period, thrived in that relationship, later labeling it the "ideal student marriage." Then, as she grew a bit older and was developing a reputation as a world-famous anthropologist, she fell in love and married again. In this marriage she and her husband developed a satisfying professional partnership. Then in her late thirties she found herself being drawn to the more mature intimacies of an intellectual companion and "soul mate." While on a field trip, she met and soon married Gregory Bateson, an English anthropologist and in her words got the "perfect intellectual and emotional working partnership." At 38, in her third "succcessful" marriage, she had her first and only child, Mary Catherine.

When life was short, we barely had time to live one adult role with one compatible mate. With longer life, we have the time and the resources to "be" many different people during one extended lifetime. Some of us will continue to grow in tandem with our spouses throughout our lives, but many of us will grow apart. In the past, death nearly always intervened before a typical marriage had run its natural course. Now, many marriages run out of steam with decades of life remaining for each spouse. When people could expect to live only a few more months or years in an unsatisfying relationship, they would usually resign themselves to it. But the thought of 20, 30, or even 50 more years in an unsatisfying relationship can cause decisive action at any age.

Many people find that as they grow older and their needs and expectations change, the essential purpose of marriage shifts from child rearing to companionship. Whereas, at the turn of the century, the average couple could expect to live only a year or two beyond the time when the last of their children left home, today, 18 to 30 years of an empty-nest marriage is becoming the norm. The average couple can now expect to spend more years *after* parenting then *during.* As a young bride or groom, you might choose a spouse partly because you feel he or she would make a good parent to your children. As an older newlywed, you might prefer to choose a spouse more on the basis of shared social, leisure, and intellectual interests.

As Mead's example suggests, seen in this way divorce and remarriage are less an admission of failure than a shedding of a skin, a breaking of a chrysalis, a moving on to the next stage. According to sociologist Gary Lee, "The rising divorce rate does not mean that people are losing faith in marriage, but that they believe marriage can be better than it often is. When marriages fall short of expectations, people have become more willing to try again. Giving up on *a* marriage is very different than giving up on *marriage.*"

Lee also believes that with each passing decade, divorce is becoming an increasingly accepted process: "Divorce, like other social customs, feeds on itself. As it becomes more common it becomes more visible, and this visibility means that more people will consider it to be a possible, if not entirely normative, solution to marital difficulties." This acceptance is reflected in the statistics.

For the past 15 years in America, for every two couples that have married, one couple has divorced.

Studies show that current older cohorts still resist divorce a great deal more strongly than younger cohorts. Having a longer exposure to more traditional values, with marriages that have often lasted for decades, they are less inclined to "give it all up" for an uncertain new life. In contrast, younger cohorts who are more accustomed to life changes of all kinds —from changing majors in college, to shifting jobs, to moving regularly from one neighborhood to another—view divorce and remarriage, however unsettling, as a more normal, acceptable alternative to staying in an unsatisfying relationship. Whereas the divorce rate for women currently in their fifties is 24 percent, the rate for women in their thirties is 60 percent.

However, even older Americans are increasingly opting for divorce. Recent figures show that in the past two decades the rate of divorce among the elderly has increased three times as fast as the rate of growth of the older population as a whole.

The rate of divorce for people over 60 is now increasing as rapidly as that of younger age groups.

Eighty percent of those who divorce remarry, and fully half of those second marriages also end in divorce. Nearly 10 million American households are already being run by remarried couples. And according to the Census Bureau, the number of Americans who have married three or more times increased by over 56 percent in the last ten years, going from 2.3 million to 3.6 million.

The younger cohorts will take their more casual attitudes toward marriage with them into their later years, causing the "average" older person's perspective on marriage to change even more in the decades ahead.

Divorce: Liberation or Nightmare?

For some, late-life divorce is a taste of freedom, a liberation from an unhappy or unsatisfying union. For others it is a terrifying nightmare of loneliness and rejection.

Several years ago I was developing a course on life planning for a community college in the Chicago area. Designed to assist older men and women find new directions in their lives after retirement, the ten-week program focused on the relatively straightforward issues of financial planning and

health management. There were approximately 40 participants in the program, including a very friendly and attractive
couple: Hank, 81, and Frances, 78.

Six weeks into the program, after a particularly lively
group discussion on interpersonal relationships, Frances took
me aside and said, "I need to talk to you in private, and I'd
really like to talk to you soon!"

"Fine," I said. "Let's go into my office and talk right
now."

In my office, Frances closed the door and told me, "Hank
and I first came to your program to learn about financial
planning. But after I heard your statistics on how much longer
I was probably going to live, I came to a very important
realization, and I've decided to divorce Hank. I haven't told
him about my decision yet. I just wanted to thank you for
giving me the courage to free myself from a marriage I'm not
happy with."

I was shocked. It had never occurred to me that by explaining the rise in female longevity, I was causing Frances to
rethink her marriage. "How long have you been married?"
I asked.

"Fifty-two years."

"Why do you want to divorce him?"

After a short pause to reflect, she answered, "Several
reasons. First, I don't really love him anymore. I've searched
my heart, and there's no love there. Second, I think he's a
complete jerk!"

Wondering if the couple might just be in the middle of
a particularly trying period, I asked, "How long have you felt
this way?"

Without hesitation, she said, "Twenty-two years."

"Twenty-two years? Why didn't you divorce him 22
years ago?"

"Twenty-two years ago," she explained, "I was 57 years
old. Back then, life expectancy was only 62. So I figured, I'm
an old lady, I'll be dead soon. Why bother?

"But now here I am, 78 years old, and healthy as a horse.

I know I've got another 20 good years left in me, and I'll be damned if I'm going to spend them with that jerk!"

Several months later, shortly after celebrating her seventy-ninth birthday, Frances divorced Hank.

Afterward, she called me up to let me know that she was feeling more alive and liberated than she had felt in decades.

For others, late-life separation can be a nightmare. In addition to the monumental task of learning how to function as a single person, the pain of rejection can make separation a particularly difficult time.

Clinical social worker Nicholas Chamberlain, who runs therapy groups for older divorcés in San Diego, California, comments on the anxiety felt by many older singles:

> Some of them immediately want to remarry. They have difficulty accepting that it's okay to be alone, to be themselves. Some people have been miserable for 35 years or more and are finally coming to admit it. They have tremendous fears—of loneliness, of poverty. The saddest cases are the women who were kept sheltered by their husbands. Even after the divorce, he says, "Don't worry, I'll provide for you." Then he remarries, and the support stops coming. We tell them to wise up. We encourage them to start working and to learn to take care of themselves.

For women, the economic fears accompanying late-life singlehood are not unfounded. A recent study of divorce in California showed that in the first year after a divorce the standard of living for older women dropped 73 percent, while the standard of living for men *rose* by 42 percent.

The increase in emotional problems created by later-life divorce is so marked that self-help groups for divorced seniors have begun to spring up all over the United States. These groups provide emotional support to their members, who sometimes call themselves "the gray divorcés." They give their members access to information and professional help, encourage research into late-life divorce, and lobby for legislation promoting equity between older men and women in divorce settlements. The first such group, "Divorce after Sixty," was started by Patty Clare in Ann Arbor, Michigan, after her divorce in 1981. When a wire service ran a story on the group, Clare received hundreds of requests for information and for guidance in starting similar support organizations.

In the years ahead, increasing shares of the practices of psychotherapy, marriage and family counseling, and clinical social work will be focused on helping middle-aged and older people make the sometimes stormy transition from marriage to singlehood and possibly back to marriage again.

THE NEW DATING GAME

If you are 60+ SWF [single white female], enjoy life, including music, dancing, camping, beach strolling, quiet dinners by firesides, I would be happy to hear from you. Write Box 5553 . . .

It shouldn't surprise us that singles ads for people over 50 proliferate. So do social groups, dances, and nightclubs designed as meeting grounds for singles in late adulthood who are looking for some peer romance.

A Tampa television station runs a commercial for a dating service, with no specific age group mentioned. The ad talks about the joys of companionship and shows a man driving home to be greeted at the front door by his loving wife. But the actors have white hair, and—what may tell us more about the commercial's intended market—the man is not driving a car but an electric golf cart.

Even Club Med, which initially marketed its "swinging" resorts to young men and women in their twenties, now finds that the median age of its guests is approaching 40. Environments and activities that were created primarily so that men and women could meet and find romance are all growing older with the Age Wave. Nearly every community in America now offers singles dances for middle-aged or older people, with regular standing-room-only attendance. Several years ago, Jerry Rubin, former draft-card burner and 1960s radical, capitalized on the increasing interest in adult mating by organizing "networking gatherings" in New York City. At these after-work parties, single yuppies can sip Perrier, argue about the current stock index, and exchange business cards with other eligible singles. When it's time for the baby boomers to arrive at Golden Pond, they might be surprised to find that they are met by an activities director sporting a name badge.

Sixty and Single

The rise in the interest in forming new relationships later in life comes at a time when the pool of possible partners is growing at an astonishing rate. In the two decades between 1964 and 1984, rising divorce rates and increasing late-life widowhood led to an increase of 123 percent in the number of older people living alone—over two and a half times the growth rate of the older population in general.

Of the total population of older Americans, 43 percent are single.

This situation affects not only individuals but also nearly every segment of our society—from housing (should complexes be designed around couples or around single women who share common kitchens and living rooms?), to leisure (should resorts, cruises, and activities be geared to couples or to groups of single older women?), to the marketing of financial services (are bankers and insurance agents ready to focus their services on the needs of single men and women instead of couples?). But the impact of late-life singlehood shows up most dramatically in the realm of dating and romance.

Older single people share many of the same dating/ mating enthusiasms and anxieties of younger singles. According to Kris Bulcroft and Margaret O'Conner-Roden, two sociologists who have studied the dating patterns of senior citizens, "The question of whether older people date, fall in love, and behave romantically, just as the young do, occurred to us while we were observing singles dances for older people at a senior center. We noticed a sense of anticipation, festive dress, and flirtatious behavior that were strikingly familiar to us as women recently involved in the dating scene."

For today's older men and women interested in new romance and companionship, there are a variety of ways to approach the problem of finding satisfying love relationships. Possible combinations include a younger woman and an older man; an older woman and a younger man; an older man and an older woman, who perhaps live together without getting married; several women sharing one man; and same-sex friendships and/or romantic liaisons.

Of the various alternatives, only the first one—younger woman, older man—has traditionally been considered acceptable within our system of social values and mores. But for the 60 percent of women over 65 who are alone, the odds against finding an available older man are high:

- Each woman is competing with a great many other older women for the attention of a proportionately smaller group of men.
- In addition, because men tend to marry women younger than themselves, the older woman is also competing with single women in their fifties or even forties.
- Of the men in this age group, nearly four of every five are already married.
- Some 4 percent of the male population is exclusively homosexual throughout life.

The other options have been either frowned upon or considered altogether taboo. However, if intimacy and sexuality are going to survive in our aging society, it's obvious that we are going to have to change the rules. This is now beginning to happen, with men and women of all ages redefining the possibilities for satisfying adult relationships.

SEXUAL AND LIFESTYLE EXPERIMENTATION

Romance without Marriage

In interviews with dozens of dating couples between the ages of 60 and 92, sociologists Bulcroft and O'Conner-Roden found that many of the older couples have few clues about what constitutes "appropriate" dating behavior for elders. Often, what they are doing in their new, later-life romantic involvements goes against their own lifetime patterns of traditional social and sexual behavior. In some instances, their biggest concern is that their new sexual adventures might shock their children:

> As one 63-year-old retiree said, "My girlfriend [age 64] lives just down the hall from me. . . . When she spends the night she usually brings her cordless phone . . . just in case her daughter calls." One 61-year-old woman told us that even though her 68-year-old boyfriend has been spending three or four nights a week at her house for the past year, she has not been able to tell her family. "I hide his shoes when my grandchildren are coming over."

Despite the fact that marriage would solve part of the problem of public acceptance of older singles' relationships, many progressive older couples, although interested in romance and companionship, resist tying the knot. Some had assumed when they began dating that they would eventually marry, but as time went on they discovered that they weren't willing to give up their independence. Many say that they do not have the same family-building reasons for marriage that young people do. For women especially, divorce or widowhood may have marked the first time in their lives that they had been on their own, and many now enjoyed their independence.

As my wife's 85-year-old grandmother told me, "I'm not going to wash anybody's dirty socks. I did it for my husband for almost 50 years, and that's enough. I want to be with a man when I feel like it, and by myself or with my lady friends when I choose."

Another major reason some elders are reluctant to marry is the possibility of their new mate's deteriorating health. They would not want to become a caretaker for an ill spouse, especially if they had been through this emotionally draining ordeal before.

By and large, older Americans mirror society's increasing acceptance of singlehood. More than 10 percent of all adult Americans currently live alone, three times the percentage in 1960; some 1.9 million couples live together without being married, four times the number in 1960. As reported in the *Population Bulletin*: "Attitudes toward marriage and remaining single have changed markedly along with the changes in marital patterns. The legitimacy of remaining single is increasingly accepted by both young people and their parents; Americans no longer regard getting married as necessarily better than remaining single."

Older Woman, Younger Man

Currently, older women make up the fastest-growing singles group in America. This phenomenon is relatively recent. At the turn of the century, there were 102 men for every 100 women in America. As recently as 1930, there were roughly as many men as women over the age of 65. But today, for every 100 women between the ages of 65 and 69, there are 83 men. After the age of 85, the ratio doubles, with only 42 men alive for every 100 women.

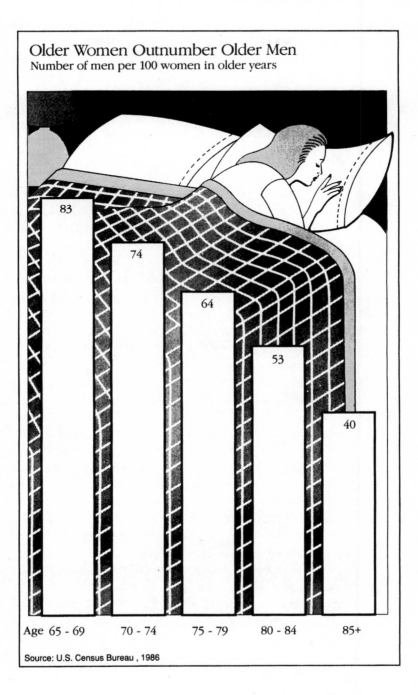

Older Women Outnumber Older Men
Number of men per 100 women in older years

83

74

64

53

40

Age 65 - 69   70 - 74   75 - 79   80 - 84   85+

Source: U.S. Census Bureau , 1986

In 1984, there were 10.4 million single women over 65, but only 2.7 million single men over 65.

The mismatch between available men and women is further skewed by the tendency in every stage of life for men to seek younger women, and women to seek older men, as companions and mates.

The tendency for husbands to be older than wives is directly related to the economic circumstances of earlier times, when women were primarily wives and mothers and men were providers. In those times, it made good sense for the man to have a few years' head start to "build a nest," making himself into a reliable provider, before he married and started a family.

There are now five times as many widows as widowers, and fully half of all women over 65 are widows. Another 6 percent have never been married, and 4 percent are divorced. Only 40 percent of older women are married and living with their husbands, in contrast with the 75 percent of older men who are currently married and living with their wives. The trend also carries over into remarriage: among women who are divorced at any time in their lives, roughly one-third will never remarry. After the age of 65, remarriage rates are about eight times as high for men as for women. How will the emotional needs of the single older woman be met?

While society has always been comfortable with the sight of older men escorting or marrying women much younger than themselves, we are not nearly as tolerant of the reverse situation. Even the classic "coming-of-age" film *Harold and Maude* was as much odd as it was entertaining. Many women and men are beginning to ask whether this prejudiced view of female/male relationships is fair.

With women and men now marrying later in life and having fewer children, the male-female dynamic is undergoing a great restructuring. Increasing numbers of women are deciding to choose men substantially younger than themselves as mates. One of the recent harbingers of this trend has been the growing number of women in the public eye whose marriages and relationships with men considerably younger than themselves have been celebrated in the press. But celebrities are just the more public exemplars (and possibly the role models) of a much larger shift. The most recent Census Bureau statistics show that almost 3 million American women are married to men who are at least 10 years younger than they.

Share-a-Man Relationships

Over a generation ago, Dr. Victor Kassel argued energetically in the prestigious medical journal *Geriatrics* that men over 60 should be allowed multiple wives. If they were allowed to marry two, three, four, or even five women over 60, he pointed out, they would provide the women some measure of needed companionship, assistance around the house, and sexual fulfillment. The expense of a home would be shared, and there would be more people to help in the event of sickness or other crisis.

Although most would scoff at the notion, and it's unlikely that this would ever be a legally sanctioned lifestyle, Kassel's idea has some historical basis. Records of Mormon and Islamic societies and of other civilizations that have permitted polygamy show that it is far from the male-chauvinist heaven we might imagine it to be. Meeting the needs of several women—be they sexual needs, companionship needs, or needs for someone to fix the plumbing—is not easy. With the exception of the Mormons, these societies are not marked as a group by their extreme male dominance, but by their demography: they were warrior societies. Because so many young men were killed in battle, there were chronic shortages of husbands. In fact, it was not usually the men who wanted polygamy; women themselves demanded it for the status, protection, and economic help that the marriage bond could offer them, even as one of several wives.

In some parts of today's man-short elderly society, a form of polygamy is already proliferating. As I have visited hundreds of senior centers and retirement complexes across the country, I have discovered that this practice is much more common than outsiders would ever suspect. I have been repeatedly amazed by how often a single older man in one of these environments will divide his time among several "girlfriends," with the situation acknowledged either openly or tacitly.

Although these relationships are often very intimate, they are not always sexual in nature. Typically, the man might have dinner with his different girlfriends on different nights of the week and might occasionally go to the movies with one, go bowling with another, and go dancing with a third. It's also not uncommon for one older man to escort several women at once to a particularly engaging social activity. Although the women involved have him only part-time, they count two distinct advantages. The first is obvious: the alternative may well be no male companionship or socializing at all. But beyond that, such a relationship allows the women to maintain their independence.

When our society has begun to fully confront the loneliness and isolation that accompany the unavailability of full-time male companionship, we might find ourselves being more accepting of share-a-man relationships for older people, just as we have come to accept unmarried younger people living together.

Several years ago, my wife and I were strolling along the beach during a visit to Miami when I recognized one of the nearby shuffleboard players as a former high-school math teacher of mine, Ed Phillips. At 67, he looked terrific, tan, fit, and filled with energy. I called out to him, and after a friendly chat, we decided to meet later for dinner.

I remembered that Phillips had been a bachelor earlier, and that evening I asked him if he had ever gotten married. "No," he said. "No need to. I have an unending stream of friendships and romantic encounters with wonderful women that leave me quite satisfied." When I probed a bit further and inquired as to how he meets these women, he told me one of the most unusual "dating" stories I have ever heard—for any age group.

One night several years earlier, while turning his radio dial, he had happened upon a talk show that consisted of nothing but interviews with eligible older bachelors. For about 20 or 30 minutes, an older man would talk about himself, his situation, and his interests. Then the telephone lines would open up, and women would call in and ask questions. When the interview ended, the radio station would announce a special mailbox number through which women could get in touch with the gentleman who had been interviewed.

As a recently retired transplant to Florida at that time, Ed hadn't been doing very well in locating desirable companions. Seeing himself as a relatively pleasant, attractive man, he decided to get on the show. Several weeks later he was on the air. In his self-presentation, he took care to emphasize what he felt were his good points: he was "healthy, educated, and neat, a good conversationalist." He was "not destitute, he had a master's degree, and he could drive."

The switchboard lit up with the calls of interested women. At the end of the show, the station gave Ed's special mailbox number, and the women wrote. And wrote. And wrote. Ed received letters from more than 60 women in the Miami area who wanted him to come to dinner.

So he did. He had dinner with nearly all of them, and with a few of their friends as well. "I started out looking for someone special, someone to settle down with," he said. "But then I figured, what for? I'd never met so many interesting and attractive women in my life!" Did he sleep with them? "Usually not. Mostly, these were pleasant, intelligent women who were hoping for some companionship, an evening of lively conversation, socializing, and some fun. A lot of them were terrific cooks and prepared wonderful meals. Now, I never took advantage of these women. I always treated them in an honest and decent fashion. But I must tell you I was stunned by their reaction to me. It was like I had become the pasha of Miami!"

Another example of the acceptance of a share-a-man arrangement is found on some cruise lines, such as Royal Viking and the Royal Cruise Line. Because of the shortage of available male cruise passengers, these lines are actively searching for older male "hosts." In exchange for their services—*not* including sexual activity, which is strictly prohibited for hosts during cruises—the hosts receive free cruise passage, complimentary shore excursions, and $100 bar credit per trip.

According to Bruce Kline, director of special programs for Royal Cruise Line, "Our hosts dine with ladies, dance with them, join them on shore excursions, and make sure everyone is having a good time. Most are retired businessmen, doctors, lawyers, professors, or military officers." Since the hosts play such an important function in the success of the cruise, their behavior is critical. Says Kline, "[The hosts] are rated by the passengers, and they must be above average to be asked back."

Whether on a cruise in the Caribbean, at a singles dance in Miami Beach, or at the local senior center, it is impossible to say just how common share-a-man dynamics are. People do not tend to advertise these situations, and few quantitative studies of elder sexuality have been carried out. The *Starr-Weiner Report* on elder sexuality did show that 38.7 percent of older Americans would like to try new sexual experiences, and 9.9 percent felt that women should deal with the shortage of men through "maverick arrangements" such as several women sharing a man.

Same-Sex Relationships

I remember attending my first dance at age eleven. It was held one rainy afternoon in our school gymnasium. As my mother helped me pick out the special shirt and tie I would wear, I recall wondering why we were bothering with such an odd activity—being forced to dance with girls. Most of the boys figured we could have a lot more fun if we could clear the gym, put our sneakers on, and play a good game of tag or basketball.

Instead, our teachers and parents had every intention of introducing us to the world of boy/girl relations. What I remember most about this childhood dance was how it began. As the hundred or so kids filed into the gym, we all nervously wandered into small clusters with our closest friends.

The boys were asked to line up on one side of the gymnasium. The girls were then asked to line up facing us on the other side. Then the master of ceremonies (the girls' gym teacher) asked the boys to remove one shoe each and place them all in a pile in the middle of the dance floor. After much moaning and complaining, we complied. The girls were told to pick a shoe from the pile, find the boy to whom it belonged, and dance with him. Voilà: instant relationships!

Although we all felt nervous and foolish, we ended up having a lot of fun. But what I remember vividly was how there was a partner for everyone. As a young boy, it never would have occurred to me that this boy/girl ratio would someday break down—that as we all grew older, aging and sickness would remove more males than females from the pool of potential partners.

At any senior center, retirement community, or adult recreational outing, you can observe clusters and groups of women talking and laughing with one another. These same-sex friends might travel together, share shopping responsibilities, and even live together.

In an increasingly "feminized" older society, it's likely that many women will extract those nonromantic social and companionship needs that were fulfilled by a heterosexual mate and learn to satisfy them with their women friends. Pairs and groups of women will increasingly band together for companionship, for mutual support in times of need, and for the economic advantages that cohabitation and lifestyle sharing offers.

According to Edith Bankster, a resident of a retirement village in New Mexico:

> Since my husband passed away, I have learned to make close and intimate friendships with other women who live in my community. In fact, one of the main reasons we initially moved in to this village is that my late hus-

band wanted to make sure that I wouldn't be alone or isolated in my later years.

My girlfriends and I like to get together several nights each week for dinner, and we occasionally pile into one of our cars and go off to a movie or show. On several evenings each week we gather in one of our apartments to watch television. We especially enjoy "The Golden Girls," and we sometimes have conversations about the topic of each show that go on for hours into the late evening. Last year when I was terribly sick from chemotherapy treatments, my girlfriends took over all of my household responsibilities, nursed me around the clock, and then joined me in celebrating my recovery.

Next year, five of us are planning an eight-week gourmet tour of Europe, something I have been wanting to do all of my life. Because one of our friends is a bit short on money, we're all going to pool our resources so that she can join us. It's kind of like the group of us have become one big happy family!

With the unavailability of traditional male/female relationships, some basic affection and intimacy needs may also be satisfied in these same-sex relationships. Gerontologist Pauline Robinson says that "sensuality as a broader experience than sexuality is not confined to heterosexual relationships. Women have always enjoyed greater license than men to express affection physically to friends and family members through such gestures as walking arm in arm, hugging, and kissing. . . . Sensual, but not strictly sexual, touching relationships may substitute for or complement heterosexual relationships."

For a small percentage of older women, same-sex intimacies will cross the line into sexual involvement. For some, lesbian relationships may be a satisfying alternative to the previously described options. This is reflected in the fact that Starr and Weiner found that while few older people mentioned practicing homosexuality or bisexuality (none of their questions directly inquired), 63.8 percent nonetheless approved of it. One 72-year-old woman reported that she had moved toward bisexuality in the later years when she found herself alone. As women seek out love and affection in their later years, the definite and growing lack of available men may well cause a rise in intimacy of all varieties among women. In fact, the growing presence of same-sex elder relationships has caused the emergence of social and professional associations that offer support, friendship, and counseling when needed.

In 1977, Senior Action in a Gay Environment (SAGE) was formed in New York City as an educational and counseling service for gay and lesbian seniors. Today, the organization has more than 3,500 members. Similar associations, both for-profit and nonprofit, have sprung up across the country during the past decade. These include the National Association of Lesbian and Gay Gerontologists (NALGG), in San Francisco; Golden Threads, in Quincy, Massachusetts; Gay Rights for Older Women (GROW), in Buffalo; Slightly Older Lesbians (SOL), in Denver; and Legacy, in Chicago. Through public-education programs, newsletters, political advocacy, and active social services, these organizations and dozens like them help older men and women with nontraditional sexual styles cope with the challenges of growing older.

REDEFINING LOVE

The tendency for elders to accept more unusual ways of relating and mating is apt to grow rapidly in the future. According to researchers Starr and Weiner: "Much more open and uninhibited about sexual practices from an early date, the year-2010 generation of older women will have few hesitations about exploring whatever workable lifestyles are available. They will not sit back and accept their lot, abandoning their sexuality. This has not been their style in the past, and there is no reason to expect it to be their style in the future."

Dating and mating among single older Americans will become an increasingly prominent part of the American scene in the years to come. We can expect more television programs to follow in the footsteps of "The Golden Girls," more movies and romantic novels on the same theme, and more romantic hideaways, nightclubs, dating services, and social clubs that cater to older singles. And, especially in light of the marked imbalance in the number of older single men and women, we can expect that this new freedom will lead to deeper changes in our social and personal behavior.

CHAPTER 9

Reinventing the Family

With the coming of the Age Wave, we will witness a dramatic evolution in the structure and purpose of the American family. Shifting from a nuclear, child-centered orientation, the new "matrix" family will be adult centered, will span three, four, even five generations, and will be bound together as much by friendship and choice as by blood and obligation. With this shift, the essential family-oriented human needs and activities such as love, caregiving, friendship, and support won't change. Instead, the form of the family will shift somewhat to better meet these needs in our changing times.

The evolution of the family isn't new to history. This basic social unit has been continually changing in size, shape, and focus in keeping with the unique tone, style, and emphasis of the economics and demography of the times.

In primitive times, the primary focus of the family was survival. Groups of individual families usually banded together into a tribe, with every member doing whatever he or she could to keep the others alive. In a hostile, life-threatening environment, men pursued the role of hunters and warriors, and women assumed the functions of child rearing, food gathering, and camp keeping. High infant-mortality rates and the desperate need for human labor fostered large families, the creation of which preoccupied all of the parents' adult years. During this period, the average life expectancy was around 20, and the median age is believed to have been in the low teens.

Centuries later, with the shift toward an agrarian lifestyle, farming and the performance of a myriad of home-maintenance tasks became the new focus of family life. Men were responsible for the heavy labor required in farming and livestock management, while women were responsible for the household as well as for the rearing of children, of which four or five might survive into adulthood. By the time the last of the children were old enough to have families of their own, both parents had usually passed away. At this stage, the median age was approximately 17.

During this period in history, the family model was extended patriarchal, with several generations living under the same roof, ruled by the *paterfamilias.* This family structure was a kind of pyramid: a large number of children, fewer adults, and very few, if any, old people. These various generations usually arranged themselves in a rigid hierarchy, based on bloodline and ordained by the obligations of tradition.

With the rise of industrialization in the late nineteenth century and the historic separation of work and nonwork activities, the family became less of an economic unit and more of a source of intimacy and personal support. For the first time, work usually took place outside the home, and money became the regular unit of exchange. In this new circumstance, men were expected to work at paying jobs, while women extended their earlier roles by keeping house and raising the children.

Now the model family became nuclear, or child-focused: mother, father and two+ children under one roof, with grandparents living close by. The nuclear family became dominant during the first half of the twentieth century, not because it was a "perfect" kind of family unit, but rather because it was appropriate to the economics, demography, and life pattern of the times. The child-centered family was the inevitable result of our youthful, child-focused culture. By 1960, the median age had risen to approximately 29.4.

Due to low fertility, high longevity, and the shift to a postindustrial economy, the nuclear, child-focused family is becoming transformed into a new form, more appropriate to the needs of an aging society.

The nuclear family, which fulfilled a unique function, was one of the shortest-lived family metamorphoses in history. According to Dr. Matilda White Riley, president of the American Sociological Association, "As four (or even five) generations of many families are now alive at the same time, we can no longer concentrate primary attention on nuclear families of young parents and their children."

The Matrix Family

Just as the shift from an agrarian to an industrial lifestyle transformed the patriarchal family into the nuclear family, the gift of extended life is causing the emergence of a form of family structure entirely new to history, one that will be referred to here as the matrix family.

In attempting to describe the unusual dynamics and complexity of today's family, we borrow the concept of a "matrix" configuration not from the traditional realm of family studies but from modern organizational theory. Today, in thousands of growing organizations, the traditional hierarchical power structure is being replaced by a more fluid "matrix" of project-oriented teams. In this manner, skills and priorities are overlaid and organized as needed to meet various personal and work-related project goals, then disbanded and reorganized again as needs change. In many ways, this flexible matrix approach accurately describes the new model that the Age Wave is creating in the American family.

There are several characteristics of the matrix family that distinguish it from the family models of days past. Whereas earlier family forms were focused around the survival needs of a youthful tribe, the economic and social challenges of extended family farming, and the work and child-rearing tasks of the industrial age, the matrix family is uniquely matched to the characteristics of the Age Wave. It is:

- **Adult-centered.** With declining fertility, extending longevity, and the rise in median age we are experiencing, the majority of family relations are no longer between young children and adults, but between adults and adults.
- **Transgenerational.** Relationships that combine, cross, and even skip generations become increasingly possible in our long-lived era.
- **Bound together by friendship and choice as well as by blood and obligation.** With increasing lifestyle independence and mobility, friendship and shared concerns become as much the basis for family-type relationships as bloodline.

In the following pages, each of these aspects will be examined in turn.

THE MATRIX FAMILY IS ADULT-CENTERED

In an aging society like ours, the cultural center of gravity—the population "hub"—is migrating from youth to the middle years of life. By 1988, the median age in the United States had

climbed to 32, its highest point to date. As a result, the pre-
ponderance of all interpersonal relationships, family and
otherwise, are now among adults. This shift has caused the
family to change its basic nature. What was once essentially
a nest for raising children has increasingly become a network
of adult relationships.

**In the future, interpersonal relationships among the gen-
erations are less likely to be among parents and their
small children and more likely to be among several generations of parents and adult children who have essentially become peers.**

"For example," says Dr. Riley, "my daughter and I have
survived together for 45 years, of which only 18 were in the
traditional relationship of parent and child. Unlike our
shorter-lived forebears, my daughter and I have been able to
share many common experiences, although at different stages
of our respective lives."

Small signs and symptoms of our increasing adult orientation are appearing all around us: the growing trend toward
"adults-only" housing, something no landlord would have
dared whisper in earlier decades; the decline of youth-oriented membership clubs like the Boy Scouts, at the same time
as the membership of the American Association of Retired
Persons has expanded to nearly 30 million; the shift in the
primary orientation of health care from acute to eldercare and
long-term care; the growth in the number of books and movies that reflect the aging of intrafamily concerns—for example, the books *My Mother, My Self* and *Making Peace with Your
Parents*, and the film *Nothing in Common*; disputes that spring
up among generations when older Americans want to convert
empty schools into senior recreation centers; and the growing
social confusion about how to cope with aging parents.

Whereas television shows such as "The Little Rascals,"
"Leave It to Beaver," and "Ozzie and Harriet" reflected the
child-focused orientation of the fifties and sixties, in the seventies we watched as media parents learned to cope with their

children's coming of age in such popular shows as "All in the Family," "Maude," and "The Jeffersons." With the eighties, the landscape of the American family on television opened on "Dynasty," "Dallas," "thirtysomething," "L.A. Law," and the "Golden Girls," as the adults—the parents—took center stage. As we shall see in later chapters, in the nineties the cultural center of gravity will migrate even farther into the realm of mid- and later-life concerns.

Already, 10 percent of today's senior citizens have children who are also senior citizens.

The Sandwich Generation

Among the broad spectrum of problems and opportunities that the new, adult-centered family brings, one of the most difficult social challenges is the rise of "the sandwich generation." These women and men "in the middle" are increasingly finding themselves caught between the needs of their children on the one hand and of their aging parents on the other. Not only are more adult children caring for their parents, but there are relatively fewer caregivers for the task than there used to be. For the first time in history, the average American has more parents than children.

Five social and lifestyle factors have converged to make the sandwich generation such a phenomenon:

Longer lives.   The over-85 group, the segment most in need of care, makes up the fastest-growing segment of the population. Today, there are 3.3 million people in this group; in the next 50 years that figure is expected to increase to nearly 13 million.

Chronic disease.   Whereas the diseases of previous centuries tended to take people quickly, today's chronic diseases tend to keep older people suffering for years. Many of today's prevalent diseases (such as arthritis and Alzheimer's) don't offer an immediate death sentence, but rather lifetime imprisonment.

Lower ratio of children to parents.   In 1900 there were 13.6 adults between 18 and 64 for each person 65 or over. By 1990 the ratio will drop to 4.8 to 1. The demand for care is going up, and the supply of caretakers is, in relative terms, shrinking. As the baby boomers advance into their own frailty, the children they did not have in their youth obviously won't be there to care for them in their old age.

The great increase in widowhood.   People who could survive nicely as one-half of a married couple often find life to be a real struggle once they are alone. The gap that has opened up between the life expectancies of men and women has left many aged women with no one to help them through the challenges of independent living.

Increased entry of women of caregiving age into the labor force.   The burden of caring for aged parents and in-laws has traditionally fallen on nonworking women. As more and more women have taken jobs and embarked on careers, it becomes increasingly difficult for these women to be as available to aging parents on a day-to-day basis as they once were.

Learning to lovingly care for our older family members and friends without overwhelming ourselves will become a commonplace challenge in the new matrix family.

Being a Caregiver to Parents

The greatest form of help that caregivers provide is direct, personal care for parents who have lost some of their ability to care for themselves. Although there are many popular misconceptions about this theme, as a culture we care very deeply about our parents. As sociologist Gary Lee of the Social Research Center of Washington State University puts it, "As a category, the American elderly are afflicted by many social and personal problems. Collective neglect by their families is not one of them."

Although some caregiving requires around-the-clock bedside attention, most support is usually a matter of occasionally helping with the housekeeping, food purchasing, assisting with transportation around town, and providing some caring companionship. However simple these activities are, they require time, compassion, and the willingness to sacrifice some aspects of one's own life for one's parents. We see people facing this dilemma across the country:

- An only son drives hundreds of miles every week to the next state to look in on his mother, spend an afternoon talking with her, take care of bills, and arrange for the plumber, the insurance payments, and the social worker's visit.
- A family moves grandpa's daybed into the living room so that he can see and be seen most easily. The teenage children begin asking their friends not to drop by.
- A librarian drops out of her graduate studies so that she can spend every lunch hour and an hour each evening at the local convalescent home with her mother-in-law.
- A struggling couple pays for their parents' mounting health bills with their steadily depleting savings.
- A construction worker leaves work early two days each week to cook dinner for his father.
- Siblings argue over who will take care of Mom now that Dad has passed away.

Of all older Americans who need care today, 80 percent will receive that care from their families.

Caring for a needy, aging relative has never been so difficult, prolonged, or common. As Lillian Troll of Rutgers University has written, "Adult children now provide more care and more difficult care over a much longer time than such children did in the 'good old days.' " A recent *Boston* magazine cover story that was devoted to parental caregiving had as its subhead: "You know you're really an adult when your parents need you more than you need them."

The weight that falls on those millions of caregivers is enormous and growing. That burden is made even greater by the fact that it is your *parents*—the very pillars of strength upon whom you leaned for decades—who are now frail, vulnerable, and dependent. "Parenting" your parents can be a powerful emotional experience that brings up a myriad of questions, such as these: Are you comfortable dressing and undressing your father? Can you feed adults who fed you as a child? Are you ready to have your mother or father come live with you? Can you deal with the psychological perplexities of seeing your parents suffer in their old age? What does an unequally shared burden of parental care do to sibling relationships? Are you prepared for the distress that adult caregiving may cause you and your marriage?

Here, as elsewhere, aging is to a great degree a women's issue. Currently, of all adult-children caregivers, it is estimated that nearly 90 percent are women. The average age of these caregivers is 57, and more than one-third are 65 or older.

The average American woman can expect to spend more years caring for her parents than she did caring for her children.

Elaine Brody, director of the Department of Human Services at the Philadelphia Geriatric Center, calls the caregiving daughter or daughter-in-law "the woman in the middle." According to her studies, "The data so far indicate that working women are just as responsible as nonworking women in that role. What they give up is their own free time and opportunities for socialization. They don't give up on caring for their parent. They don't slack off on responsibility to their jobs or their husbands. They take it out of their own hides."

American women of all ages will increasingly find themselves in a difficult situation, filling the multiple roles of mother, professional woman, wife, and caregiving daughter. There is no historical precedent for the combined effect of these complex and stressful roles on the average woman.

Caregiving children often give money as well as time. Because most long-term illness is not covered by Medicare or other government insurance programs, adult children often find themselves paying crippling medical expenses, or the expense of a stay in a convalescent home, which averages $20,000 to $40,000 per year.

The problem is even greater for minorities. The proportion of older blacks, Hispanics, and Native Americans is growing at a much faster rate than that of older white Americans. The poverty rates of older minorities are far higher; in addition, their health is, on the average, worse, and they have less access to health care and helpful community programs.

The general pattern in American families is to be mutually available and helpful in caring for older relatives. But when the older person becomes frail and dependent, that burden can easily go far beyond the family's financial and emotional capacity. According to a recent AARP report, "the average length of home care for a severely dependent person who is over 70 is between five and six years," and "in many cases the caregivers are only slightly more able than the dependents."

In fact, one recent study showed that parent-caring is becoming a major source of stress in family life. The institutionalization of a family member usually comes only after the family has already done everything they could possibly do. This has caused large numbers of families to be stretched to their limits caring for older people, stripping themselves of economic, social, and emotional resources in the process.

Jacqueline Lelong, who directs a counseling and education agency in Austin, Texas, says people who find themselves responsible for the long-term care of an aging relative often feel like prisoners: "You can't leave. You have someone wandering around who doesn't know where the bathroom is, who can't feed himself. No one knows what it's like unless he's been there," she says. "We must be very careful before we pass judgment."

Under such strain, marginal families can often push themselves into dysfunction, and personal care can become personal neglect or even abuse. According to Gloria Cavanaugh, executive director of the American Society on Aging, "Elder abuse is one of the fastest-growing crimes of our times, but it is mostly unreported and almost totally neglected in the budgets of local, state, and national government."

In 1985, when Congressman Claude Pepper's House Subcommittee on Health and Long-Term Care held hearings on elder abuse, shocking reports surfaced. For example: a 75-year-old Massachusetts man, disguised in the hearings as "Mr. Smith," whose son had attacked him with a hatchet; a 74-year-old New Jersey woman whose son-in-law had beaten and raped her and whose daughter then threatened her, saying, "You won't have a home to sleep in if you say anything about this." Pepper's subcommittee estimated that, counting all forms, including unintentional neglect, "over 1,000,000 older Americans are physically, financially, and emotionally abused by their relatives or loved ones annually." Surveys indicate that approximately 86 percent of the abused aged are victims of their own families.

Just as often, abuse takes the form of neglect. This neglect can be unintentional, when the caregivers don't have the knowledge, competence, stamina, or money to continue to carry the burden of care. A study by the University of Maryland found that passive neglect, usually manifesting as abusive inattention or isolation, was the most common form of elder abuse, followed by verbal abuse, physical abuse, and financial abuse.

Many elders fall victim to financial exploitation when a child or other relative offers to "help out" with the finances and then siphons off the elder's assets for his or her own use.

Abuse occurs most often in families under strain—with a history of violence, alcoholism, or drug addiction—and families pressured by unemployment or financial stresses.

When we look at the future, we see an increasing number of frail elderly and a decreasing number of adult children to care for them. We see pressure on Medicare, Medicaid, Social Security, and every other public source of help in the care of the aged. All of this adds up to a huge number of families under strain, and a mushrooming potential for abuse of the elderly.

"Parent Care" Programs

In response to the emotional and financial burdens of elder caregiving, and as a strategy to prevent abuse, a variety of innovative forms of help are on the way.

Many aged people simply require help around the house. Here the narrowness of government services, which provide nonmedical chore assistance only to the very poor, has provided a considerable opportunity for programs sponsored by profit as well as nonprofit organizations. For example, the century-old charitable Visiting Nurse Service in New York operates a "Nursing Home without Walls" for the poor, as well as a for-profit subsidiary called "Partners in Care." In the latter, middle-class older people are provided companionship, escorts to the doctor's office, and assistance with cooking, cleaning, shopping, and other nonmedical tasks. Founded in 1983, Partners in Care had expanded by 1986 to 2,000 aides providing more than 2 million hours of home assistance. Major private companies like Upjohn Healthcare and Kelly Services now offer services aimed at this same market.

For those older men and women whose health problems require more than home assistance services, a huge home-care industry is rising across America. It is estimated that each year more than 3 million older Americans, representing more than 10 percent of the elderly, receive some sort of long-term care assistance at home or in the home of a family member. In 1977 there were 2,496 Medicare-certified home-care agencies nationwide; 3,289 new agencies have sprung up over the past decade. And as social policy experts predict that health-care reimbursement will increasingly shift away from expensive institutional services and more toward less costly home care, this industry is expected to multiply in the years ahead.

Perhaps the greatest challenge is seeing to it that an older loved one has trustworthy assistance in accomplishing the various tasks and activities of independent living. Making sure that Mom has a reliable ride to and from the doctor's office, gets assistance with her grocery shopping, has someone to clean the house each week, and has someone nearby to call 24 hours a day in case of emergencies can be a challenging task, especially if the caregiver lives in a different town or even a different state from the person they're caring for—an increasingly common occurrence.

One poignant fact stood out from a study recently conducted by the Travelers insurance company: a large fraction (36 percent) of the "sandwiched" caregivers reported that they did not know where to turn to find out about resources in the community, about public or private insurance that might be useful, about how to care for specific illnesses, or even where they might find professional home care.

In response, both public and private sectors have begun to attempt to fill this gap with the development of local and national *care managers*. For example, under a federal pilot program, at least 12 states have started programs in which care managers steer clients through the bureaucratic maze of available medical and social services.

One entrepreneur in Virginia offers a comprehensive package, at a cost starting at $75 per month, that includes everything from a personal ombudsman to deal with governmental bureaucracies to monthly medical checkups. Another company, Rothschild & Britt Resources in California, provides planning and decision-making guidance, referrals to prescreened and monitored residential-care homes, arrangements for respite care, and companionship programs. In all, some 200 firms have entered the field in the last few years, charging from $10 to $85 per hour for their services.

One highly successful venture deals exclusively with the problems of scattered families, with parents living in distant states. Since 1982, Aging Network Services, based in Bethesda, Maryland, has linked clients with more than 200 care managers (in this case, psychiatric social workers in private practice) in scores of cities across the country. A son in California might be trying to care for his mother, who lives in Chicago; perhaps, with the right services, she can stay in her own home. The dozens of problems that need to be solved and the selection of the right services can be impossible to manage from out of state, even for a trained expert, but Aging Network Services can help in such a case. Founder Barbara Kane or one of her coworkers would have a one-hour phone interview with the son and call other relatives to get the full picture. Then, she would contact a care manager in Illinois and refer the case, with a complete set of notes on the mother and the family, along with a recommendation. The care manager would then do whatever was necessary for the mother, including acting as an advocate for her; counseling her and her children; coordinating resources that she might need; serving as a liaison between her, her doctor, and her family; and monitoring whatever services she uses.

Between 1986 and 1988, Aging Network Services doubled its individual client business. Other organizations have sprung up to fill the gap, including Pathfinders in Scarsdale, New York; Elder Care Management in New York City; and Living Better, a pilot program sponsored by several East Coast hospitals. In fact, it's estimated that, whereas five years ago there were less than 100 care-management agencies nationwide, there are now more than 600 private firms, approximately 1,000 nonprofit hospitals, and more than 500 government offices that offer some type of comprehensive care-management services.

Like child care, parent care will increasingly become a corporate problem.

The problem of caring for one's aging parents is becoming so widespread that many insightful employers and community agencies are beginning to recognize that the family problems brought on by an elderly population are going to profoundly affect their companies and programs. The next wave of significant growth and support for care management will thus likely come from corporate contracts. In the years to come, employees may be granted a specific number of "caregiving" or "parent-care" days as a standard element of benefits packages.

In 1984, the New York Business Group on Health asked its member companies whether they were experiencing any problems caused by employees taking care of frail elderly relatives. Two-thirds to three-fourths of the companies reported a number of problems, particularly absenteeism, lateness, unscheduled days off, increased phone use, and general increased stress levels. Michael Meyer, a prominent New York–based health-care consultant, has estimated on the basis of the Travelers survey that the average 500-employee company loses $220,500 per year through the absenteeism and lateness of caregiver employees.

In a recent Travelers study of its employees over the age of 30 it was found that:

- One in five spent some time caring for an older person every week.
- The average time spent was about 10 hours per week, but one in 12 spent 35 hours or more.
- Eighty percent said that their duties interfered with their social, emotional, and family needs some or most of the time.
- Eighteen percent said that they had not taken a vacation from those duties in two years or more.

On any given day, an estimated 5 million Americans spend some time caring for a parent, and within the next two decades that number is expected to double. In 1985, various studies reported that 11 percent of middle-aged and older working women had to leave their jobs to care for an aging relative.

As the problem mushrooms, we will see corporations becoming involved with parent-oriented care-management organizations like Kane's. American Express has initiated studies to determine the feasibility of company-sponsored parent-care services. Similarly, the Center for the Study of Aging at Connecticut's University of Bridgeport has started a Corporate Eldercare Project with three clients—Pitney Bowes, Remington, and People's Bank of Bridgeport—to set up a telephone hotline, lunchtime discussion groups, and, in the future, a respite program that will give employees an off-hours break from the routine of care. Ciba-Geigy has sponsored seminars on caregiving. The Travelers insurance company has sponsored a caregiving information fair and a support group. Pepsico has sponsored seminars, a hotline, and a community resource book.

Such services are the vanguard of a huge private-sector boom. Dana Friedman, the Conference Board's expert on work and family, identifies caregiving as *the* employee benefit of the 1990s.

U.S. Commissioner on Aging Carol Fraser Fisk concurs:

> We are going to see some dramatic changes in how we take care of our older population. Look what happened in child care when the baby-boom generation began to put the pressure on business. We got very positive results. Now that the boomers are beginning to care for their parents, that's starting to happen in caregiving.

> When I can't find someone in my office in Washington, it's not because a child fell down. It's because of a crisis with an aging parent. And that is happening in corporations now. In time the structure of caregiving will include benefits from the employer such as day-care centers for adults instead of just for children.

> The structure of caregiving will come to include a range of options. Different kinds of insurance packages will help cover the costs of the kind of assistance needed for independent living. In time the new structure will

change the way we look at benefit packages, and it will change the way we plan our own later years.

Taking an innovative step forward, in 1988 American Express and Procter & Gamble became the first major U.S. corporations to offer their employees long-term-care benefits, covering nursing home stays and the like. Although employees pay for the coverage, the companies have arranged significant reductions on these long-term care programs. Ford, General Motors, and Chrysler will soon be piloting similar programs in which they will foot the bill.

Eventually, comprehensive, custom-designed personal care-management services will form part of national elder-care networks. As the number of older Americans who need some type of lifestyle assistance increases, a new professional service system will evolve to help give the love, attention, and care that were once the exclusive domain of the family.

Caring for the Caregiver

In addition to professional care-management services, other programs that help the "sandwich generation" help themselves have begun to appear.

For instance, at the turn of the decade, self-help groups for the children of aging parents began to spring up across the country under names like "Children with Aging Parents," "You and Your Aging Parents," and "Generations." There are now hundreds of such programs, involving more than 12,000 people across the country.

Such groups help inform caregivers about alternative geriatric services that are available in the area and educate them to give better care. But perhaps most important, they help the caregivers feel supported and more prepared to handle the challenges of caring for an aging loved one.

ECHO Housing: A Clever Solution
to a Growing Problem

One of the first challenges people face in intergenerational caregiving begins when an older parent moves in with an adult child's family. Although many young and middle-aged families enjoy this special opportunity to have mother or grandfather close by, for others, the problems can sometimes be troublesome for all involved.

An ingenious solution to this dilemma, referred to as ECHO (Elder Cottage Housing Opportunity) housing, or "Granny flats," initially sprouted in Australia and then moved to the British Isles. It has now taken root in a few spots in the United States.

It works like this: you think your aging mother, grandfather, or friend might be more comfortable, better cared for, and less lonesome if he or she lived close enough for you to keep an eye out, to visit, or to take over a hot meal. But your home is too small, or your family is unwilling to accommodate such an arrangement. Call the local ECHO company, and within hours they'll come by with a truck and place a lovely cottage in your backyard, complete with a bedroom, living room, bathroom, utility nook, and kitchen. The cottage has a heating system and a stacked washer and dryer. Your "significant elder" has privacy and can come and go as he or she pleases, but is only steps away if the kids want to drop by and visit, if there's any problem, or if he or she wants to join you for dinner.

In the Australian state of Victoria, the Ministry of Housing installs and rents the units, then comes out and picks them up when they are no longer needed. This has proven equally popular in the Canadian province of Ontario.

In this country, ECHO housing—or elder cottages, as these units are sometimes called—are built as prefabricated housing by a few companies and sold in the $14,000–$22,000 range. One of the principal sources here is in Lancaster, Pennsylvania. This is not at all random: for centuries, Amish families in this part of Pennsylvania have been building what they call *Grossmutter* (grandmother) houses on their farms.

Although there was some initial concern over zoning and the aesthetics of such manufactured housing, most local governments that have taken a serious look at ECHO units have come out feeling positive about them. One builder says, "Every time it has actually come to showing it to a local board, letting them see the model so they can see that the aesthetics are not jarring, explaining that it is, in fact, temporary and can be dismantled and removed later, it has been approved." Such places as Frederick County, Maryland; Colerain Township and Lancaster County, Pennsylvania; and Tucson, Arizona, have specifically allowed elder cottages as exceptions to the zoning in certain areas. California has passed legislation that encourages local governments to allow elder cottages.

ECHO cottages are catching on: statistics show that 13 percent of all prefabricated "manufactured" houses are currently located not in mobile home parks but on the property of families and friends.

THE MATRIX FAMILY IS TRANSGENERATIONAL

In our agrarian past, we became accustomed to a kind of vertical hierarchy of family relationships. Kids were kids and lived in their own world; they were the least in charge and were expected to take orders from their elders. Parents inhabited a different universe of needs and activities, usually as power figures to their children, while at the same time respectfully deferring to their own parents. And grandparents, because of their perceived greater wisdom and experience and their control of the family property, usually assumed the highest position of authority.

Extended life will allow people to reach beyond the bounds of the nuclear family to form meaningful rela-

tionships with friends and relatives across two or three
generations.

Today, more than 8 percent of all American children
have more than four living grandparents or step-grandpar-
ents. And with the continued rise in divorce and remarriage,
there will be a proliferation of blended families, which bring
together sons and second wives, sisters-in-law and half-broth-
ers, grandparents and great-granddaughters-in-law.

When three or four family generations are adults at once,
sharing many of the same ego, social, sexual, and power needs
common to the adult years of life, the vertical power and
control hierarchy dissolves into a more horizontal network of
multigenerational family members who are, in many ways,
peers.

The proliferation of transgenerational families will generate a host of previously unexplored ethical issues. When
you are in a conservative marriage and your mother is dating
promiscuously, how does this affect the way you relate to her?
Does she need to confer with you before she sleeps with her
new boyfriend? When son and father are competing for the
same job in the family business, who defers to whom? If you
want to use your savings to take a two-year trip around the
world but your child needs your "inheritance" to capitalize
her new business, who decides what is more important? If
your father lives alone in a five-bedroom home with no mortgage payments and you're struggling to subsist with your two
children in a four-room apartment, should he take out a second mortgage on his home and make you the recipient of the
property value? If a granddaughter and grandmother are
competing for the resources of the mother, how does the
"sandwiched" mother decide who should get her attention?
If the summer home you purchased with your spouse's parents was built with only one private master bedroom, who
gets it? If your son wants to take over the family business but
you are getting a second wind and decide not to retire, is this
fair?

As the old lines of power and obligation dissolve, it

becomes hard to fall back on rules and priorities geared to another era and a different social order. The Age Wave will cause each of us to come up with new choices based on our own family's values and circumstances. Out of these new child/parent challenges, we can expect the arrival of a host of new books, educational courses, and therapies geared to help millions of adult Americans learn to relate with and, if needed, care for their loved ones without spoiling their own lives in the process.

Grandparents/Grandchildren: The Ties that Bind

One of the signs of the growth in grandparenthood was the initiation in 1987 of a pilot for a magazine called *Grandparents*. Apparently, editors and publishers feel that the time is coming when they'll be able to fill whole magazines with regular how-to articles on the subject. For example, the fall 1987 issue contained such articles as "Your Grandkids' Education," "When a Grandmother Fills a Mother's Shoes," "Are Your Children Problem Parents?" and "When Divorce Steals Your Grandchildren."

Of the 72 million Americans over the age of 45, nearly 50 million are grandparents. Already, about one-half of all individuals over 65 are *great*-grandparents.

At the same time that an increasingly large number of people are becoming grandparents, there are a diminishing number of grandchildren to relate to. *Toy Trade News* recently trumpeted the fact that what they refer to as the "grand ratio" (the number of grandchildren under 10 per grandparent) had dropped from 2.4-to-1 in 1950 to 1.2-to-1 today, and that it will continue to fall, to an estimated 1-to-1 in the year 2000. This means that each grandparent has only half as many grandchildren, and each grandchild has twice as many grandparents alive as was the case just a little over a generation ago.

In 1987, *Grandparents* magazine ran the following letter from Lela Goodell of Hawaii:

When my first grandson, Noel Miller, was born in 1981,
he had seven living grandmothers:

1. His mother's mother (me)
2. His father's mother
3. and 4. Both paternal great-grandmothers
5. His divorced maternal grandfather's new wife
6. One maternal step-great-grandmother
7. One paternal step-great-grandmother

Grandparents ran the letter under the title "Can you top this?"
But although little Noel's case may seem unusual, in the
future such a collection of relatives will be commonplace.
These complex multigenerational relationships will be the
source both of new forms of family bonding as well as an
assortment of thorny social problems spurred by divorce, intergenerational conflicts, and debates over the fair distribution of family wealth.

Grandparents As Caregivers

A key function that grandparents are increasingly called upon
to perform is caregiving and support in times of family crisis.
In periods of economic difficulty, sickness, or divorce, grandma and grandpa often step forward to help out in every imaginable way—from occasional baby-sitting and assistance with
child care, to financial support, to actually assuming interim
responsibility for the troubled household.

In a study published in 1986 that involved a nationwide,
three-generation series of interviews over seven years, Frank
Furstenberg and Andrew Cherlin found that in the case of
divorce, three out of ten grandparents said that the grandchild
had come to live with them, often accompanied by the parent
who had custody. This is not necessarily a bad thing. Many
grandparents, parents, and grandchildren report that even
though the transition can be difficult, they receive a good deal
more love and nurturance in this arrangement than when they
were all living separately.

One way that grandparents are reaching out across the generations to help their families is by providing direct financial support. Carol M. Kornhaber, who cofounded the Foundation for Grandparenting with her psychologist husband, Dr. Arthur Kornhaber, says, "The grandparent generation is far better off financially, and the family structure is fragmented. Grandparents are helping financially as a way to get involved in their grandchildren's lives."

Grandparents are beginning to take an active role in helping to pay for their grandchildren's education. A case in point is Pittsburgh's Duquesne University, which projects an average annual increase of 7 percent in its current tuition of $5,000. It recently gave its alumni a chance to prepay, at a discount, four years of tuition for children under college age. The price varied from $4,500 for a 1-year-old to $14,500 for a 16-year-old. Of the 482 alumni who took advantage of the offer, 55 (more than 11 percent) were grandparents paying for their grandchildren. Similarly, Benny Walker, director of financial aid at Furman University in Greenville, South Carolina, and president of the Southern Association of Financial Aid Directors, reports, "The gap between [the financial aid] schools provide and what parents provide is often filled by grandparents."

The Grandparent Marketplace

As these new grandparents demonstrate a willingness to dig deep to help their grandchildren, a powerful intergenerational purchasing phenomenon is emerging. The grandparent market is going to be an Age Wave market par excellence. Retailers of toys and children's clothing were the first to spot it and have already begun to target their advertising and locate their stores to reach grandparents. Grandparents are the buyers who will buy the big-ticket items most freely. It's no wonder that Mattel not only came out with Grandma and Grandpa versions of Ken and Barbie for its Heart Family of dolls but made sure that the dolls came equipped with presents for their doll grandchildren.

The Saks Fifth Avenue store in Palm Springs, California, a town populated mostly by adults, nevertheless does a brisk business in children's toys and clothes (the children's section of the store is referred to by some as "the grandmothers' boutique"). Margot Holland, associate fashion director for the chain, says, "If it's an expensive item, the grandparents will buy it." At the top-of-the-line toy chain F.A.O. Schwarz, the name "Grandparents' Boutique" is featured over one section, and the chain goes out of its way to hire grandparents as salespeople. John G. Flood, the company's vice-president and general manager, says, "Our customers can relate to them. . . . We get a lot of phone calls from the retirement states—Florida, Arizona, and the like—to send out orders to what we assume are grandchildren."

In 1987 and 1988 grandparents accounted for nearly 25 percent of all money spent on toys in America.

A Tearing at the Seams

This deep involvement across two and three generations can have an unpleasant downside when crossed with today's rising divorce rates. One of the saddest outcomes of the separation of families is its effect on the grandparents. Some divorcing parents divorce not only the spouse but the spouse's family as well. They cut off all contact between the children and the parents of the ex-spouse. The effect can be devastating on the grandparents as well as on the grandchildren. Such separation can also happen because of other problems in the middle generation, such as the death of one of the children's parents, problems with drugs or child abuse, or even a simple conflict of values.

The numbers are hard to accurately track, since many grandparents keep these kinds of troubles to themselves. It is estimated that, across the country, hundreds of thousands of grandparents are being deprived of contact with grandchildren they love because of some problem in the middle generation.

For example, 61-year-old Robert Ross Wylie was deeply shaken when divorce removed his granddaughter Melissa from his life:

> Melissa had big blue eyes, blonde hair, and a wide smile of bright sunshine. She could get anything she wanted from Grandma and me. The drumstick at Thanksgiving seemed almost as big as she was. She grasped it in her tiny hands and had such fun trying to bite into it with next to no teeth at all, and when it slid out of her hands, she squealed with sheer delight. Then, in her swing chair, she made happy little sounds as a music box lulled her to sleep. I loved to hold her when she napped.
>
> The day came when I picked up what was left . . . a broken toy car without front wheels . . . the leg of a doll. . . . There was no more music from the music box, no golden laughter. Only silence. I looked out the window, and the window started to blur. I choked back the tears. Grandpas aren't supposed to cry.

Wylie's beloved granddaughter was 3 at the time. He hasn't seen her since. She is now 11.

In response to the sadness and frustration at losing their grandchildren, many older Americans have begun to fight for their rights to be active grandparents. Support groups and advocacy organizations such as the Foundation for Grandparenting and Grandparents'-Children's Rights, Inc., are surfacing nationwide. A typical group, Human Rights for Grandparents and Grandchildren, has 2,000 members in its California chapter alone.

As a result of struggles by groups like these, in the past decade laws allowing grandparents to petition the courts for visitation rights have been enacted in every state, with the exception of the District of Columbia.

Why Not "Adopt" a Grandparent?

What if you have no grandchildren, or your children have no grandparents? Such seemingly insolvable circumstances can now be corrected.

Nine years ago, the Generations Together program was created at the University of Pittsburgh as a model program to link the friendship and interpersonal needs of older people and young children in a kind of "adopt-a-grandparent" program. In this innovative service and several hundred others like it that have surfaced throughout the United States, old and young who are not joined by heredity are brought together to share, nurture, and enjoy one another.

One older participant in the Generations Together program, Robert Kennedy, was drawn to the program nearly a decade ago when he "came across the disturbing statistic that 30 percent of the third-graders in wholesome, middle-American Avalon [Pennsylvania] were living with only one parent." When he learned this, he said, "I made a vow to myself that if I could ever do something to help that problem, I would. And when this [program] came along, I did."

Kennedy spends time each week with the several children he and his wife have taken under their wings as "grandchildren," and he enjoys every minute of it. The children he has befriended have grown to love him and his wife, and the Kennedys feel that their lives have been enriched by the experience. "I think [the children] get a brand-new view of life when they have someone on their side," he says. "If they don't get this love and affection, they'll miss so much in life."

The success of the initial programs sponsored by Generations Together has led this forward-thinking organization to expand its range of activities. For instance, at the Point Park College Day Care Center in a downtown Pittsburgh high-rise, four older people are paid under a government grant to provide child-care services to the residents of the building. At Pittsburgh's High School for the Performing Arts, elder "artists-in-residence," as they like to be called, help young students develop their budding artistic skills. At the Eastern District Area School for Exceptional Children, a team of older volunteers help teach emotionally disturbed and disabled children many of the basic skills of independent living.

The Generations Together programs appear to be highly successful. One study of 360 elder participants found that these older men and women found their lives a great deal more satisfying as a result of their experience in helping younger people.

The children benefit as well. Kids who have participated with elders in these programs show significantly improved behavior and grades. For those without actual grandparents, the loving contact with elders opens them up to a whole world of pleasant intergenerational relationships. According to Generations Together program director Sally Newman, "Many of the children we've interviewed were afraid to grow old. But we have found that their work with the older people gives them a positive notion of the continuity of life."

THE MATRIX FAMILY IS BOUND TOGETHER BY FRIENDSHIP AND CHOICE

The sweeping changes that the Age Wave will bring may alter the way we define what a family is and who its members are. Until now, the bases of the family have been bloodline, genetics, and economic obligation. According to *Webster's Ninth New Collegiate Dictionary*, a "family" is "a group of persons of common ancestry." Traditionally, the family has been the group into which you were born. It was not something you chose, and you had no control over who your relatives and family members would be.

According to sociologist Dr. Gunhild O. Hagestad of Pennsylvania State University, a key difference associated with the new matrix family is the fact that within our time, increasing individual independence has rendered emotional needs more important than economic needs as the basis for family bonding:

Over the last century, economic needs have given way to emotional needs as the main family "glue," especially in relationships among adults. Over the same period, we have seen a shift in emphasis from the needs of the family as a group to the needs and wishes of individuals. Individual choices, such as decisions about when to marry and leave the family, were once guided by the needs of the family as a whole. The twentieth century, with its pension and health-care plans, has "freed" generations from many of the economic dependencies.

In its fall 1980 issue, the respected *Journal of Home Economics* offered a progressive new definition of the family geared more toward the unique needs and characteristics of our aging society than the anachronistic *Webster's* version: "The *family* is a unit of intimate, transacting, and interdependent persons who share some values and goals, responsibility for decisions and resources, and have a commitment to one another over time." There is no mention here of blood relationships, of obligation, or even of marriage. Such phrases as "a unit of interdependent persons" and "shared values, goals, and responsibilities" form the core characteristics of the new matrix family. The operative word is *commitment*, reflecting a purely voluntary relationship.

According to sociologist Matilda White Riley, "Today's kinship structure, which has no parallel in history, can be viewed in a new way: as a latent web of continually shifting linkages that provide the potential for activating and intensifying close family relationships. These relationships are no longer prescribed as strict obligations, but must be earned—created and re-created by family members over their lives."

When I was growing up in Newark, New Jersey, my parents, grandparents, 15 first cousins, dozens of aunts and uncles, and scores of second and third cousins formed a very close-knit extended family. More than 100 members of my family lived within 30 minutes of one another, and we got together regularly.

I grew up loving these family gatherings. I loved it when

we all went out for a picnic; we played softball and ate barbecued chicken and told family stories.

Now that I live in Berkeley, California, with my parents in New Jersey, my wife's parents in Los Angeles, and most of my relatives dispersed throughout the United States, we don't have large family parties anymore.

However, my love and appreciation for these kinds of gatherings haven't diminished at all. And so, in my attempt to share with my wife and daughter the joy and security I experienced as part of such a lively and involved extended family, I have attempted to duplicate some of the festivities and relationships that nurtured me when I was growing up.

For example, last April when our daughter Casey had her first birthday party, nearly 100 members of our "family" were on hand to celebrate this happy occasion. But that day, I couldn't help noticing that of the 100-plus "family" members present, only three were blood relatives. The others were friends, neighbors, and work associates . . . the collection of humanity that has become our "family."

Roommate Matching and Shared Housing Experiments

A practical example of how friendship and acquaintance networks are replacing some of the historical functions of blood relatives can be seen in the area of housing.

Many older people don't want, or can't afford, to live in special retirement communities, and they also don't want to live alone. It can be lonely rattling around a big house all by yourself: there's no one to debate the news with, no one to cook breakfast for, no one to steady the stepladder while you change the light bulb. And for many of the 30 percent of today's elderly who live alone, a big apartment or house can be very hard to keep up.

Living alone denies millions of older men and women the friendship, support, and love that can come from sharing a home with a loved one or with family members. Since not all older people have the luxury of available relatives to live with, several clever solutions, such as roommate matching and shared housing, have begun to pop up around the country.

As the number of older men and women with large "empty-nest" houses or multibedroom apartments grows, roommate matching and shared housing may prove to be the simplest of all the schemes for solving a wide variety of the physical, financial, and social needs of many of America's elders. In the state of California alone, an estimated 200,000 people live alone in houses that have three or more bedrooms. That's 400,000 empty, paid-for rooms in one state alone.

Over the past decade, agencies that specialize in matching older homeowners who have spare rooms with older potential tenants have begun to spring up. One of the first, the nonprofit Project Match in San Jose, California, reports an impressive 70 percent success rate in matching some 1,800 roommates since 1979.

According to Janet Witkin, executive director of the Alternative Living for the Aging project in Los Angeles, "It's a big leap" to move into a shared house. It requires an ability to take risks [and to] give up control. But it's worth more to them to be with someone than to have everything their own way."

When roommate matching works, it can turn people's lives around. For example, 78-year-old Ben Himmel was recently matched with 88-year-old Victor Arkin. Himmel summed up what having a good roommate can mean: "We didn't have any common interests at all. He was a mechanic involved with tools, and I was interested in the arts all my life. And yet I find I am so pleased to be with this man. Since he moved in, I have never felt like being alone in my room. . . . I used to dread getting out of bed in the morning because I was so lonely. Now getting out of bed is a real pleasure."

In other instances, several individuals join together to buy or lease a large house. These ventures, often sponsored initially by churches or other public or private agencies, usually bring together between 3 and 15 residents. Ordinarily, residents have their own bedrooms and share the common rooms.

The secret to successful shared housing, according to a report in the journal *Challenge*, "seems to be the small scale of the projects in combination with the flexibility and active participation of the residents."

In a house started by Boston's Back Bay Aging Concerns Committee, for instance, each resident is required to share the responsibility for tasks that fall within her or his abilities. All residents attend weekly group dinners as well as a weekly house meeting, at which all decisions are made. According to a report written after the house's first three years of operation, 15 people shared the house. This group was comprised of 12 older people, a young couple who acted as "house facilitators," and a young handicapped woman. The report said:

> Members of the house help each other with meal preparation, dressing, and other activities, as help is needed. Frailties and illnesses are dealt with as in a family or among good friends. . . . Most of the residents claim that, at first, they were fearful. They were all strangers to each other and had chosen this option simply because it seemed slightly better than other options available to them. None was expecting to find the love and support that have developed.

Does this kind of shared-housing arrangement seem familiar? The son of one of this house's residents figured it out immediately: "My 75-year-old father lives in a commune. I guess he's become a hippie!" In fact, there are many similarities between adult-oriented shared-housing arrangements and the hippie communes so prevalent in the late sixties and early seventies. Because of this, it's likely that when the boomers find themselves to be empty-nesters, they will readily turn to house sharing and roommate matching for live-in companionship and convenience, just as they did during their college years.

Some shared-housing arrangements are intergenerational. Mary Gildea, clearing-house coordinator of the National Shared Housing Resource Center in Philadelphia, estimates that as much as 50 percent of roommate matching for seniors matches people of different generations.

For instance, Boston's Shared Living Project, founded by several churches and the Gray Panthers, now manages two houses with a total of 38 residents and is building a third for 30 more people. This is an experiment in a different kind of living: a group home that seeks the special synergy that can arise when several generations live in the same household. When the first project was opened in 1980 in a converted Boston mansion, it became home to 16 people, ranging in age from 24 to 82. One of the members of the steering committee, Reverend Merlin Southwick, commented at the time: "The beauty of the concept is that each generation has something to offer. Young people do much of the physical work needed to keep a place going, while older residents provide stability and emotional support."

These alternatives are growing rapidly in popularity. As Mary Gildea says, "This trend continues to grow. It meets the financial, companionship, and security needs that older people have. Five years ago there were about 40 roommate-matching and shared-housing programs around the country. Today there are about 400."

THE METAMORPHOSIS OF THE FAMILY

Whether in your role as grandparent, parent, friend, lover, or son or daughter, the length and vigor of your life will profoundly affect all of your relationships and the decisions you make about them. The longer life expectancy you can anticipate affects what sort of friends you are likely to make. It can turn your expectations of marriage inside out and restructure your family. And it can alter all the relationships within your family, as generations find themselves interacting in unexpected ways.

As America ages, not only will we relate most closely with those blood and marital relatives with whom we feel the greatest affinity, but we will find in our networks of close friends, workmates, and neighbors the love, support, and companionship that our relatives cannot provide.

These are, in a way, the deepest issues we can face—who we love, how we love them, and how we all care for one another. Challenged by the Age Wave, the interpersonal matrix of family, friendship, and intergenerational relationships is undergoing a profound metamorphosis.

The Maturing Marketplace

Until now, most businesspeople have operated on the belief that the youth market is filled with free-spending consumers and that anyone over the age of 50 is staid, crusty, and tight with what little money he or she has.

For example, advertisers have considered the most desirable television audiences to be those in the 18-to-49 age bracket, and they have paid $10 to $12 per thousand for audiences in this age group, as opposed to only $4 per thousand for those over 60. One statistical study of 100 randomly selected television commercials found that, although people over 55 constitute 22 percent of the viewing audience, the messages have almost always been delivered by young actors and actresses. Older people—especially older women—have rarely been shown.

Until recently, the absence of older models in advertising was just as pronounced in magazines as on television. One study looked at every ad in every January issue of

Vogue, Ladies' Home Journal, Ms., Playboy, and *Time* from 1960 to 1979. The researchers guessed the apparent age of every person pictured. What they found was a clear bias: at a time when 21 percent of the adult population was over 60, less than 2 percent of the adults in the ads were in that age bracket. The bias against older women was even stronger: while at the time 57 percent of American adult women were over 40, only 4 percent of the women in the ads fit into this age category.

But the Age Wave is beginning to pull American business in new directions. The national economic picture is now shifting, and the 60 million Americans over 50—one-fourth of the total U.S. population—will turn out to be the most powerful and affluent consumer group in history. It's likely that decades from now, historians will look back on the 1980s and wonder why American industry worked so hard to sell to the youth market when it was their parents and grandparents who had most of the resources.

Although they represent only 25 percent of the total U.S. population, Americans over 50 now have a combined annual personal income of over $800 billion and control 70 percent of the total net worth of U.S. households— nearly $7 trillion of wealth.

Today, members of the 50+ population:

- own 77 percent of all the financial assets in America.
- own 80 percent of all the money in U.S. savings-and-loan institutions.
- purchase 43 percent of all new domestic cars and 48 percent of all luxury cars.
- spend more money on travel and recreation than any other age group.

- purchase 80 percent of all luxury travel.
- spend more on health and personal-care products than any other age group.
- spend more in the drugstore than any other age group and purchase 37 percent of all over-the-counter medicinal products.
- purchase 37 percent of all spa memberships.
- spend more per capital in the grocery store than any other age group.
- eat out an average of three times a week.
- purchase 41 percent of all food processors and toaster ovens.
- purchase 25 percent of all alcoholic beverages.
- gamble more than any other age group.
- join more auto clubs than any other age group.
- watch television more than any other age group.
- read newspapers more than any other age group.
- spend more on quality children's clothing for their grandchildren than the children's parents do.
- account for a whopping 40 percent of total consumer demand.

Gordon French, vice-president of the National Association of Senior Living Industries, believes that the "prosperity among older Americans is no sudden revelation. It's more a product of evolutionary changes in our society: population changes, economic changes, lifestyle changes, and changes in attitudes." French pinpoints the key factors that are directing marketplace attention to the needs of the mature consumer: "a heightened awareness of the market's growth and characteristics; the discovery of its true economics; and the advent of diminished profits from other, younger segments of the consumer marketplace."

A NEW BREED:
THE "SEASONED CONSUMER"

Madison Avenue has constructed a smoke screen of myths about the older consumer that have kept most businesses away from this potentially powerful market segment. We have been led to believe that all older people are poor and therefore cannot purchase new products or services, even if they want to. And we have been told over and over that older men and women are fanatically loyal to their brands and too set in their ways for advertisers to bother marketing to them.

These notions may have been true at one time with an earlier generation of elders, but they are not accurate descriptions of today's new breed of mature American. As we have seen, men and women over 50 are now spending disproportionately to their numbers. And what is being attributed to "brand loyalty" may be an entirely different phenomenon— the good judgment and concern for quality of seasoned consumers.

Because of their greater experience, older consumers are often more thoughtful purchasers than younger buyers and are less inclined to follow fads or to buy on impulse. A man who has bought ten cars has a more critical eye than someone who has bought one, and he is more likely to look for things that are not evident to the novice buyer. Older people are also likely to keep in mind the positive experiences they have had with particular products or merchants. To be turned into new buyers and repeat customers, they need to see quality that can be demonstrated and service that is reliable, friendly, and efficient. They pay attention to price, but they are more willing than younger people to pay for quality and service that will make their purchase cost-effective in the long run.

According to a study conducted by the Daniel Yankelovich group for *Modern Maturity* magazine, 50+ con-

sumers show a higher concern for quality over cost than consumers from all younger age groups.

Older consumers want information that will allow them to take charge of their own lives, including their buying decisions. They want to play an active role as consumers and expect to be responded to in this regard. The sales message should thus be based on facts, not emotions.

Since older people have been seen as not easily swayed, few advertisers have tried to sway them. Only a handful of businesses have gone out of their way to design new products and services for them. No one is trying very hard to change their minds, so their minds go unchanged. As a result, in this self-fulfilling prophecy, they may remain committed to products that were promoted to them when they were younger.

To respond most effectively to the switch from the young to the mature consumer, businesses will need to retool and refocus their imagination and skills. Richard Balkite, director of senior marketing at Donnelley Marketing, reports that "while business is clearly aware of the importance of targeting the changing needs, desires, and lifestyles of consumers over the age of 50, marketers are woefully lacking in an understanding of who they are."

According to Carol Allen, one of the nation's first experts on the 50+ marketplace and director of Allan Associates, a market-consulting firm in Chevy Chase, Maryland, one reason Madison Avenue has been slow to respond to the older market is that "people in advertising are still so young themselves. They can't imagine how 50- and 60-year-olds can even be alive!"

As the number of older consumers grows and their marketplace clout multiplies, advertising strategy will steadily change. John B. Sias, the president of ABC Television, describes this shift: "As the market imperatives of the Age Wave dawn on many companies, as they begin to grasp it and target it, the whole market will begin to turn toward it."

THE MATURE CONSUMER:
SEVERAL MARKETS WITHIN A MARKET

Often, marketers lump everyone over the age of 50 into one amorphous group. Professional market-research companies don't differentiate older Americans with the degree of sophistication that they apply to younger, less financially potent groups. For example, the highly respected Simmons Market Research Bureau, which analyzes marketplace preferences for nearly all of the major magazines in America, compiles separate statistics on 18-, 19-, 20-, and 21-year-olds. In contrast, it provides data on older age groups in four-year increments and then puts everyone over 70 into one category. Similarly, the influential Nielsen ratings don't isolate any subgroups over the age of 55 in their ratings considerations.

But older Americans are far from being homogeneous. As we have seen, they are more diverse in every regard. In the years to come, heightened interest in the mature consumer, combined with new breakthroughs in market research and data analysis, will allow us to isolate and correlate buying needs and preferences with such interacting characteristics of the 50+ population as these: gender, educational level, health status, values and lifestyle, financial niche, previous spending patterns, occupational status, geographic orientation, family circumstances, and daily activities. New market-analysis systems will make it possible to precisely target the various adult segments in America by key lifestyle and purchasing variables in order to clearly determine who the different adult groups are, what they want and need, what they will pay, and what kinds of commercial messages they will respond to. The Age Wave Institute for Population Studies (a subsidiary of Age Wave, Inc.) was recently formed specifically for this purpose.

However, for our more basic purposes here, we will segment the 50+ consumer by age into three separate groups:

1. 50–64: Middle Adulthood
2. 65–79: Late Adulthood
3. 80+: Old Age

Although this particular kind of segmentation serves many useful purposes, there are always exceptions to any standard based on age. For example, there are 50-year-olds whose tired point of view and low energy make them seem old, while some 90-year-olds are very youthful in spirit and full of life.

50–64: Middle Adulthood

Men and women in this age group are, in many ways, at the high point in their adult lives. The children are grown, the mortgage is paid, and they have the highest disposable income of any age group. This particular cohort is better educated and more affluent than their parents were at the same age.

Since those in the 50–64 age bracket can expect to live longer, on the average, than any previous generation, their major issues are those of health, self-fulfillment, a broad spectrum of social activities, comfort, and what to do with their increasing spare time.

This lifestyle focus has prompted some advertisers to refer to them as "suppies"—senior urban professionals—or "opals"—older people with active lifestyles. Then as they grow a bit older, they become "rappies"—retired affluent professionals.

Whatever trendy name they are given, men and women in this age group are an excellent market for financial services, health promotion, wellness and nutrition products and services, luxury travel and tours, personal-care products, adult education, second homes, and recreational products and services. Most are eager to spend money on themselves, since the financial burdens of raising a family are now behind them. Some experts, such as James Gollub of Stanford Research International, think that as these affluent adults in their fifties continue to retire over the next few years, the spending of retirees could jump by as much as 80 percent. As new grand-parents, they are interested in buying gifts for their grand-children at the same time that many are curious about what products and services they can purchase in order to help care for their aging parents.

65–79: Late Adulthood

Today, most people in this age group are living active and independent lifestyles. They are not yet "old" by usual soci-etal standards, and they are interested in many of the same social, health, and leisure activities as the 50-to-64-year-old group. However, during this period there is a greater concern for health and a growing fear over the limitations that a seri-ous illness could cause. Their utilization of medical and long-term health-care services rises dramatically, as does their reliance on family and friends for assistance with the tasks of daily living. Like their 50-to-64-year-old counterparts, they are an excellent market for financial services, estate planning, health promotion, wellness and nutrition products and ser-vices, adult education, travel, personal-care products, second homes, and recreational products and services.

People in the 65–79 age bracket are very interested in long-term care insurance, retirement and lifecare hous-ing, local health-care club membership, and senior-oriented social activities.

Because many in this group have been removed from the activities of the workplace for some time, they are very sensi-tive about being excluded from society. They most definitely do not want to be "put out to pasture" by the young. Many men and women in this age bracket have active social and friendship networks and often remain quite involved in the community. The death of close friends or loved ones, likely during this period, can be very unsettling. And at this stage in life, the number of female-headed households begins to climb.

80+: Old Age

With the average life expectancy now in the seventies for both men and women, the number of older Americans over 80 is less than the numbers in the other 50+ groupings. At this point in life, many older men and women have lost a good deal of their health and personal independence. Less than 2 percent of these people are working, compared with 10 percent in the 65–74 range and 41 percent of those 55–64. They also have the highest poverty levels of any age group in America. For example, according to the Social Security Administration, in 1983, 21.3 percent of the 85+ group lived in poverty, compared with only 11.9 percent of those between 65 and 74.

Although some 80+ men and women remain active in the community and a few are still working, most have retreated to a more reserved life of daily self-care and contact with a small group of family and friends.

Approximately two-thirds of the 80+ population is female.

Members of the 80+ age have the hardest time shopping and getting around town and often have difficulty with tasks and activities that younger people take for granted, such as carrying suitcases or shopping bags, putting food away on top shelves, or cleaning the bathroom. Because of the steady loss of physical vigor and independence, these men and women are an eager market for a wide range of services they used to perform themselves—for example, finance management,

food and medicine purchasing, gardening, home maintenance, housecleaning, cooking, and driving.

Guess Who's 50 Next:
The Migrating Boomers

Just when we think we have described the basic characteristics
of the current mature-marketplace segments, we discover a
challenging fact. Because of the steady progression along the
life line that aging brings, the average 50-, 70-, or 85-year-old
changes with every day that passes. Each year, the older
groups are replaced by more contemporary cohorts, as each
generation takes its turn at being old.

**As powerful as they are today, consumers over 50 have an
invading horde at their backs. Within a decade, the
boomers will make the over-50 group the fastest-growing
and most powerful buying block of our times.**

Cheryl Russel, editor-in-chief of *American Demographics*,
paints a vivid picture of what is already happening as the
boomers migrate out of their twenties and into their thirties
and forties:

> In the next ten years, the number of people aged 18 to
> 24 will fall by four million, down 15 percent. In spending
> power, the youth market is shedding more than $3 bil-
> lion a year. In the next ten years, the number of 25-to-34-
> year-olds will drop by nine percent, a loss of more than
> four million people. The spending power of this group
> will decline by fully $67 billion.

> In contrast, the number of people aged 35 to 44 will
> increase by 26 percent in the next ten years. The spend-
> ing power of this group will grow by more than $195
> billion, to $900 billion by 1997. . . . Households headed
> by 35-to-44-year-olds spend 28 percent more than the
> average household, and they spend more than younger

households in almost every category, including furniture and appliances, entertainment, and personal care.

There will always be a youth market, but it won't always be powerful relative to other markets. In the future, American business has got to learn to love the middle-aged.

As the boomers grow older, they are destined to continue their role as the dominant age group in the United States, from the other side of 50. As adults, they have learned the lessons well that were taught them by television. They have made a complete about-face from the traditional Protestant ethic of saving, self-sacrifice, and delayed gratification. They have learned to spend their money fast and to borrow rather than save; they more readily use their checkbooks than their savings passbooks. While every index of real income for young couples has dropped during the past fifteen years, boomers' consumer spending actually went up by 15 percent. There are two reasons for this seeming paradox: first, more women worked, and second, the boomers turned out to be more willing than their parents to go into debt. Whereas their parents and grandparents were cautious and reserved about spending money, even when they had it, the boomers are exceedingly comfortable spending money, even when they *don't* have it. And it's likely that the boomers will take their spending style with them into their older years.

The Cohort Effect

Social research has demonstrated that each generation, or "cohort," tends to form its own unique point of view with regard to numerous key preferences, such as choice of clothing, food, and music, as well as with regard to more serious issues, such as social values and the making and spending of money. Many of the most influential forces that shape these styles and preferences occur during the first 15 to 20 years of life, when basic adult beliefs and goals are being developed and tested. These patterns of generational values and preferences are illustrative of what sociologists call the "cohort effect," a useful system for understanding the various likes and dislikes of each unique generational group as it migrates from youth to old age.

For example, most people develop their tastes in music during the years when they first begin dating and having sex. Once established, these preferences often persist throughout the adult years. One generation may have always liked the big-band sound of Glen Miller, another the exciting beat of Elvis Presley, another the driving guitar of Eric Clapton, and another the electrifying rhythms of Michael Jackson. Of course, radio programmers have known about the cohort effect for years. And successful advertising experts usually key the pace, sound, and mood of their commercials to the particular cohort they're trying to reach.

When analyzing the financial styles of any particular generation, there are two basic issues to consider: whether they have money, and how they feel about spending it.

Some of the more fascinating aspects of these generational preferences relate to the making and spending of money. Not surprisingly, members of most cohorts form their core values with regard to how they will relate to money during the influential years when they first start working.

For instance, today's 65+ consumers were deeply influenced in their youth by the terribly hard and financially frightening times of the depression. Their point of view is "Save, save, save. Something terrible could happen, and you must be prepared for that rainy day."

The next generation of elders, those who today are in their fifties and early sixties, were influenced by the great prosperity that followed World War II, as well as by the trying times of the depression. Their point of view, therefore, is a blend: "Save some, spend some."

The boomers, try as their parents did to inculcate in

them a sense of financial practicality, were fully immersed as consumers in the free-spending, affluent decades following World War II. Their point of view about money is thus somewhat different from that of their parents and is totally at odds with that of their grandparents. Essentially, their attitude is this: "If you have no money in the bank but you have at least two credit cards that aren't over the limit, you're doing fine."

Better educated than any generation before, and possibly since, they have been trained in rational decision making. They may spend freely, but they do so with increasingly good judgment and business savvy. They are less likely to become imprisoned by brand loyalties, and they make careful comparisons of the quality of competing products.

RETOOLING THE MARKETPLACE

If business and industry are to meet the needs of the increasing population of men and women over 50, they will first have to learn what those needs are. This section will explore the following six key consumption-oriented psychological and lifestyle characteristics of the mature consumer:

- Mature consumers don't like to be thought of as old.
- Mature consumers prefer to be reflected in an attractive, positive fashion.
- Mature consumers are more interested in purchasing experiences than things.
- Being comfortable is a key psychological need of the older consumer.
- Security and safety are key psychological factors in the older consumer's decision to buy.
- For an older consumer, convenience and access may be just as important as the product itself.

Through an understanding of this purchasing profile, we can begin to catch a glimpse of the broad range of product and service needs that a mass population of older men and women will have. In the next chapter, "Redesigning America," we will take a glimpse into the future to examine many of the exciting new business opportunities that the Age Wave brings.

Mature Consumers Don't Like to Be Thought of as Old

Perhaps it's a reflection of our cultural gerontophobia, or merely a desire to be thought of as young and attractive, but the truth is that many older people would prefer not to be referred to by age at all. According to Robert Wood, publishing director of *Modern Maturity* magazine, "Senior citizens don't think of themselves as old, they think of themselves as people." This makes for a difficult challenge to marketers. How do you target products or promotions to members of the mature population when they are somewhat uncomfortable with being identified as part of that group in the first place?

There are two effective ways to solve this problem: first, targeting the self-perceived "cognitive age," and second, bypassing age altogether and instead targeting lifestyle "affinities" that are both common and important to the older consumer.

Targeting self-perceived cognitive age vs. chronological age.   According to David Wolfe, national consultant to industry on the mature consumer, "If you ask older people how old they think they would be if they did not know their own age, about three-quarters of them give an answer that is 75 to 80 percent of their chronological age."

Studies conducted throughout the United States have consistently shown that once people pass their fiftieth

birthdays, they tend to feel 10 to 20 years younger than their actual age.

Companies that pitch straight to the age of the audience that they mean to hit will find themselves missing the market. A few years ago, for instance, Johnson & Johnson designed a shampoo called Affinity that was created especially to deal with the problems of over-40 hair. And that's exactly how they marketed it. It struggled in the marketplace for several years, until finally Johnson & Johnson eliminated all age references from the ads. As one ad executive put it, "How many women want to walk into a drugstore and say, 'Do you have that shampoo for women over 40?' None."

Companies wishing to cater to this audience, therefore, should target to the age that is 10 to 20 years lower. Helena Rubinstein put out a product group called "Madame Rubinstein," aimed at the older market. The ads used the tag line, "Beauty doesn't have to end at 50!" The ad was a big hit—with women over 60.

When Frances Lear, then 62, decided it was time to create a popular women's magazine for "women her age," *Lear's*, she targeted the 40+ woman. "I can't tell you how strange it seems to be 64," she told us. "I don't relate to that age at all."

Bypassing age, targeting lifestyle affinities.   The other solution is to bypass age altogether and focus instead on some issue, concern, or "affinity" that older men and women will have that is likely to get their attention and draw them to the product. For example, just as acne-medicine commercials attract the attention of teenagers but are nearly invisible to anyone over 25, antiwrinkle-cream ads will go over the heads of kids but will instantly capture the attention of their parents.

Quaker Oats recently launched a national campaign to more aggressively promote its breakfast cereals to older men and women. The tack they took was simple and direct: "Quaker Oats is nutritious, low in sodium, has no cholesterol, and is good for digestion." Since heart disease and good digestion are very likely to be concerns for an older person, the ad hit its mark. Similarly, by promoting aspirin products for their prophylactic effect in preventing second heart attacks, as Bayer is now doing, an affinity is immediately created with 50+ men, who are at the highest risk for heart attack.

In a recent meeting I conducted with a prominent New York–based magazine publisher, the senior management wondered how to title a new magazine that will deal primarily with matters of personal finance management for wealthy people over 50. Convinced that any reference to age in the title would have a negative effect on sales, the group brainstormed for hours until arriving at an ingenious title, one that they felt would attract the attention of exactly those whom they wanted to target: *Assets.* While most young or poor people won't even notice the magazine on the stands, wealthy older people will.

Another way to create an affinity with a consumer is by having the product promoted by an individual who is an easily recognized celebrity or authority figure to the generation you're focusing on. For example, several months ago, while visiting my parents, I watched a football game with my father. During the commercial break, a Michelob beer commercial appeared featuring rock-guitar legend Eric Clapton. Having been a fan of Clapton for years and never having seen him before in a commercial, I turned excitedly to my dad and said, "Can you believe that Michelob was able to get Eric Clapton to appear in their ad?" My father turned to me and said, "Who's Eric Clapton?" On the other hand, had the commercial featured a popular singer from years ago, the conversation would likely have been reversed.

By targeting self-perceived cognitive age or focusing on relevant lifestyle affinities, savvy marketers can appeal to older consumers without having to deal with consumers' psychological acceptance or rejection of their chronological age.

Mature Consumers Prefer to Be Reflected in an Attractive, Positive Fashion

Older people are very sensitive to being portrayed negatively. When Wendy's fast-food chain featured Clara Peller in its "Where's the beef?" ad campaign, many older people were insulted by the commercial. "We don't look or act like that!" they angrily responded. They felt that Peller's performance fostered images of older people as silly, cranky, and funny looking.

With increasing concern about health and personal well-being, older consumers want products and services that will make them feel and look better physically, mentally, and socially.

According to industry observer Len Albin,

> When a TV commercial shows older people acting like dopes (having a nervous breakdown because of loose-fitting dentures) or a little fuzzy in the head (as in the old Country Time Lemonade ad, which was subsequently changed), it doesn't move older viewers to try the product. In fact, any sort of advertising which segregates older people as "different" is insulting.

The world of advertising is swiftly opening up to a more positive image of aging. We can see this trend reflected in the increasing use of older Americans in commercials as authority figures, as lovable grandparents, and simply as people who have their own full, rich lives. According to Clay Edmonds, marketing director at Ogilvy & Mather Partners, "Rather than youth being the ideal in advertisements, as it used to be, health, vigor, alertness, and doing the most with what you have are now the ideals."

A good example is a recent Clairol commercial featuring middle-aged "Dynasty" beauty Linda Evans. The opening line? "Let's face it—40 isn't fatal." And an advertisement promoting *Lear's* magazine reads "If You're under 40, Lie about Your Age!"

More and more commercials now show attractive and vital people of all ages. A middle-aged man in a bran commercial does aerobics while his wife cheers him on. A mature beauty in an Oil of Olay commercial says, "I'm about to wash a whole day's worth of aging away." A distinguished gentleman with thinning silver hair sells Reunite wine. An over-50 Sophia Loren sells perfume named after her, as well as eyeglass frames. A glamorous mature model describes Cover Girl's "Replenish" for "changing" skins, and then asks, "Who says you ever have to stop being a cover girl?"

Even Pepsi, which built its reputation on the youthful baby-boom generation, is growing up. The initial image of the Pepsi Generation—with the product touted as being "for those who think young"—reflected Madison Avenue's infatuation with youth. Although all of the original Pepsi ads featured lively, energetic, and youthful actors, more recently Pepsi has begun to reach out to the older consumer. Now, the "Pepsi Spirit" campaign presents consumers who span at least three generations, enjoying Pepsi side by side. According to Alan Pottasch, senior vice-president for creative services for Pepsico, Inc., in the 1960s "Everyone wanted to 'think young.' . . . More recently, we've tried to take the Pepsi Generation from meaning the group frcm 15 to 25 and expand it to mean the group from 15 to 75, provided their attitude toward life is a vital one."

Cutty Sark recently based a successful advertising campaign on three people: a man and a woman who looked about 40, and an elegant, well-dressed, silver-haired man about 70, appearing together as symbols of sophistication, good taste, and affluence. According to Warren Berger of the Food and Beverage Marketing Association: "The Cutty campaign wasn't specifically directed at older consumers, though they are important Scotch buyers. Instead, the older gent was used both as a model for success for younger buyers, and one who would also play well with older drinkers." According to Don

Klein, president of the Howard-Marlboro agency, which created the ad, "The objective was not to show an older person, but to communicate the feeling of achievement. . . . The reviews from the trade were positive—and, apparently, so was the response from consumers. Cutty was the only brand that grew in share last year."

When AT&T, MCI, and GTE Sprint went head-to-head in competition over the long-distance telephone market in 1985, many consumers were confused about which service was better. To calm their anxiety, the long-distance companies all decided to use older, more mature spokespersons. AT&T hired 63-year-old Cliff Robertson as their primary spokesman. MCI used 75-year-old Burt Lancaster and 51-year-old Joan Rivers for its ads, while GTE Sprint went for a sophisticated, seductive lady with obvious lines of experience in her forehead.

A successful series of California commercials for the Pacific Bell telephone company featured a positive look at two older men calling each other long distance to reminisce about the course of their 60-year friendship. According to Robert Black, the creative director of Foote, Cone and Belding, the ad firm that created the commercials, "I enjoy older people, and I think they're a natural for this kind of campaign. You have 60 years of life to portray; they give you a natural storytelling device."

Two of the most clever and popular television ads oriented toward the 50+ market were created for the McDonald's Corporation. One, entitled "The New Kid," depicts an older man experiencing his first day at work at a McDonald's restaurant. In his new job, he has a grand time pleasing the customers while showing the younger workers a thing or two about his seasoned skill and stamina—to their great pleasure. Perhaps it was the positive feelings that this ad engendered that caused it to be named one of the five favorite commercials of the year in 1987.

The second was entitled "Golden Time" and was created by the Leo Burnett Advertising Agency. According to Gene Mandarino, senior vice-president/creative director, "Everything on the tube is so 'up' and youthful. Everybody's jiving around in their Levi's. So when I was looking for an idea for McDonald's, I thought, 'Let's throw a change-up at them.' One-third of McDonald's customers are older people, but nobody talks about them."

The idea for "Golden Time" did not come from Mc-Donald's, or from focus groups, surveys, or other market-sampling techniques. It sprang from Mandarino's own experience. "When I was living in the city, I used to see dozens of older people on the verandah of the McDonald's nearby," he says. "The people were so happy, the place was clean and comfortable, they could afford it. And I found myself wishing my dad had had a place like that in his neighborhood when he was alive. My father had lost my mother and was alone. He spent his last 15 years wandering through life, trying to find some companionship, feeling very clumsy about it."

Mandarino feels that "Golden Time" was a "sweet classic." He explains: "An older man walks into a McDonald's, past an older woman sitting alone in the corner. It's filmed close, intimate. There's music; he's seen her there before, he'd like to meet her, but he doesn't know what he'll say. He's as nervous as an adolescent. She's noticed him, too, the song tells us: 'I'm too old to be smitten; besides, it's not fittin'.' But this time he does work up the courage. He asks her if the space is taken, and as the curtain comes down, they are beginning a relationship.

"It was a commercial that people noticed, because it treated older people not as buffoons, but as real people."

Mature Consumers Are More Interested in Purchasing "Experiences" Than Things

We are used to thinking of consumers as being interested in "things"—but there are only so many things people can buy before they have filled up their houses.

**Older men and women are drawn to purchasing products
or services insofar as these create a desirable experience.**

Having the money and time to travel, to learn, and to
explore new areas of their lives, mature consumers have as
their goals satisfaction, personal well-being, and self-fulfillment.

In a recent study on the 55+ market conducted by Jordan, Case and McGrath, researchers discovered: "As an extension of the 'me generation' phenomenon, society has come
full circle. The concentration on youth and self has filtered up
to the older population. They are no longer content to altruis-
tically live their lives for their children or grandchildren, but
instead for their *own* fulfillment."

A similar conclusion was reached by the Daniel Yankelovich Group in its 1987 study of mature Americans: "They
show a strong commitment to spending on products and services that enhance their personal enjoyment of life. Most have
successfully fulfilled family and financial obligations and feel
a sense of accomplishment. With children launched and
homes in many cases paid for, the over-50 Americans feel
entitled to a certain amount of self-indulgence; and many of
them now have sufficient discretionary income to act on the
new agenda."

I was recently visiting a posh travel agency in an exclusive area of Beverly Hills, and was amused by a sign on the
wall. It said, "Go first class. Your heirs will."

Dr. James Ogilvy was director of research for the prestigious Values and Lifestyle Study at the Stanford Research
Institute. As he examined the changes taking place as a result
of the maturing of the population, he realized that "the success of the industrial revolution has satisfied most of the demand for tangible goods like housing, clothing, and cars.
. . . The growth of our economy is no longer driven by the
desires of consumers to accumulate goods. It is driven by the
consumer's quest for vivid experiences."

According to Ogilvy, "The experience industry cultivates through education, broadens through travel, allows escape through entertainment, heals through psychotherapy, numbs through drugs and alcohol, edifies through religion, informs through reading, and enraptures through art."

A practical example of the mature preference for satisfying experiences can be seen in the world of retail banking. During the past decade, in response to the preference of busy young people for off-hours banking and to their need to get in and out of the bank as quickly as possible, automatic tellers have multiplied throughout the land. The problem is that most older customers don't use them. The reasons are simple. First, having more time at their disposal, older people no longer have speed of service as a primary concern; in fact, many are looking for ways to fill up their hours. Second, for many of today's older cohorts, computers are puzzling, uncertain equipment, not something they want to entrust their life savings to. Third, and most important, they prefer having human interaction with the bank teller to a "conversation" with a computer screen.

For these consumers, the interpersonal experience matters a great deal. In fact, in many retirement-area locations, banks offer refreshments and a comfortable air-conditioned lounge. They encourage people to visit and to take as much time as they'd like at the bank. This concept would never occur to a retail-banking manager who had cut his or her teeth on busy yuppies.

One of the first attempts to design specialized banking services for the older customer is under way at Bank Five for Savings in Burlington, Massachusetts. According to Robert Collins, vice-president of marketing, "Banks can bundle and cross-sell services in countless ways, but a promotional effort aimed at the seniors market calls for a different kind of 'relationship' banking." In its first year of operation, Bank Five's "Presidential Group" sponsored four cocktail parties, four dinner/theater parties, an investment seminar, and trips to New York City and Bermuda. During that year, the bank opened 450 Presidential Group accounts for more than 700 members. The average account balance was $63,000, and 20 percent of the total deposits—approximately $5,670,000—represented new money to the bank as a result of the "relationship" program.

Beyond enhanced customer service, banks hold the further possibility of helping older men and women transform their possessions directly into satisfying experiences.

As we have seen, many older persons are "brick-rich and cash poor": that is, their principal financial asset is the equity in their homes. Today, older Americans own an estimated $700 billion of home equity. That's a median of $48,000 in equity for every older homeowner. This enormous amount of home equity has so far not been available to support many of their lifestyle needs. In the years to come, a variety of innovative and practical financing schemes will focus on freeing these resources as a means to make life more comfortable and satisfying while unleashing a flood of elder assets into the marketplace. One of the most promising of these financial strategies is the reverse mortgage, a concept that originated in the 1970s.

Putting your house to work.   Consider, for example, a 70-year-old retired couple who own a decent house, paid off, but are struggling to survive on Social Security. They are anxious about using up their savings and prefer not to have to sell their home for a source of income. If a bank or lending institution were willing, they could take out a traditional second mortgage on the house and live off the proceeds. But since traditional second mortgages depend upon one's ability to repay them out of current income, this couple probably wouldn't qualify.

But there is another possibility. After evaluating the equity in their house, future trends in interest rates, and how long the actuarial tables say the couple is likely to live, the bank could offer them an arrangement by which they would be paid anything from $100 to several thousand dollars per month for the rest of their lives. In essence, they could continue to live in their home while drawing an ongoing "salary" from their property. This way, they'd never have to worry about the payments ending, they'd have extra money to finance their various needs, and they could remain in their home as long as they liked. For the lender, the money is a long-term, fixed-interest loan. The principal grows with each payment, and the interest accumulates. When the homeowners pass away and the wills are probated and the house sold, the lender would receive the principal and the interest back as well as any appreciation on the property.

Or, if the homeowners preferred, they could work out a "term" arrangement that might give them a balloon payment up front, more money per month, or leave any appreciation in the house to their heirs, but would be limited to a certain number of years.

By early 1987, there were 1,500 reverse mortgages (RMs), Home Equity Conversions (HECs), and Individual Retirement Mortgage Accounts (IRMAs) operating in the United States, representing over $50 million. In comparison, Great Britain has moved more swiftly with this innovative strategy and already has some 17,000 reverse mortgages operating.

Studies have shown that if the United States created the right legal framework for RMs, and if the general public were to become more comfortable with this idea, at least one-fifth of America's 3.5 million elderly poor could move above the poverty line and live comfortably in their own homes, supported by steady cash withdrawal of their property assets.

In response, the U.S. government has begun to set the reverse mortgage wheels in motion. The Federal Housing Administration is studying strategies for the emergence of a practical reverse mortgage program. In legislation passed at the end of the 1987 legislative session, the FHA was instructed to insure some 2,500 RMs in a demonstration project over the next few years. As they become better known to the public, and as more financial institutions become more familiar with the idea, RMs and other similar arrangements may turn out to be the solution to many later-life financial concerns that have historically fallen on family members or on the government.

Being "Comfortable" Is a Key Psychological Need of the Older Consumer

As we age, we become more interested in being comfortable. One of the most telling manifestations of this need is reflected in the increasing interstate "gray migration" that is taking place throughout America. "The migration of older people across state lines has increased by 50 percent in the last decade," says Charles Longino of the University of Miami's Center for Social Research in Aging, "and I'm guessing that it will increase another 50 percent in the coming decade."

Knowing why these people are leaving, and where they are moving to, provides a useful insight into the "quest for comfort."

Half of all Americans over the age of 65 who relocate are leaving familiar neighborhoods to move south and west in order to be warm and comfortable.

This great migration to the Sun Belt has some solid grounding in physical realities: older bodies don't retain heat as well, and the inconveniences of winter—shoveling walks, driving on icy roads, and having to stay indoors much of the time—all weigh more heavily on the old. And they have fewer reasons than the young to put up with these inconveniences and discomforts.

As a result of this quest for comfort, the Sun-Belt states are repeatedly rated as among the most desirable places for retirees to live. The top four states that older people move to are Florida, California, Arizona, and Texas, in that order. Together, these four states account for nearly half of all the older Americans who move to new states.

But the desire to be comfortable goes far beyond relocat-

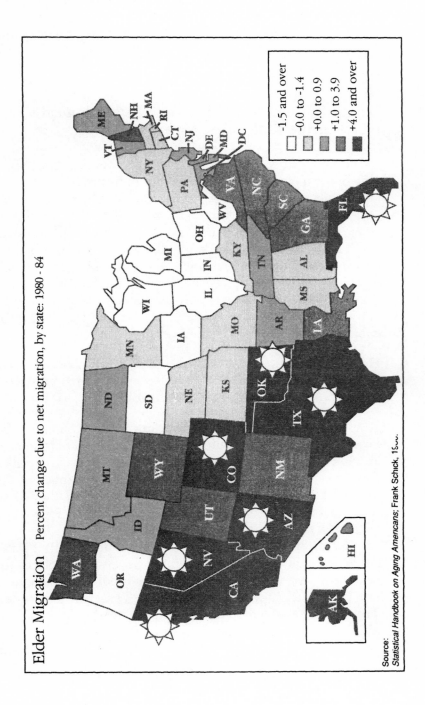

Elder Migration   Percent change due to net migration, by state: 1980 - 84

Legend:
- -1.5 and over
- -0.0 to -1.4
- +0.0 to 0.9
- +1.0 to 3.9
- +4.0 and over

Source:
Statistical Handbook on Aging Americans; Frank Schick, 1986.

ing to a warmer climate. As we age, we come to feel that we have had enough hassles. We feel less inclined to conform ourselves to products that were not designed with ease of use in mind. At the same time, we are less concerned with showing off; we are less impressed by what looks good and more by what feels good. While young women will walk around in high-heeled shoes that kill their backs but look sharp, older women will likely opt for comfort over fashion.

It's no coincidence that the most successful mail-order catalog for yuppies is entitled *The Sharper Image,* while the popular new catalog among their parents is called *Comfortably Yours.*

In 1983, when New Jersey catalog entrepreneur Elaine Adler started *Comfortably Yours*, she intended to develop a modest business geared to providing hundreds of items, gadgets, and clothes to help the elderly stay comfortable, independent, and involved. In three years the company has experienced astounding growth, expanding its staff from 3 employees to 80.

With the coming of the Age Wave, many products and services will be newly designed to meet the comfort requirements of the older user. To catch a glimpse of a world of products designed with the older body in mind, wander through Adler's catalog. Some of the items are for people who are quite frail or who have lost some specific function: walker attachments, adjustable beds, special tables and desks for the bedridden, dressing hooks, cutting boards and weed pullers that can be controlled with one hand, adapted garden tools for those whose grips have been weakened by arthritis, guardrails and nonslip mats for the bathroom, and special telephone speakers for the hearing impaired.

There are items here, too, for people who have just lost a step or two: "catapult" spring seats that help you get up out of a chair, shovel and rake handles specially designed so that you don't have to stoop, automatic card shufflers, indoor exercise equipment, lightweight irons, and extenders for bathroom mirrors.

Finally, there are quite a few products that you don't

have to be impaired at all to appreciate: comfortable foot warmers, easy-off clothing with Velcro tabs, muscle-relaxing moist heating pads, garden "scoots" (wheeled seats that allow people to sit as they do garden work), needle threaders, ergonomically designed back cushions for automobiles, easy-to-hold hammer handles, and portable whirlpool baths.

Regarding psychological, as opposed to physical, comfort, market research has shown that older people are not active buyers of various kinds of new technology, such as home computers. Is it that they aren't interested, or that they aren't comfortable with the new technology? Computer companies think that older people aren't interested in computers and won't use them—a profound mistake. Every computer company in America is trying for 1 percent, 3 percent, or 6 percent of the 40-and-under generation, when they could have 50 percent of the 50+ market just for the asking. Not one company has identified itself as the one that has people over 50 in mind.

In order to effectively market computers to an older population, some redesign is needed (for example, larger screen graphics and easier software). More important, however, is that the consumer feel comfortable with the product. Older people may be somewhat intimidated by computers, and many would like to have assistance in bringing computers home, setting them up, and learning the basic steps for effective usage. Weekly or monthly brush-up lessons in their own homes or at a senior center would go a long way toward creating a sense of ease with this technology. In addition, a 24-hour, 800-number help line would be invaluable for the older user, who doesn't always have access to work mates or on-the-job assistance.

It might also make good sense for computer companies to train a legion of older customer-service representatives—possibly volunteers—specifically for the task of helping older users get comfortable with their hardware and software.

Security and Safety Are Key Psychological Factors in the Decision to Buy

If you were to visit most retirement communities, you would notice first the walls that surround them. As we grow older we tend to feel somewhat more physically and socially vulnerable. Twenty-four-hour security is one of the basic requirements for age-segregated housing. The commanding presence of walls, alarm systems, guards, and passkeys reflects the internal anxieties regarding the possibility of physical, psychological, or financial harm to oneself or a loved one.

This psychological concern for security is also reflected in the disproportionately high purchase of luxury cars by those over 50. In addition to being a sign of status, such cars are usually seen as being more sturdy, more reliable, and safer than smaller, less "substantial" models.

Older men and women tend to seek security in two ways: through products and services that directly protect them from harm, and through products and services that simply make them *feel* more secure.

For example, Johanna Varma, vice-president of operations for the lifecare and elderly-housing centers being developed by the Marriott Corporation, explained that her company had given a great deal of thought to the importance of security to people 65 and older. Specifically, the firm wasn't sure whether to fit each apartment with deadbolt locks and standard metal keys or with perforated plastic cards, like the ones that have become standard in most new hotels. Marriott had planned to use the cards because of their effectiveness and ease of use, Varma said, "but our research showed something interesting. The two systems are equally secure. But we found that older people tend not to trust the plastic cards. They grew up in an era when security was reflected in big steel locks with brass keys. So that's what we give them."

New applications of technology now offer a means for older people to feel even more psychologically secure in their homes, especially if they live alone. For instance, approximately ten years ago, Boston University psychology professor Dr. Andrew Dibbner conducted research into the psychological concerns of older men and women in the Boston area who lived alone. He discovered that one of their greatest fears was the thought of falling down or otherwise needing help without being able to call out or reach the telephone to dial for assistance. Although these people enjoyed living independently in their own homes or apartments, this particular anxiety had many of them terrified.

In response, Dibbner developed an ingenious piece of equipment that connects directly to a standard telephone and is controlled by a tiny wireless transmitter that can be worn on the wrist or around the neck, or placed in a pants pocket or purse. Some systems also include large "panic" touch pads on the walls of the most frequently used rooms, such as bathrooms, bedrooms, kitchens, and living rooms. Should the older person need help of any sort, he or she need only press the button on the transmitter or wall pad, and it signals the telephone to dial a preprogrammed number for immediate assistance. Today, more than 50,000 older men and women have such a system—known as Lifeline—in their homes.

Recently, Lifeline introduced a new model, which includes a "Dick Tracy"-like two-way voice-transmission capability. This way, the office monitoring the system can carry on a conversation with the subscriber, regardless of whether or not that person can pick up the phone.

AT&T markets a similar system, which also has the ability to monitor water, electrical power, and temperature conditions and to sense fire or smoke, and can respond to a hand-held medical or accident beeper (all for less than $500).

Recently, such a beeper saved the life of a 93-year-old woman who was attacked in her Los Angeles home by young thugs. They woke Eulalia Newsom from a nap, held a knife to her throat, and demanded money. When she wouldn't give them any, they threw her in a closet. One of them ripped a pendant from around her neck, saw it was worthless plastic, and threw it back in the closet with her before he slammed the door. Although they broke into her safe and removed her $17,000 life savings, Newsom found the pendant and pressed the panic button.

The remote transmitter dialed Emergency Response System, Inc., and within minutes paramedics and sheriff's deputies had arrived. Newsom's assailants had escaped, but the paramedics were just in time to get her to the hospital and save her from death due to the shock of multiple fractures and contusions. Later, she told reporters from her hospital bed, "That pendant saved my life. I just might have given up." The system cost her only $25 a month to rent.

But even more remarkable applications of technology may be just around the corner. Picture an elderly man with a heart condition out for a walk in the park. Suddenly, he grabs at his chest and bends over in pain. He begins to stumble toward a nearby bench, but he has hardly reached it when a police car roars up the park walk. The policemen jump out and begin to administer oxygen and perform CPR. Moments later an ambulance arrives, and the man's life is saved.

The technology that would make this scenario possible—a portable life monitor—would be a combination of a miniaturized heart monitor and a tiny communications device, an emergency locator that is similar to (but much smaller than) models now in use on airplanes, trucks, and boats. Miniaturized monitors for various critical body readings (such as heart rate, blood pressure, and blood-sugar level) are already being developed, and cellular-telephone technology has already been implemented in most cities. These monitors will be combined with a miniaturized transmitter that signals when vital signs exceed some preset parameters. Then a tiny, low-power homing signal sends police and other emergency workers precise and instantaneous information about the subscriber's location and needs.

A related concern is financial security. Older men and women have spent a lifetime working hard for what they have, and they are at a point in their lives when they want to feel secure financially. Knowing that they might not get a second chance to accumulate these hard-earned resources, they are more inclined to take risks and try new things *only* with the credible promise of trusted authorities or institutions, and ideally with a complete money-back guarantee. They will not respond to user testimonials from unknown consumers or to store displays that spur impulse buying but are not associated with any clear positive benefits.

Home Savings of America recently launched an engaging television advertising campaign that features George Fenneman, who has been one of their spokesmen for decades. During this no-frills commercial, Fenneman earnestly explains that after all his years of association with Home Savings of America, he has come to understand how important your money is to you. He assures you that with Home Savings of America, your money is *safe,* and he gives his word that your hard-earned savings will not be exposed to any foolish risks. Home Savings of America, Fenneman concludes, knows who its customers are and what's on their minds.

The importance of financial security to the older consumer has been reflected in the past ten years in the phenomenal growth in the number of 65 + subscribers to health-maintenance organizations (HMOs).

HMOs provide medical care on a "capitated" basis—that is, rather than billing for each procedure performed on a patient, they bill a set fee for each patient ("per capita") each year. Whether you need a mole removed or a heart bypass operation, once you're a member, you simply walk in, hand the person at the counter your card and a nominal fee, and you're taken care of. Regardless of the severity of your health problem, there will be no additional charges. In the last three years the number of Medicare enrollers at HMOs has tripled. When asked why he joined this new form of insurance program, Joseph Carlisle, 72, of Minneapolis, reflecting the concerns of many of his age peers, commented, "At my age, with the continually rising costs of health care, I'd rather go to sleep each night knowing exactly how much I'm going to have to spend on health care this year, instead of always worrying that a serious illness could drive me to the poorhouse."

Many experts predict that the same psychological and financial concerns that have motivated such a dramatic rise in HMO participation will force a major restructuring, perhaps a nationalization, of the American health-care-funding system. A public opinion poll conducted for the Los Angeles *Times* in 1987 shows that, fed up and frightened by the rising costs of health care, nearly two out of three Americans now support the idea of national health insurance.

Convenience and Access May Be Just as Important as the Product Itself

With age, the concerns for comfort, satisfying purchasing experiences, and a minimum of hassles translate directly into a greater need for convenience.

Products and services will need to reach out a bit more to older consumers than they do to younger people.

One approach to convenience enhancement, a high level of personalized customer service, is very old-fashioned.

According to John Pellegrene, senior vice-president of marketing for Dayton-Hudson department stores,

> The older market has a need to feel appreciated, to be treated special. But if you're going to capture that market, the treatment of the older person is going to have to improve. The contact on the floor of the department store is going to have to improve. The actual consultant [salesperson] is going to have to know a whole lot more about the needs and interests of older buyers. If you don't have a bonding with your customer, you're going to have trouble with the over-50 market. Our approach is to offer service, service, and service, in that order.

Robert Beck is currently executive vice-president of Bank of America and was the director of benefits at IBM during its phenomenal growth years in the late 1970s and early 1980s. Because of his work involvements, Beck—who is middle-aged—has become very capable at using a wide variety of computer and electronic technologies. It should not have been surprising to him when his 78-year-old father commented one day that he wished he could have a VCR like his son's. "You can, Dad—all you need to do is go out and buy one," said the younger Beck. "Easy for you to say," replied his father. "First of all, even though I'd like to own one, I wouldn't know which one to buy. Second, I could never carry it into my house. Third, I wouldn't know how to set it up. And fourth, I'm not sure that I could follow the instructions on how to use it, and I wouldn't want to buy something I couldn't use." For the elder Beck, money wasn't the issue; the inconvenience of purchasing, setting up, and using was.

As a solution, the son went with his father to an electronics store and helped him buy a good, easy-to-use VCR. Then they worked out a deal with the store manager whereby one of the technicians would deliver the VCR to Mr. Beck's home and set it up for him. In addition, for an additional $25, they arranged for the technician—now Mr. Beck's "personal customer-service representative"—to give him three lessons, spaced one day apart, on how to use the VCR. Once he got the feel for this new technology, Mr. Beck quickly became a big fan of prerecorded videos and now boasts the largest collection of movies on his block. In fact, he has begun a weekly movie-watching club for his retired neighbors and friends.

As a postscript, he has come to enjoy his VCR so much that he recently returned to the electronics store himself and worked out similar arrangements for the purchase of a quadraphonic stereo set with remote controls, a cordless telephone, and a coffeepot that turns itself on to make coffee before he wakes up. For Mr. Beck, making the purchase more convenient and being helped to learn how to use his new equipment was every bit as important a part of the sale as the product itself.

Home deliveries of everything from pizza to furniture and health-care services will be making a comeback, as thoughtful merchants and service providers look for ways to attract and assist the older shopper. For example, New York's Doctors on Call and Washington, D.C.'s Geodan Medical House Calls, Inc., are bringing back the old-fashioned house call at a cost to seniors of $50 per visit. Physicians with Doctors on Call visit more than 50,000 patients per year, 35 percent of them seniors. If needed, the company will even bring traveling labs to your door for blood and urine samples, X-rays, EKGs, and ultrasound.

Perhaps you don't need a doctor, but just want to have a few health-related questions answered. For routine information needs, you can call one of the hundreds of local Tel-Med hotlines. After you have identified your particular area of concern, a three-minute, medically approved tape will come on to answer most of your questions. Tel-Med provides prerecorded tapes on nearly 300 topics.

For those who would like to talk directly to a health authority about their concerns, the Adventist West hospital group, headquartered in Roseville, California, recently put into action a service called "Ask-a-Nurse." If you have a health question, you can call a toll-free number and speak to a nurse. There is no charge, and you don't even have to be a member of an Adventist West system. The hospital benefits from the good public relations, from the data base of potential customers it can build, and from the referrals that its doctors get when a caller needs a physician.

Another increasingly popular strategy among the 50+ population for convenience-oriented buying involves membership buying clubs. Membership clubs, of course, are not new; there are already many successful clubs that satisfy the needs of consumers of all ages, such as the AAA automobile club, American Express, AARP, and Book-of-the-Month Club.

In an attempt to form a closer relationship with its mature consumers, Sears now runs a club for people over 50 called "Mature Outlook," offering a mail-order discount pharmacy service, free home evaluations from Coldwell Banker, financial portfolio analysis from Dean Witter Reynolds, discounted insurance from Allstate, and discount travel packages from Greyhound and Budget Rent-a-Car, as well as discounts of up to 25 percent on products ranging from eyeglasses to lawn mowers. Sears researched the over-50 market: what they need, how they see themselves, and how they like to shop. Sears found that these consumers would like a closer identification with one company, that they would trust the Sears name, and that they would respond well to intelligent treatment.

Using direct mailings as large as 40 million pieces per year, the club has enlisted more than 1.6 million members, who each pay a $7.50 annual fee during its first three and a half years. Those members have shown their loyalty by responding twice as well as nonmembers to direct-mail solicitations for membership in the Allstate Motor Club, by responding better than any other group to offers from Allstate Insurance, and by using their Sears credit cards 14 percent more than nonmembers.

Beyond the realm of consumer products, some of the most innovative new membership clubs have emerged from the field of health care, an industry with a disproportionately high usage by older people: while people over 65 make up 12 percent of the population, they purchase nearly 40 percent of all health-care services.

Perhaps the nation's most successful health-oriented senior membership club is the Baylor 55+ Club at Baylor Medical Center in Dallas, Texas. Through extensive market research, Baylor discovered that in addition to the skills of the physician and the quality of hospital care, a key element in health-care utilization is the level of ease and convenience with which older people can access the diverse, and sometimes confusing, collection of community health and social services.

In response, Baylor set out to create a wide spectrum of added-value offerings that would make their hospital system completely user-friendly. Members of their 55 + Club receive special rates at the hospital, assistance in handling Medicare paperwork and in purchasing inexpensive medicines, free delivery of drugstore purchases (home delivery of all products will be a must in an increasingly older society), free transportation to and from the hospital, free room upgrades, free telephone service, free parking for patients and their families, access to the hospital's community-based Aging Resource centers, several complimentary home-health-care visits, free or discounted health screenings, daily "telephone reassurance" calls for shut-ins, and a complete care-management service for older members and their families.

When the program was started in January 1987, Baylor's goal was 8,000 members. In Baylor's commitment to becoming the "hub" of their community's eldercare services, older consumers instantly spotted a more sensitive approach to their needs. In the first 12 months of the program, 44,176 residents of the greater Dallas community signed up. What is even more incredible is that 42 percent of the members switched hospitals to gain access to Baylor's program.

New services will also emerge to make transportation more convenient for older people who do not own or drive cars. For example, if you're an older person living in Omaha, Nebraska, you can sign up with Community Connection. Then, if you need to go somewhere tomorrow, you can give them a call. They will come to your door at the appointed time, with anything from a station wagon to a 17-passenger bus, and will help you into it, take you wherever you need to go, and pick you up when you are done. The cost is only a fraction of the price of a cab, and it isn't necessary to have the fare with you: they'll bill you at the end of the month. Similarly, Mount Sinai Medical Center in Miami Beach, Florida, transports more than 300 passengers a day in its 15 vans and one minibus.

The modes of transportation assistance that are popping up throughout the United States include shuttle minibuses, volunteer driving fleets, dial-a-ride jitneys, and valet parking at large institutions for elders who find walking difficult.

For this "paratransit" market, companies such as Care Concepts of Phoenix have begun to build or convert minivans that have front-wheel drive, front engines, lowered floors, and simple ramps that provide a flat entrance from a curb. Care Concepts currently has between 200 and 250 such minivans on the road in transit use, and it is now planning a larger model.

Dutcher Motors of Maryland takes it a step farther: its "TransiTaxi" is a minivan built from the ground up to serve both as a seven-passenger urban taxi or airporter and, with no modification, a van for the disabled. Its rear engine and rear-wheel drive provide for an unusually low, flat floor. High, wide doors on both sides make the minivan extremely easy to enter and exit. A wheelchair ramp can be pulled from under the vehicle. The seats flip up or down to accommodate passengers, luggage, or wheelchairs. Such a sensible, roomy van would be welcomed not only by the disabled but also by the more active, as an alternative to the traditional low sedan.

Several innovative drug and grocery stores are designing convenience-oriented shopping systems so that older customers will not need to walk up and down the aisles, pick up products that are sometimes heavy or hard to grasp, and then carry them to the cashier and transport them home. Instead, the customer will be able to call up the product on a specially designed television screen and, simply by pushing a button, send the product to the checkout stand. Should a drugstore customer need assistance in making a selection, a pharmacist or nurse will be available to answer any questions.

According to food expert Phillip Lempert, "By the year 2000, the purchasing and bagging process—the primary source of consumer complaints—will be streamlined. Technology will allow products to be scanned and packaged automatically. Coupon scanners also may come into widespread use. Customers will insert a card that will determine whether they have enough money to cover the purchases and [that can] then electronically debit their accounts."

Some retailers are taking steps to ease the shopping difficulties of older customers. For example, the K-Mart chain created special hours during a recent holiday season, during which the stores were open only to those 55 and over. A company spokesman called the promotion "extremely successful" and said it will be offered again this year. And K-Mart makes sure that all of its ads include a toll-free telephone number or some other way for customers to obtain information easily.

Convenience-minded older men and women who prefer to handle their about-town needs without having to drive at all will have their social world expanded through the use of "viewdata," interactive television, and similar systems. These systems connect the household television, a standard telephone line, and sometimes an inexpensive keyboard to a computerized service network that allows you to shop, pay bills, seek emergency medical advice, hear the latest news, make reservations at hotels and restaurants, reply to polls, take part in panel discussions, or play computer games with other subscribers. These systems are already being implemented in many communities and may in the future become quite common, especially in communities with higher-than-average concentrations of the homebound. Digital television, which has recently appeared on the scene, will greatly aid the growth of these systems.

Whether through value-added customer services, membership clubs, mail-order catalogs, or clever store design, making buying convenient and accessible to the older consumer will become a key theme in all business marketing in the years ahead.

WAKING TO POWER

Although slow to venture very far, business and industry have begun to wake up to the marketplace power of the mature consumer. The reason is straightforward; the famous bank robber Willie Sutton may have put it best: when asked why he robbed banks, he replied, "Because that's where the money is."

Companies that once catered exclusively to the young are now redirecting toward the mature consumer.

Gerber Products, for instance, was first listed on the New York Stock Exchange in 1956 at the height of the baby boom. By the 1960s, Gerber controlled an incredible 65 percent of the massive baby-food market. Remember the tag line of their ads? "Gerber—babies are our business. Our only business." Not anymore. As the boomers grew up, Gerber expanded into an array of products that stretched to include everything from baby food, children's centers, and dry cereals to farm products, display motors, graphics services, insurance, and even interstate trucking.

Similarly, Johnson & Johnson started out as a manufacturer of baby powders, shampoos, and oils. In the 1950s the company promoted its products heavily to the mothers of the boom babies. As the babies grew up, the products were increasingly sold to adults. Ads showed construction workers using baby powder. Retired quarterback Fran Tarkenton became a commercial spokesman for baby shampoo; the ad's tag line was "No matter whose baby you are." Johnson & Johnson's baby oil grew up and turned into an adult skin product. Now the company's Ortho Pharmaceutical division is attempting to capture the antiaging market with its new anti-wrinkle skin product, Retin-A.

A similar change has been occurring in the fast-food industry. Built on the tastes and styles of the teenage boomers, this industry has had to retrench by searching for broader markets and redesigning for the needs of older patrons. For example, when the boomers passed their teens, they began to prefer to sit down with their friends or children while eating at fast-food establishments. Kentucky Fried Chicken and McDonald's, which were long geared to a young, fast-moving crowd and had thousands of take-out windows but very few seats, have had to revamp. Gone are the garish, Pop-style oranges, reds, and greens; in their place are pleasing yellows and warm, earthy browns, more comfortable to the mature customer. In recent years, fast-food restaurants have expanded to include dining areas, salad bars, and even fenced-in playgrounds for diners' kids and grandchildren.

To keep up with the Age Wave, the publishing industry has also had to adapt or fail. Many of the specialty publications that grew up with the baby boom have either changed their images or folded. Previously popular magazines such as *National Lampoon, Crawdaddy*, and *Seventeen* have struggled to keep their subscription bases as the interests of the boomers have turned to *Money, Esquire*, and *Working Woman.* During the 1980s, *National Lampoon* suffered a 32.2 percent drop in readership. *Seventeen* magazine, trapped within its age-specific title, has nevertheless tried to grow up by revising its motto to "Today, she's really 18–34." Even *Playboy* has gotten into the act by featuring 50+ Vicki LaMotta and Joan Collins and by offering several 30+ centerfolds. When *Playboy* began, the median age of the men who read the magazine was in the early twenties. Today, the median age of subscribers is 37.

Even movies and television are beginning to wake up to the Age Wave. According to Jack Valenti, president of the Motion Picture Association of America, "The figures are statistically confirmable. In 1987, men and women over 40 bought 71 million more movie tickets than they did in 1986. . . . This ought to give some heft and weight to producers who are looking for material adults will find interesting." This aging of the cinema is a welcome occurrence to many movie producers who have felt stymied by the traditional youth orientation. "Thank God," says Leonard Goldberg, president of the 20th Century–Fox Film Corporation. "If we don't have to rely on teenagers as much, it will allow us to make a wider range of movies."

Television has always been a reflection of marketplace interests, and it has long been the bastion of the young. Even though people over 65 make up more than 12 percent of the population, less than 3 percent of the characters on TV are over 65. But the demographic slices are beginning to be rearranged. In dramatic disproportion to general population ratios, 42 percent of the 99.48 million viewers in America who watch television between 8 and 11 P.M. are now 45 or older. And these older viewers have significantly higher per-capita and discretionary incomes than do those under 45.

According to Steve Radabaugh, manager of Broadcast Services for AARP, "I think it's significant that three of last season's top-rated shows starred older people: "The Golden Girls," "Murder, She Wrote," and "Matlock." That wouldn't have happened three years ago."

Perhaps the most extraordinary breakthrough in the mat-uration of broadcast television is the fact that NBC's "The Golden Girls" was voted best comedy series two years in a row, with Rue McClanahan, who plays the sexually assertive Blanche, winning as best actress. According to Jane Porcino, director of the National Action Forum for Midlife and Older Women, "The show is doing much to end the myth that we are a 'Noah's Ark' society, serenely walking hand-in-hand with our mates into aging. It is also endorsing a relatively untried shared-living arrangement that has a lot of potential in real life."

Spurred by the success of these shows, all three networks have offered shows that prominently feature mature charac-ters: NBC's "JJ Starbuck," with 64-year-old Dale Robertson; ABC's "Buck James," with 63-year-old Dennis Weaver, and "Slap Maxwell," with 55-year-old Dabney Coleman; CBS's "The Law and Harry McGraw," with 52-year-old Jerry Or-bach, and "Jake and the Fatman," with 67-year-old William Conrad.

David Poltrack, vice-president of marketing for CBS Tel-evision, says, "The older audience has always watched a more than average amount of TV. But the advertisers have not always been interested. As they become more aware of the power of the graying of America, television programming will be getting older as well."

In the field of clothing and fashion, a realm long known for its avoidance of people over 30, the wall of gerontophobia is melting as well. High-fashion model Kaylan Pickford broke into modeling a decade and a half ago, when she was 44. She did not dye her gray hair or try to hide her age because, she says, "I don't want to look young, just beautiful." She was annoyed and frustrated by "the mysterious myth that men as they grow older become more attractive, while women just get old." According to Pickford, "The fashion industry lives in a world of pretend. In advertising terms, it pretends that there are no women in the country over 30 or 35. But the facts are different. The mid-life woman is the major clothes buyer today, and she spends the most money. Her dollar has four times the buying power of that of the young, and that amount is increasing every year."

It is perhaps a sign of changing times that it wasn't until Pickford was past 50 that she began getting a few big ads—for example, for De Beers diamonds, Piper Heidsieck champagne, Bergdorf Goodman, and Smirnoff Vodka, among others. Approaching her sixtieth birthday, Pickford is now considered the top 50+ model in America. The agency she works with, Eileen Ford's "Today's Women" group, was begun in 1978 with 9 women between the ages of 32 and 70. Within three years it carried more than 50 women under contract, and business has been booming. Recently, *Vogue* trumpeted that "age is becoming less and less a factor in fashion" and called this "one of the biggest changes in modern dressing."

We can see the look of older fashion, too, in the increasing acceptance of gray hair. According to Carol Kingston of Germaine Monteil cosmetics, "Hiring silver-haired model Tish Hooker three years ago has absolutely put us on the map." Already, one in four of us is gray, and the silver look is becoming very popular in fashion circles. "When you're surrounded by a flood of people who are graying at the same time you are, it's no longer dowdy to stay gray," says Robert Crane of Revlon, which recently introduced Glis'n, a shampoo designed to add sparkle to gray hair.

In 1988 I had the privilege of becoming a consultant to CBS, Inc. As part of this relationship I was invited by CBS chairman Larry Tisch to conduct a seminar for senior management on the impact of the aging of America on CBS's various businesses. For hours we reviewed the demographic changes the nation was undergoing, the shifts that could be expected in lifestyle, in the family, in politics, in communications, and in entertainment. When the seminar was winding down, I managed to get a few minutes to visit with Mr. Tisch privately, and I asked him what he made of all that I had covered.

After reflecting for a few moments, he responded, "The amazing thing about what we reviewed today is that this has never happened before. Throughout history, most social phenomena have repeated over and over again. We have had political movements shift from the left to the right, good leaders and bad; social behaviors have become more liberal, and then conservative again. But we have never before had a mass population of middle-aged and older men and women before. . . . It's no wonder we're all so baffled by what to make of it. Just think of all the problems!" And then after pausing for a few seconds, he smiled and said, "But just think of all the opportunities!"

CHAPTER

11

Redesigning America

As the country ages, a broad assortment of products, technologies, and environments will need to be redesigned—"retrofitted"—to match our changing needs.

Next time you're at a traffic light, ask yourself how we decided on the length of time needed for people to walk across the street. Next time you read a newspaper, look at the size of the typeface, and ask yourself how it was determined that this was the right size. How do we decide on the colors for a cereal box, on the brightness of the images on a computer monitor, on how much strength it should take to open a bottle of soda, or on how high the steps on a bus should be?

We have woven a physical world for ourselves that has been as suited to our needs and activities as a beehive is for its bees. And it has been woven on the form and physiology of youth.

According to Margaret Wylde, director of Advanced Living Systems at the University of Mississippi's Institute of Technology Development, "The average five-foot, eight-inch-tall, able-bodied male is the nemesis of everyone who *isn't* an average five-foot, eight-inch-tall, able-bodied male, since products designed around this 'Everyman' don't take individual differences into account." And as people grow older, their individual differences intensify.

The physical changes of aging cause thousands of mismatches in the way we interact with the world around us, changes so subtle that we often don't notice them at first.

Cara McCarty, curator of the New York Museum of Modern Art's spring 1988 exhibit, "Designs for Independent Living," says that "while previously the tendency was to view people with physical limitations as dependent on others, today the emphasis is on designing environments that help integrate people into the community and enable them to live as independent and normal a life as possible." In the past, such design-related problems were solved through the use of unattractive equipment or clumsy homemade versions of such equipment. McCarty believes that the new trend in "gray design" will be to create products, appliances, and environments that will be attractive and aesthetic as well as functional.

In this chapter we will explore a wide variety of changes that the Age Wave will bring in the design of the products and appliances we regularly use, as well as in the physical environments—our homes, cars, and community centers—that surround us. In addition, we will examine how an assortment of futuristic applications of ergonomic design, aesthetic surgery, exercise physiology, and bioengineering will increasingly allow us to redesign our own aging bodies, from the texture of our skin to the functioning of our nervous system.

MEETING THE NEEDS OF OLDER BODIES

In an attempt to determine how the standard physical environment becomes less form-fitting to an older person, the Gallup Organization recently asked 1,500 noninstitutionalized people 55 and over what they might need help doing in order to stay self-sufficient and feel comfortable in their environments. The idea behind the research was that determining what obstacles to independent living exist in our environment would enable us to make changes to improve the ergonomic "fit" of the environment. When asked what they considered to be the main problems of everyday life, those surveyed identified the following 16 areas:

1. Opening medicine packages
2. Reading product labels
3. Reaching high things
4. Fastening buttons, snaps, or zippers
5. Vacuuming and dusting
6. Going up and down stairs
7. Cleaning bathtubs and sinks
8. Washing and waxing floors
9. Putting on clothes over one's head
10. Putting on socks, shoes, or stockings
11. Carrying purchases home
12. Using tools
13. Being helpless if something happened at home, since no one would know
14. Using the shower or bathtub
15. Tying shoelaces, bows, and neckties
16. Moving around the house without slipping or falling

What these problems have in common is that they are minor inconveniences that can rapidly make life impossible as we age, as our mobility is reduced, or if our senses are impaired. And they are inconveniences born of improper product or environmental design.

To envision how we will need to redesign our environment for physical comfort, convenience, and maximum independence, it is essential to first understand the specific bodily changes that occur with aging. We will review the shifts that occur in the second half of life with regard to such physiological characteristics as vision, hearing, touch, temperature, taste, general mobility, skin and hair, heart and lungs, and internal organs and bones.

Vision

Our eyes begin to change when we are still in our mid-40s. The lens tends to harden, thicken, and become more yellow. Its surface becomes less even. The pupil becomes smaller, and the muscles that control its opening and closing become increasingly slow to respond. This can make it difficult to perceive quick-moving images—yet the production tempo of most of today's television programming relies on such images. In television commercials geared to young people, there are changes every few seconds. In the future, we're likely to see a slowing down of the speed with which scenes are shifted on television and in the movies.

Because a smaller pupil lets in less light, a person over 80 may need three times more light than a 20-year-old in order to see clearly. The eyes also take longer to adjust to the dark with age—three times longer at 70 than at 25. In addition, the yellow film that forms over the lens of the eye with age changes color perception—for instance, light blue, pink, and salmon, seen as very distinct shades through the eyes of youth, may become difficult to differentiate, just as black, gray, dark blue, and dark brown begin to seem increasingly similar. Thus, an advertisement or container that seems very striking to a young designer might miss the mark completely with the older people for whom the product is targeted. In the future, publishers and ad agencies will use more contrasting colors and will steer clear of overly cluttered pages. Type sizes will also grow larger.

Because the lens of the eye thickens by as much as 50 percent with age, only one 75-year-old in seven has 20/20 vision, even with glasses. Because the aging lens is less even and less elastic, the older eye is much more sensitive to glare from automobile headlights and from shiny floors, walls, fixtures, and countertops.

These changes in the capabilities of the eyes will generate a wide assortment of redesign concerns. For example, many public environments have smooth floors waxed to a high gloss. These surfaces can resemble ice-skating rinks to the older individual with failing eyesight. The problem of glare, for instance, can be avoided by covering floors and surfaces with carpeting or some other textured surface. In addition, many interior designers now attempt to simplify color schemes by exactly matching the colors of two elements that are seen together. This can be dangerous for older people with impaired vision, who may not recognize subtle differences between cabinet and wall or table and floor. Again, contrasting colors will offer the most functional support.

Automobile designers might be wise to incorporate the following elements:

- Front windows that automatically adjust in tint to eliminate all glare and are specially treated to accommodate a full range of weather and light conditions
- Dashboards with fewer metallic or reflective surfaces
- Larger side mirrors and large dashboard display numerals
- Controls in the center of the steering wheel for the lights, the heating and cooling system, and the radio
- Liquid crystal displays that project the car's rate of speed and other crucial information directly onto a corner of the windshield so that the driver can access key information while continuing to look straight ahead. This would take care of the problem of rapidly readjusting the eyes from near to far and back—very difficult for the older eye.
- Warning systems that would sound when any object came too close to the car. This would be particularly useful in foggy or bad weather, in parking lots, or when backing

out of driveways, and would help compensate for the limited peripheral vision and slower reaction time of the older driver.

Older people often have difficulty seeing in low light, and their range of vision tends to be more narrow than that of younger people. As a result, they may not be as quick to see landmarks, exit signs over doors, items on high shelves, overhead direction signs in airports, high billboards, overhead freeway signs, or elevator floor numbers.

In the future, public environments will be lit with bright and diffuse bulbs, and glaring fluorescent tubes will be shielded or eliminated. All signs will be enlarged for easy reading, and lettering will be simplified.

Another solution to sign problems could be redundant cueing, which would give the same information to two or more senses—for example, bell tones or beeps in addition to a car's fuel gauge to indicate that the tank is low. This approach would be particularly useful in public environments. For instance, the Dallas–Fort Worth airport's rapid-transit system uses a machine-generated voice to announce terminals and airlines and to give safety warnings.

And many people would benefit from having talking appliances, such as ranges that could say, "The right-front burner is on high heat" or "The oven has now reached 350 degrees." A talking or whistling car could let you know where it's parked. A talking camera could tell you if you needed more light or if you hadn't focused quite right. And talking exit signs that announce "fire," "power failure," or "exit" (depending on the situation) are already on the market in a choice of several languages.

Hearing

Unlike problems with vision, which are fairly obvious to other people, partial deafness is not so evident. Today, more than 30 million Americans have hearing problems of varying degrees. These problems become more common with age, affecting 25 percent of the over-65 population. In the future, bulky hearing aids will be completely replaced by micro-auditory enhancers that can be tucked into the ear canal. These tiny devices will respond to commands for frequency control from wireless transmitters as small as credit cards.

Hearing loss manifests itself in several different ways. For instance, we may find it increasingly difficult to isolate significant sounds from background noise. As a result, air conditioners, electrical hums, "mood" music, vacuum cleaners, and traffic noises all tend to create a blanket of sound that can make it difficult to listen to music, participate in a class, watch television, or even hold a conversation in a public environment.

As we age, we begin to lose the higher frequency ranges of our hearing—the range in which most warning signals and public-address systems are usually projected. We tend to raise our voices when talking to a person who is hard of hearing. Unfortunately, we not only speak louder but also in a higher register, thus making it more difficult for the person to hear us. Similarly, older adults often increase the volume on television sets in an attempt to hear more clearly. However, the issue is usually not one of volume, but of tone.

Some of these problems will be alleviated through differential adjusting of the bass tones in contrast to the treble in radio and television broadcast signals. In the future, all public-address systems will have their sound geared to accommodate the hearing range of the older listener, just as all music and video recordings will be engineered to match and satisfy the specific hearing characteristics of the older ear. Radios, television sets, and telephones will have more sophisticated capabilities so that every user can custom-program the equipment for his or her unique auditory profile.

Age-related changes in hearing will also cause changes in other areas of ergonomic design. For example, people with hearing problems have an easier time communicating with others when there is direct, face-to-face contact. The standard park benches and couches of today will be replaced by seats that are angled toward one another or that are clustered around small tables. In New York's Washington Square Park, many of those seated at the park's permanent chess tables aren't playing chess; they simply find the small table a more comfortable place to sit and chat than the nearby park bench.

Manual Dexterity

Increasing stiffness and loss of dexterity in the fingers can pose a constant and annoying problem to many older people. More than half of those over 65 have some arthritis in the finger joints. In a 1987 study conducted by Donnelly Marketing, seniors were asked about their likes and dislikes on a wide range of consumer products. Incredibly, the thing that concerned them the most was not whether the product was of good quality, but whether the container was easy to open.

Medicine bottles, food containers, cutlery, computer keyboards, appliance controls, and purse clasps will need to be redesigned to better accommodate the needs of older hands. Similarly, clothing manufacturers will use more Velcro tabs and will switch to larger buttons, eliminating the small buttons and tiny snaps that can be difficult for older hands to manipulate. Sears already has a line of "Fashioncare" clothing that features Velcro closures, deep pockets, and large armholes.

The possibilities for redesigning commonplace tools, utensils, and appliances are endless. Some useful examples that have begun to appear include:

- Comb and brush extenders
- Long-handled sponges and dusters for hard-to-reach spots, such as high shelves
- Long-handled, easy-grip zipper pulls for back zippers
- "Foot mops," handy sponges that slip on over a foot or shoe and make it possible to clean up spills without bending over

- Easy-to-grab wall extension mirrors for shaving and grooming
- Large-faced clocks, kitchen timers, and thermostats
- Talking clocks that announce the time when touched
- Lightweight, motorized scrubbers for pots and pans, for hands that have trouble with the chore of scrubbing
- Cutting boards with an attached, saw-handled knife
- Nonskid slippers and socks to help prevent falls
- Stretchable elastic shoelaces to make shoe removal easier
- Frying pans and pots with angled grips for easier lifting
- Automatic electric teapots with inexpensive weight sensors that turn them off when the water has boiled away
- Attractively designed large or contoured-handle eating utensils for people who have difficulty gripping small objects tightly
- Electronic-touch lamp converters that allow lights to be turned on and off simply by touching any part of the lamp, thereby eliminating the possibility of burning a finger by reaching up under the shade
- Automatic light switches that turn on when there is a sound in the room, and off when there has been no sound for a while
- Key chains that beep when you blow a whistle for them
- Tap turners that fasten over faucets and stove-top controls to make turning easier and more precise
- Lightweight or motorized garden tools
- Jumbo-button or voice-activated telephones to make dialing easier and calling errors less likely
- Remote-control units, already on the market, that can turn several appliances on or off from one location. Such units can be made to respond to voice commands with currently available microcomputer technology

Temperature

As we age, there is a gradual increase in the body's fat content and a decrease in its water content. Because water has the capacity to hold large amounts of heat, older people have a more difficult time tolerating temperature extremes and sensing changes in temperature.

Because the metabolic and temperature-controlling processes become less efficient with age, it can take the older body longer to adjust to changes in temperature. A young person, for instance, can typically detect a change of a single degree in temperature, while someone 65 may not notice anything less than a five-degree change.

With the diminished circulation that often accompanies age, it can become much more difficult to keep warm. Older people often find themselves putting on sweaters when younger people in the room feel perfectly comfortable.

In the years ahead, it will be standard for homes and hotels to have individually controlled thermostats in each room. In addition, a space-age material developed by NASA to enable astronauts to retain body heat is now being incorporated into coats so that older people can have warmth without bulk. In the future, perhaps we will see self-contained heated clothing, heated furniture, or heat-producing foods.

Taste

The average 30-year-old has 245 taste buds on each little bump (papilla) on the tongue. By the time that person reaches 80, he or she will have only 88—a 64 percent decrease. As a result, it becomes harder to discriminate among the four basic taste sensations: sweet, bitter, sour, and salty. Sweet taste buds diminish the most, and sour the least. Older people who don't feel like eating may not be depressed or ill, but perhaps simply uninterested because food doesn't taste the way it used to. More commonly, older men and women add more and more spices or sweeteners to their food in an attempt to recapture a pleasing taste they remember from their youth.

Because of these significant taste changes, all of our foods will have to be, in a sense, redesigned to offer enjoyable flavorings to less capable palates. This will present an interesting challenge to food manufacturers and restaurateurs, especially in light of the various food sensitivities and nutritional needs the older eater might also have. In all likelihood, entire lines of specialty foods geared to an individual's unique taste capabilities will emerge.

In addition, with the aging of the population, there will be a significantly increased sensitivity to the nutritional make-up of popular foods. Since 83 percent of those in the 65+ population already have at least one chronic degenerative disease, they must be very careful that what they consume will not aggravate or worsen their condition.

The simplest way to learn more about the nutritional needs of an aging population is to invite ten 70-year-olds out to dinner and take note of what they order. Those with hypertension will steer clear of foods with sodium and will keep an eye out for fats and cholesterol. Those with diabetes will try to avoid all sugar and other refined carbohydrates. Those who have difficulty with digestion will be sure to order high-fiber foods, and the arthritics might avoid citrus or gluten, depending on which restrictive diet they follow. And regardless of specific dietary restrictions, on the average, older people are very savvy about the relative nutritional levels of the foods they eat.

According to Joseph Eastlack, Ph.D., of the Campbell Soup Company, "Older people, more aware of their body's frailties than their younger counterparts and fearful of endangering their independent lifestyle, perceive nutrition as a means of promoting good health and resistance to illness." In an aging society, foods that are unhealthy will be avoided; those that promote well-being, vitality, and longevity will flourish. As a result, according to Eastlack, older men and women will be significantly more inclined to "increase consumption of vitamins, fruits, fruit juices and vegetables, especially 'fresh' vegetables."

In a 1987 study conducted by Donnelly Marketing, seniors identified cholesterol, salt, calories, and caffeine as the dietary factors they were most concerned about limiting or eliminating.

Age-related dietary concerns and restrictions will be the foundation for profound revolutions in the ways we grow, manufacture, and distribute food.

Several years ago, in anticipation of these dietary changes, the Campbell's Soup Company created a multimillion-dollar business by offering low-sodium versions of its most popular soup products. In the area of cholesterol reduction, NutraSweet and Procter & Gamble have both recently announced "fake fat" products—substances that look like fat, can be cooked like fat, and taste like fat, but *aren't* fat. NutraSweet's Simplesse is low in calories and cholesterol. P&G's Olestra has no calories at all, since it is not absorbed by the body. When this product—which actually sweeps up stray bits of cholesterol—is fully tested and introduced, that next order of french fries may be just what the doctor ordered.

Along similar lines, Michael Foods, Inc., of Minneapolis recently obtained the rights to new technologies that researchers say make it possible to remove up to 90 percent of the cholesterol in egg yolks.

Staying lean and reducing the risk of heart disease are the motivations in this low-cholesterol revolution. As reported in the February 1988 article "Quest for Fake Fat" in *U.S. News & World Report*, "Spurred by an estimated potential of $2 billion in annual sales for truly tasty fat substitutes, the food-marketing war of the 1990s will be under way, making the low-fat, Lean Cuisine, diet-soda, light-beer revolution of the 1980s look like small potatoes."

But the concern for healthy nutrition goes far beyond an interest in fat substitutes. Today, fitness foods are the fastest-growing segment of the $300 billion retail-food industry.

According to Al Clausi, senior vice-president for research and development at General Foods, "People have realized that they are what they eat. We are gearing up in a great rush to meet this interest."

Even the conservative National Institutes of Health is now recommending that Americans cut their fat-consumption level by 25 percent. Reflecting the growing popular interest in healthy nutrition, the per-capita consumption of beef fell from 94 to 75 pounds per year during the decade from 1975 to 1985. During the same period, per-capita consumption of leaner poultry rose dramatically, from 43 pounds per year to 70. And during the years between 1983 and 1988, Americans ate 11 percent more vegetables and 7 percent more fruit. On the extreme end, according to a 1985 Gallup Poll, some 6.2 million Americans are now vegetarians.

The "food-marketing war" will be particularly hard-fought over the breakfast table. Although most food companies struggle to increase their share of the 25-to-49-year-old market, people in this age group consume an average of only 6 pounds of breakfast cereal each year per person. However, in the over-65 group, the average is 10.4 pounds a year, with older people preferring natural, high-fiber cereals.

Already, concern over the high caloric level of sugar has spurred a revolution in nonsugar sweeteners. The success of Aspertame, for instance, helped boost the sugar-substitute share of the total sweetener market from 4 percent in 1972 to 9 percent in 1988. More than 78 million adult Americans now consume low-calorie foods and beverages, up from 42 million in 1978.

General Mobility

Some older adults become restricted in their ability to move around, with the degree of limitation ranging from minor (for example, mild arthritis) to severe (recovering from a stroke). Some mobility limitations are caused by changes in the brain and central nervous system, with the greatest decrements in the functioning of the central nervous system observed in activities that require the coordination of a number of different organs, senses, limbs, or functions. Nerve cells, unlike most other cells in the body, are not replaced by new cells when they are destroyed through aging, trauma, or disease. There is also a decline of about 2 percent per decade in the speed at which nerve impulses are transmitted. Thus, older men and women have slower reaction times to various stimuli and are slower to perform certain tasks that require a combination of functions involving transmission of nerve impulses. This can cause problems in the performance of a wide variety of sensory motor tasks, such as driving, using a computer, or reaching for items on supermarket shelves.

A related capability that tends to decline with age is the kinesthetic sense, or the awareness of the body's position and location in space. This complex sense arises from receptors in the muscles and joints and in the semicircular canals of the inner ear. With the gradual loss of this sense, older people may experience some unsteadiness of balance and become increasingly subject to falls. In the coming years, bathtubs and kitchens will come equipped with nonskid surfaces. Chairs will have seats that are at least 17 inches off the ground and arms (which are essential) that are long enough to provide support for getting in or out of the chair.

To accommodate those who are confined to wheelchairs, appropriate entry and exit ramps, wide passageways, and easy-to-reach shelves and counters will appear in all public environments.

Because the loss of general mobility affects a wide range of ergonomic interactions, the potential for retrofitting is profound. Bathrooms are probably the area most in need of change. Here we will see:

- *Attractively designed grab bars,* strategically placed in and around the shower, tub, and toilet
- *Built-in seats* in the tub or shower

- *"Soft tubs"* made of a resilient and heat-preserving material, to provide greater comfort and safety as well as to keep the water hot longer
- *Levers* in place of faucet knobs
- *Medicine cabinets* in a less glaring and more accessible location than the bathroom, such as the bedroom or kitchen
- *Water-heater regulators* that will keep tap water from becoming too hot

In the years ahead, other common household and neighborhood features that might become standard include these:

- *Crank-operated windows* in place of the usual double-hung windows, which can be too stiff for older people to open
- *Lower windows,* so that they will be of use to someone who is bedridden or spends a lot of time sitting down
- *Storage and closet space* rearranged to provide access to people with more limited movement
- *Rampways* instead of stairs to provide easier accessibility for impaired people
- *Low-level lighting in movie theaters* in place of near-total darkness. (The brightness of the images being projected will need to be increased as well.)
- *Lower stairs or special lifting platforms* on city buses
- *Pedestrian street lights* that change more slowly
- *Midstreet traffic islands* in wide streets so that slower walkers can pause and rest

In the area of automotive design, we can expect to see standard retrofitted equipment, including:

- *Redesigned seats* that can be adjusted for individual mobility limitations
- *Seats with multiple adjustments.* Already available in some luxury cars, these seats can be customized for each individual driver.
- *Verbal command systems* that allow the driver to raise and lower windows, operate the stereo, the heater, the lights, the windshield wiper, and even the ignition simply by giving commands. Such systems can be programmed to individual voices and can thus also serve as security devices.

Even wheelchair technology is evolving. New models include a graphite wheelchair that is so lightweight and portable that it can be taken aboard an airplane rather than put in the luggage hold. Jon J. King, whose International Texas Industries (Intex) of San Antonio markets a microprocessor-based wheelchair, says, "The state of the art in wheelchairs has been the state of the art for 50 years. There is an obvious niche for a company to apply technology to improve the quality of life for the aged."

Similarly, an entirely new level of motorized transportation, the microcar, will emerge and multiply. Poised between the automobile and the wheelchair, this miniature relative of the golf cart is designed for people who don't necessarily think of themselves as disabled but who find getting around the neighborhood or walking around a shopping mall to be too taxing.

Cara McCarty of the Museum of Modern Art believes that the increasing numbers of slightly disabled older men and women will cause a renaissance in the business of manufacturing attractive and easy-to-use equipment. She comments that "it's often the equipment, not the disability, that detracts from the appearance and aesthetics of the person." In the years ahead, companies that serve the changing physical needs of the aging population with practical, aesthetically pleasing products will boom.

Skin and Hair

What has often been referred to as "the graying of America" can perhaps be more accurately described as "the tinting of America." As they age, Americans will increasingly fight to look as young as they feel. Millions of Americans are now attempting the near impossible: they are trying to take their youth with them into old age. After one of my talks, an attractive older woman told me her honest sentiments about physical aging: "I used to be old," she said, "but I didn't like the style."

Perhaps the area of greatest concern pertaining to physical aging is the health and appearance of the skin. Throughout the body, cells liquefy and disappear, to be replaced by fat, scar tissue, or droplets of liquid. As cells disappear, the body's tissues shrink, causing the skin to become dry and thin. It also tends to lose its elasticity due to changes in the structure of the body's collagen. In addition, the loss of elastic collagen fibers and of underlying muscle mass lead to wrinkling.

In the years ahead, the cosmetics industry will experience the biggest boom in its history. Cosmetics manufacturers will increasingly target the older market. Americans over 55 spend 40 percent more than the national average on health and personal-care products, according to a recent study by Jordan, Case and McGrath of New York. This includes 37 percent of all facials, weight-loss treatments, and health-spa memberships.

Of every $4 spent on cosmetics in the United States, $1 comes out of the pocket of a woman over 55; of every $10 spent in beauty parlors, $4 comes from women in that age group.

The current success of such skin whiteners as Esoterica and Porcelana—pushed by explicit marketing, which, in the case of Porcelana, claims to remove "age spots"—is estimated at more than $90 million a year. Adrien Arpel offers "Bio

Cellular Series Treatments" such as "Wrinkle Life" and "Plasma Pak B12." Coty, Neutrogena, Oil of Olay, Clinique, Christian Dior, Revlon, and other cosmetics companies are all churning out products that contain vitamins, minerals, and collagen, all clearly targeted to a population whose skin is aging.

A number of mail-order firms have jumped into the fray, including Georgette Klinger, Bee Pollen Products, and Hanover House, which created a catalog called "Mature Wisdom." Direct-sell leader Avon has introduced "Accolade," a line of four products that contain collagen and elastin. The Food and Drug Administration has already begun investigating a new generation of antiaging creams, such as Retin-A, which promise to make wrinkles and age spots disappear.

The market for products for the older man has also begun to boom. The sale of men's skin-care products is showing a 16 percent annual growth rate. One entrepreneur in this area, New York's Jan Stuart, took a $2,000 nest egg and in six years had built it into a business pulling in $10 million in sales each year.

Industry giants such as Estée Lauder, which brought out Lauder for Men, has been joined by such companies as Georgette Klinger and Elizabeth Arden. Altogether, there are now some 25 male cosmetic lines to choose from. When *Playboy* magazine offered its first feature story on men's skin-care products in 1986, it was no sissy matter: the model shown using the face masks and moisturizers was the macho actor Dolph Lundgren, straight from his tough-guy role as Ivan Drago, Rocky Balboa's Soviet nemesis.

If lotions and potions can't get the job done, the knife or laser might. In response to the coming of the Age Wave, cosmetic surgery is becoming one of the fastest-growing medical specialties in the nation. Trendy *Los Angeles* magazine features literally dozens of ads for cosmetic surgeons in every issue. According to the American Society of Plastic and Reconstructive Surgeons (ASPRS), in one typical recent four-year span (1981–1984) the number of procedures grew by 61 percent. The actual numbers make "uplifting" reading:

Face-lifts: up 39 percent, from 39,000 to 54,400

Chemical peels: up 67 percent, from 9,700 to 16,000

Eye lifts: up 31 percent, from 56,500 to 73,900

Mastopexies (or "breast lifts"): up 26 percent, from 12,800 to 16,200

Abdominoplasties (or "Belly lifts"): up 37 percent, from 15,300 to 20,900

Others are having their wrinkles injected every 6 to 12 months with animal collagen, which helps to plump them up and smooth them out (at $175 to $300 a pop). Liposuction (or "fat-sucking," as some call it), is the latest rage. In this procedure, a tiny tube actually vacuums fat cells out of the body. It is soon to be joined by microlipoinjection, in which fat cells suctioned out of one part of the body are injected into another part that might need them, such as a laugh line or a forehead crease.

This is big business. A face-lift or surgical fat removal can cost from $2,500 to $5,000, when done in a doctor's office, and up to 75 percent more in a hospital. Some surgeons perform as many as a dozen such procedures each day.

A new weapon in the eternal battle against wrinkles may be artificial skin, which is woven of collagen made from cow cartilage and was invented by Ioannis Yannas at the Massachusetts Institute of Technology. Implanted in the skin across a wound, it forms a framework on which new skin can grow, unwrinkled and unscarred.

If you are uncomfortable being covered with a bovine coating, how about cloning some of your own skin? Nicholas O'Connor, a plastic surgeon in Boston, has used new skin cloned from patients' own skin to cover up to 80 percent of the bodies of burn victims. O'Connor envisions us storing away skin in our youth to be used for cloning new skin when we are old.

Dr. John Goin, past president of ASPRS, says, "I think we would all agree that we have always lived in a youth-oriented society, but what has changed in recent years is that

Grandma is not sitting at home in a rocking chair knitting for her children. She is out playing tennis and shopping and may not want to look older than she feels."

And more men are doing it too: according to ASPRS, the number of men seeking cosmetic corrections has increased by 35 percent in the last two years. Explains Dr. Melvin Dinner, director of the Center for Plastic Surgery in Cleveland: "The 40-year-old who has lost his job is competing with a young hotshot. It's the competitive demand to look youthful."

If we can do it for skin, we'll do it for hair, too. Surgical techniques of hair transplantation to fight male-pattern baldness have been multiplying rapidly. In addition to hair "plugs," which can cost up to $20,000, a host of even more exotic techniques have appeared. These include scalp reduction—essentially, a top-of-the-head face-lift—and scalp flaps, which are swatches of hair-bearing skin excised from the side of the head and twisted into place to form a new hairline. By 1986, board-certified plastic surgeons alone were performing 2,800 hair transplants per year.

As radical as they are, all of these techniques may in time be rendered obsolete by the first actual nonquack hair restorers. In 1983, the Upjohn Company found that it was selling a surprising amount of the drug minoxidil, an antihypertensive marketed under the name Loniten. In two years its sales had quadrupled to an estimated $30 million to $40 million annually. It turned out that people were breaking open the capsules, mixing the powder with an alcohol-based solvent, and putting the resulting lotion on their bald spots. The claim was that this treatment actually resulted in hair growth.

When Upjohn issued an open call in Washington, D.C., for human "guinea pigs" on which to test the potion, 10,000 men showed up. According to the company's annual report, the unprecedented positive results were divided in thirds: one-third of the test subjects developed significant hair growth, one-third developed none at all, and the rest had partial hair growth. By 1986 the FDA had begun testing the claims. As the possibility of a cure for baldness became known, the price of Upjohn's stock more than doubled. According to Ronald Nordmann, a pharmaceutical analyst with Paine Webber, minoxidil "could easily be a $1 billion-a-year drug." Upjohn recently broke ground on a $23 million plant in Kalamazoo, Michigan, for the manufacture of the wonder drug, which it is marketing under the name Rogaine. The company already has the go-ahead to distribute the drug in 34 other countries.

Teeth and Gums

As we age, the enamel on our teeth grows thinner, and the dentin underneath becomes more translucent. But most of the changes in our mouths—gums pulling away, loss of teeth—are the result not of age itself but of disease and long-term lack of care. One hundred years ago, three-quarters of the women in America over the age of 50 had no teeth. Today, the average 70-year-old has lost only 10 teeth.

In the adult years, the focus of mouth care shifts from a concern about cavities toward a concentration on the gums. Although the major cause of dental disease under 30 is decay, a greater problem for the over-50 man or woman is gum disease. Dr. Roger Stambaugh, a professor in the department of periodontics at the University of Southern California in Los Angeles, says that "cavities are rapidly becoming a thing of the past. The dental profession is moving away from filling teeth to becoming more involved in cosmetics, periodontics, and oral surgery."

According to a 1983 report prepared for the American Academy of Periodontology, more than 90 percent of the population will get some form of gum disease during their lives. Already, more than 30 million Americans are believed to suffer from some form of gum-related disease, most of which is undiagnosed.

In addition to the increasing concern for the health and vitality of our gums, a new revolution is happening in the care of our smiles in the form of cosmetic dentistry. In the future, generations that have drunk fluoridated water all their lives and have been better educated in habits of dental hygiene will lose many fewer teeth. And when they do lose teeth, they'll be able to get lifetime replacements. A recently perfected technique allows false teeth to be permanently attached to steel posts set into the jaw. The bones of the jaw actually grow onto the synthetic bone material, which has been bonded to the small posts. An individual tooth set in this method costs about $700, and a complete set about $8,000 or $9,000.

For those adults who have their own teeth but are not completely satisfied with the way nature has arranged them, it's not too late to straighten them out. The number of adults wearing braces is soaring. Of the 4 million Americans who wear braces, more than 1 million are over 18. Dr. Craven Kurz of Los Angeles is taking the trend a step farther: for grown-ups who don't want to wait, he is developing pulsating headgear that will vibrate your teeth into place while you sleep. Tomorrow's elders will have the nicest smiles that money can buy.

Heart and Lungs

The functioning of the heart declines somewhat with age, and there is a general decrease in the elasticity of the large arteries and an overall deterioration of the blood vessels. Because the heart has to pump harder, there is a tendency toward a lower maximum heart rate and increased blood pressure. At age 75, the probability of death or illness from heart disease is 150 times the risk at age 35.

In addition, breathing capacity lessens, as does the ability to exert oneself physically. The lungs lose some of their tiny air sacs, resulting in a decreased surface area for the exchange of oxygen and carbon dioxide. The rib cage stiffens over the years, causing a reduction in its bellows action on the lungs.

Medical science is battling heart disease through such techniques as balloon and laser angioplasty, multiple-bypass operations, heart-lung transplants, pacemakers, and artificial

hearts. All developed during the past few years, these procedures are now being performed in incredible numbers.

**In 1985 alone, American surgeons performed more than
230,000 coronary bypass operations and more than
100,000 angioplasties.**

New drugs have been driving heart-attack statistics
down. One, called TPA or Activase, eats away at the blood
clots that cause permanent heart damage after a heart attack.
Heart specialists are calling this drug "the penicillin of heart
disease," and predict that it will save lives and improve the
quality of a great many others. Another new drug, Lovastatin,
can lower cholesterol levels by 30 to 40 percent.

The commitment to a healthy longevity has also caused
an explosion in the fitness and wellness movements. Today,
parks and beaches everywhere are crowded with adult jog-
gers, and many exercise clubs across America are packed to
overflowing. The following statistics attest to the current fitness explosion:

- In 1960, according to a Gallup Poll, a mere 24 percent of
  Americans (43 million people) did any regular exercise.
  By 1986, that figure had more than tripled, climbing to
  over 57 percent (136 million people).
- In 1972, Americans were spending $227 million for mem-
  bership in some 2,000 athletic clubs across the nation. By
  1984, the total had spiraled to over $8 billion spent in
  6,500 clubs.
- In 1979 the nation had 60 sports-medicine clinics; by 1986,
  it had more than 600.
- In 1974 the total sales of all home-exercise equipment came
  to $93 million. By 1986 the figure was over $1.2 billion
  (an increase of 1,200 percent in 12 years), with roughly
  another $1 billion spent on multispeed bicycles.

- In 1985, Americans spent $3.4 billion on athletic socks, bathing suits, leotards, sweatshirts, warm-up suits, tennis togs, and other athletic clothes.
- According to a survey conducted by the National Sporting Goods Association, by 1985 more than 73 million Americans swam with some regularity, 51 million cycled, more than 41 million took walks, 28 million jogged, 24 million did aerobics, 26 million did calesthenics, and 32 million used weights or other equipment.

Another aspect of the future can be seen at the Pritikin Longevity Centers in Santa Monica, California, and Downingtown, Pennsylvania. When you first enter one of these centers, you may feel that you're on familiar ground: there are the gleaming equipment, sweating habitués, treadmills, and staff dressed in warm-up suits and carrying clipboards that you might find in many other health clubs. But these are not fat farms or spas. They are, more than anything else, longevity schools with a curriculum that teaches you how to live long and well and how to make your body over so that you can go the distance.

The two- and four-week programs at the centers mix lectures, workshops, and counseling. Here, top chefs show you how to cook food that is lean and nutritious, yet tasty and filling. Nutrition experts fill you in on the ideas behind the recipes and show you how to find healthy food on a restaurant menu. Exercise physiologists design workout programs that can become a regular part of your life. Personal consultants teach you specific steps you can take to reduce your stress level.

While what you take away from such a program is long-term, many of its effects are evident immediately. According to an evaluation made by the Department of Biostatistics and Epidemiology at California's Loma Linda University (with the results published in such professional journals as *Diabetes Care* and the *Journal of Cardiac Rehabilitation*), most people who arrive at the Pritikin Centers taking medication for specific chronic conditions are able to quit their medication, without ill effect, by the time they leave. This includes 85 percent of people with high blood pressure, 62 percent of angina patients, and 50 percent of those with adult-onset diabetes. In addition, 85 percent of the smokers quit, and overweight people lose an average of a half pound a day.

Such a life makeover at the hands of experts is now only available at special clinics like the Pritikin Longevity Centers, the Richardson Institute for Preventive Medicine in Houston, the Golden Door in Escondido, California, or Canyon Ranch in Tucson, Arizona. And it is expensive; weekly costs for these programs run between $2,000 and $3,000. What was once exclusively the territory of obese women has been invaded by male and female executives intent on rebuilding their bodies for the long haul. With the growing consumer interest in lifelong fitness that the Age Wave will bring, we can expect that total wellness graduate schools like the Pritikin Centers will become much more common, and much more affordable.

Internal Organs and Bones

The digestive and reproductive systems decline somewhat with age, but in the absence of disease, they rarely do so to the point of disability. With aging comes a decline in the basal metabolism rate, about 3 percent every 10 years. The body's caloric requirements decrease correspondingly, causing fat to be more easily accumulated.

Of the major internal organs, the kidneys show the greatest decline with age. The kidneys of people over 80 perform at about 50 percent of the level of people in their twenties.

Bones have a tendency to lose density and become osteoporotic, especially in women. As a result, more than one-third of the women in America over 65 have vertebral fractures. Past the age of 80, one-third of all women and one-sixth of all men suffer hip fractures.

Until now, many of the physical infirmities of old age have resulted from the degeneration of one particular organ or system before the rest—such as when a diseased liver exists within an otherwise vital body or, as in the growing number of cases of adult-onset diabetes, when the pancreas ages or degenerates long before the rest of the body. When specific body parts wear out in this fashion, the entire system eventually degenerates, leading to premature death.

In our old age, most of us will have several transplanted or artificial parts in our bodies to enhance our health and vitality and to extend our years.

In recent years, a variety of areas of applied research beyond the realm of normal medicine have begun to produce solutions to these previously irreversible conditions of aging. Such diverse fields as bioengineering, electronics, microsurgery, and electrical engineering are involved in the development of new devices and therapies, which are increasing at a breathtaking pace. More and more pieces of the bionic man and woman are available every day—artificial inner ears; eye lenses; blood vessels and skin; knee, hip, and knuckle joints; heart valves and hearts; bone; muscle; and reinforcements for injured ligaments and tendons. These devices fall into several related categories: organ transplantation, bionic parts, artificial organs, bioelectronics, and genetic engineering, each of which will be discussed in turn.

Organ transplantation. With breakthroughs in such immunosuppressant drugs as Mercapturine, Imuran, and various synthetic corticosteroids, as well as increasing public support for organ transplantation, the replacement of failing organs with healthy ones will be increasingly common in the decades ahead. Already more than 40,000 persons alive today have had kidney transplants, and there are about 1,000 liver transplant operations performed each year. To date, transplantation technology has been hindered by the lack of available organs and by the body's tendency to reject alien tissue. However, these problems may soon be solved.

More and more research is being conducted in the field

of biological cloning, in which one cell from a donor body would be isolated and then grown in the laboratory as a whole, healthy, and completely identical twin of the donor body. While the cloning of a whole organism seems more like science fiction than science fact, successful exploration has been done into the simpler area of "single-organ" cloning. Through this process, youthful donor cells can be grown into countless numbers of identical organs. When a particular organ begins to age or degenerate, it could be easily replaced with a new one, conveniently warehoused at a local organ storage center. Since the new organ would be a perfect biological match, it would not be rejected by the body.

Organ transplantation could very well become the major life-extending technology of the future. The Rand Corporation estimates that human cloning will be successfully accomplished by the year 2005—one year before the first of the baby boomers turns 60.

Bionic parts. Although television promoted the "Six Million Dollar Man" as science fiction, in the very near future continued advances in biomedical research may allow millions of us to replace worn-out or damaged body parts with bionic substitutes.

Originally developed for its possible military applications, the science of bionics weaves together a number of different disciplines—including engineering, computer design, electronics, physics, and medicine—to produce implements for replacing or amplifying the potential of the human body.

According to author Vance Packard, in the decades ahead "the production, sale, installation, and servicing of human spare parts is likely to become the fastest-growing industry in the modern world. In dollar volumes it will rival the automobile spare-parts industry, conceivably the entire automobile-building industry."

One of the earliest developments in bionics was the hip-joint replacement. Today, this consists of a stainless-steel ball that is mounted on the end of the thigh bone and a polyethylene socket implanted in the pelvis. By 1986, more than 201,000 people had received hip-joint replacements. Similarly, there are now some 150 types of knee joints and 50 kinds of ankle joints available.

Even bone repair is now being aided by new, porous metallic and ceramic artificial-bone materials that allow the natural bone to grow into the artificial supporting structure, thereby effecting a much stronger, more integral repair than was possible with the metal plates and screws used previously. Injured ligaments and tendons can now be bionically reinforced through the use of a Dacron scaffold, and synthetic muscle has even been made using silicone rubber.

Artificial organs. Cardiac pacemakers are among the most familiar of current bionic devices—hundreds of thousands of Americans are currently being kept alive with them. And more than 260,000 people in this country, most of them over 50, have already benefited from bionics through heart-valve replacements.

In recent years, a portable artificial kidney has been developed that is small enough to wear as a backpack. Eventually, it may be possible to implant a bionic kidney directly into the body. At present, some 90,000 patients benefit directly from kidney machines each year, a tremendous increase from the 5,000 who were using dialysis machines in 1972.

A more recent development is the artificial pancreas, which supplies diabetics with insulin. A metallic disc acts as a sensor to monitor the level of glucose in a patient's blood, and a tiny pump/insulin-storage device releases measured doses of insulin into the bloodstream.

Bioelectronics. Researchers for such diverse organizations as Hughes Aircraft, Los Alamos National Laboratory, the U.S. Naval Research Laboratory, and Gentronix Laboratories (Rockville, Maryland) are working on parallel projects in this area. The goal of this research is to develop switchable computer chips that would be inserted into the nervous system to reconnect severed or worn-out nerves, as well as "smart" microcomputers that would be implanted directly into the central nervous system to help the body manage its various health-related responsibilities.

The results of success in such research would sound like a list of biblical miracles: the blind would see, the lame would walk, and the deaf would hear. Miniature "television cameras" could be connected directly to the optic nerve. Replacement of severed or worn-out nerves would allow people confined to wheelchairs to walk—and even run—again. Hearing aids could circumvent the ear entirely, plugging into the auditory nerve; already, researchers at the University of Melbourne in Australia have developed a cochlea implant, a kind of bionic ear.

Microcomputer implants connected directly to the brain could give you phenomenal memory, increase the power of all your senses many times over, and greatly extend your body's ability to monitor and correct its own functions for long life. Such devices, already under development in this country, Japan, and England, will be able to monitor as many as eight different variables at once (from heart rate or temperature to insulin level), administer the proper compensating chemical (for example, insulin, adrenalin, or hormones), and in the case of a medical emergency, send an appropriate message over the cellular phone network to the office of the prescribing physician.

Genetic engineering.   Of all the forms of biological redesign, genetic engineering is the most controversial and the most promising. Although the entire field is still in its infancy (it was only in 1949 that Crick and Watson first discovered DNA), researchers are confident that one day we will be able to decipher the codes that are programmed into each DNA molecule and, through the application of sophisticated microsurgical and biochemical manipulation, to actually redesign the genetic code.

The implications of genetic engineering for aging and disease are profound. Most late-life disease is the result of the body's increasing susceptibility to certain infections and contaminants and to cell degeneration. Through gene splicing, we could perhaps build tougher cells, ones for which cancer or diabetes would be easy foes to conquer. Or, if we had the knowledge and skills to alter the genetic code reliably, a simple application of this technology might be the reprogramming of the genetic blueprint—the "biological clock"—to set back the onset of aging by 10, 20, or possibly even 100 years.

FITTING THE NEW FORM

Many of us envision the future as a world created by and for the young, a world in which we will not fit in. This concern provokes our fear that, like Gulliver, we will become physiological outcasts in our homes and communities, as well as in our own bodies. But the Age Wave will change things profoundly.

As more and more of us grow older in new and different ways, we will change the world to meet our needs.

We will strike down the obstacles that could prevent us from living independent, fully vigorous lives. We will construct a new, more mature blueprint of psychological, physical, and lifestyle values and preferences from which a wide range of life-supporting products, services, technologies, and environments will be constructed. The Age Wave will recreate our world in a more comfortable image.

CHAPTER

12

A Great Age

About ten years ago, when I was first attempting to formulate my thoughts on the Age Wave, I was invited to present a lecture to a group of nearly 1,000 religious leaders from all denominations. The focus that I chose for my talk was the increasing health, vigor, and beauty that we could expect to see among the "new" elderly in the years ahead. The talk went very well, and at its conclusion a wave of applause filled the room.

Then, filled with the exhilaration of having delivered a well-received program, I sat down at the head table and turned to chat with the gentleman seated next to me, the prominent religious leader and gerontologist Monsignor Charles Fahey. "Well," I said, "what did you think of my presentation?"

"Very exciting talk," he said.

"Thank you."

"But, Ken, I'm sorry to tell you that I think you may be missing the most important point of the entire subject."

"Oh," I said, feeling very deflated. "And what's that?"

"If the entire purpose of old age is to be just like we were when we were young for several more decades, what's the value of that? Should the primary goal of childhood be an attempt to be an infant as long as possible? Is prolonging adolescence for a few more years the purpose of young adulthood? Should the focus of late adulthood be a longing for youth? I think not. I sure hope not!

"Think about it," he continued. "We know that even with the best of care, overall fitness will decline gradually with the years. While the strength of the senses is lessening, what if the powers of the mind, the heart, and the spirit are rising? If life offers the ongoing opportunity for increased awareness and personal growth, think of how far we could evolve, given the advantage of several extra decades of life!"

Monsignor Fahey's comments struck me very deeply. Until that moment, in both my personal ruminations and my undergraduate and graduate studies in psychology, I had believed that the inner life was essentially like a flower that blossomed in youth. Throughout the rest of life, the task was to try to keep the petals from falling off. What Fahey was proposing was that although our bodies may decline somewhat with age, our spirits have the capability of soaring to new heights in our later years. In fact, he suggested that *the growth and evolution of the inner life* may be the unique and special opportunity that the Age Wave brings.

Becoming more than we've ever been before is the point of extended life.

The topic of how to best fulfill the opportunity of long life has been explored in tales and folklore throughout history. For example, in J. R. R. Tolkien's *The Lord of the Rings*, the hobbit Smaegol discovers a magic ring that renders him both invisible and immortal. The catch is that the ring does not bring greater "quality" to his life; it just stretches out his life. As Smaegol lives longer and longer, he loses the positive attributes of life—a feeling of purpose, attachments to others, and a sense of wonder. His skin becomes waxy and pale. His voice sinks to a gravelly whisper, and he speaks only to himself. Finally, he retreats to an island in an underground lake, where he lives in darkness. By the time we meet him, he is an attenuated, whimpering, wraithlike being who goes by the name of Gollum. He has been drained of his life force; a slave to the ring, he is hundreds of years old and unable to die.

The image is poetic, but very real. Until now, history has been filled with men and women who died *before* their time. With elevated life expectancy, we increasingly meet people who seem to be living *beyond* their time, people who have outlived the purpose they established for themselves in youth and who now merely exist in an empty old age. We see it all around us: however fit they may be, men and women who have grown old with no new goals or dreams, no useful identity for their later years, but only memories of who they "used to be."

On the other hand, a "Dorian Gray" life of unending youth may not be fulfilling, either. Although most of us would hope for some measure of energy and vitality in our later years, being trapped forever in the body and spirit of youth without ever being able to mature or age has its own nightmarish qualities.

What Monsignor Fahey caused me to realize was that there are special human qualities and abilities that can only come to full blossom with age—for example, mature wisdom, experienced leadership, the ability to give back to society the lessons and resources that have been harvested over a lifetime. And if these deeper, greater qualities could come to be associated with age, then we might think of the evolution from young to old as an *ascending,* not *descending,* passage. On the other hand, if we evaluate the worth and value of age through the criteria of youth, the later years will fare poorly. By aiming at the wrong target, we will always be yearning for what we "used to be."

THE THIRD AGE

Modern Western psychology, molded as it was on the inner wars of childhood, has done little to date in the way of providing a clear blueprint for who we can become in our later years. Freud, for all his brilliance and innovation, did not even believe in adult development. He thought of childhood as the essential shaper of the psyche. He did not expect adults to grow in new directions, and he was reluctant to work with patients over 50. Of course, in Freud's era, 50 was considered very old, not the mid-life point it is becoming today.

Perhaps the first organized glimpse of the ascending psychological concerns of life's later years was offered by Erik Erikson, the "father of adult development." In his 1950 landmark work, *Childhood and Society*, Erikson insightfully outlined eight stages of human development, based on his clinical psychoanalytic research and his Freudian-oriented psychological training. He suggested that each life stage is marked by a developmental task or challenge, usually presented as a dichotomy, which the individual must successfully resolve in order to move on to the next, more mature level of development. Failure to progress results in emotional distress and a freezing of the maturation process.

Erikson's eight stages of development, their related tasks, and the inner quality each stage brings forward are listed on the following page.

According to Erikson, the key inner themes of late adulthood are not focused around the challenges of youth—issues of autonomy and the basic formulation of personal identity. Rather, the transformational turmoil of the later years is much more likely to center on two qualities: "generativity" (that is, the concern with how to pass along to future generations what one has gathered in life) and "ego integrity" (the achievement of a sense of personal wholeness in life's final stages). The practical meaning of this viewpoint was captured perfectly by Maggie Kuhn when she commented, "I continue to

	Stage	Task	Quality
1.	Oral–sensory	Basic trust vs. mistrust	Hope
2.	Muscular–anal	Autonomy vs. shame, doubt	Will
3.	Locomotor–genital	Initiative vs. guilt	Purpose
4.	Latency	Industry vs. inferiority	Competence
5.	Puberty and adolescence	Identity vs. role confusion	Fidelity
6.	Young adulthood	Intimacy vs. isolation	Love
7.	Adulthood	Generativity vs. stagnation	Care
8.	Maturity	Ego integrity vs. despair	Wisdom

realize that old age is a time of great fulfillment, when all the loose ends of life can be gathered together."

Erikson, himself now approaching his ninetieth birthday, has recently emphasized the achievement of wisdom as the ultimate stage of emotional maturation. According to Erikson, "Wisdom comes from life experience, well-digested. It's not what comes from reading great books. When it comes to understanding life, experiential learning is the only worthwhile kind." However, in Erikson's now classic eight stages of development, the greatest emphasis remains on youth, not age, with five of the eight stages in childhood.

This emphasis is repeated by other theorists who have worked to chart adult development. Such authorities as Daniel Levinson, Roger Gould, and Gail Sheehy have generally confined the core of their theories to the ages below 65; Sheehy's "passages," for example, stopped at 55.

In many ways it was the pioneering work of psychologist Abraham Maslow in the late 1950s that gave some direction to an understanding of the special purpose and opportunity offered by long life. In his well-known *hierarchy of needs*, Maslow proposed that some of our drives have precedence over others. The most basic needs are physiological—hunger and thirst, for instance. Next come concerns pertaining to safety, security, and stability. Following these are the needs for belonging and love and for affection and identification; then come concerns for self-esteem, prestige, and self-respect. Finally, at the very top of the hierarchy, is the desire for self-actualization—that is, for realizing all of one's latent awareness and capabilities. Maslow thus suggested that this last need is the ultimate goal and purpose of human existence.

This concept of an ascending hierarchy, in which coming to terms with one level of needs sets us free to tackle the next, is in contrast to Freud's and other homeostatic theories, which proposed no goal for adult human life beyond "adjusting" to reality and coming to terms with one's childhood influences. Within Maslow's point of view, the extra time and experience that come with growing older afford a historically unprecedented opportunity to come to terms with life's larger and more profound questions. However, influenced as he was by the youth-oriented perspective of the 1950s and 1960s, Maslow did not relate his theories to human aging.

The Three Ages of Man

It is from outside the realm of traditional psychology that we find a new perspective on the inner possibilities of old age. A compelling philosophy has recently emerged from the European tradition of adult education that provides a simple yet visionary orientation to this issue. Referred to as "Le troisième age"—The third age—this point of view proposes that there are three "ages" of man, each with its own special focus, challenge, and opportunity.

In the *first age*, from birth to approximately 25 years of age, the primary tasks of life center around biological development, learning, and survival. During the early years of history, the average life expectancy of most men and women wasn't much higher than the end of the first age, and as a result the entire thrust of society itself was oriented toward these most basic drives.

In the *second age*, from about 26 to 60, the concerns of adult life focus on issues pertaining to the formation of family, parenting, and productive work. The years taken up by the second age are very busy and are filled with social activity; the lessons gathered during the first age are applied to the social and professional responsibilities of the second. Until several decades ago, most people couldn't expect to live much beyond the second age, and society at that time was thus centered on the concerns of this age.

However, with the coming of the Age Wave, a new era of human evolution is unfolding, the *third age* of man. The purpose of the third age is twofold. First, with the children grown and many of life's basic adult tasks either well under way or already accomplished, this less pressured, more reflective period allows the further development of the interior life of the intellect, memory, imagination, of emotional maturity, and of one's own personal sense of spiritual identity (akin to Erikson's concept of the achievement of ego integrity and to Maslow's concept of self-actualization).

The third age is also a period for giving back to society the lessons, resources, and experiences accumulated and articulated over a lifetime (akin to Erikson's idea of generativity). From this perspective, the elderly are seen not as social outcasts, but as a living bridge between yesterday, today, and tomorrow—a critical evolutionary role that no other age group can perform. According to Monsignor Fahey, director of Fordham's Third Age Center, "People in the third age should be the glue of society, not its ashes."

Of course, this is not a new or novel perspective, just one that years of youth-focus have obscured. In other cultures and at other times, the elderly have been revered for their wisdom, power, and spiritual force. In ancient China, for example, the highest attainment in mystical Taoism was long life and the wisdom that came with the passing of years. According to social historian Simone de Beauvoir, "Lao Tzu's teaching sets the age of 60 as the moment at which a man may free himself from his body and become a holy being. Old age was therefore life in its very highest form."

Among the Aranda, hunters and gatherers of the Australian forests, extreme old age brings with it a transition to near-supernatural status. De Beauvoir writes: "The man whom age has already brought close to the other world is the best mediator between this and the next. It is the old people who direct the Arandas' religious life—a life that underlies the whole of their social existence."

In contemporary Japanese culture, a high value is placed on the unique opportunities for spiritual development offered by old age. According to Japanese culture expert Thomas Rohlen,

> What is significant in Japanese spiritualism is the promise itself, for it clearly lends meaning, integrity, and joy to many lives, especially as the nature of adult existence unfolds. It fits the physical process of aging. It recognizes the inherent value of experience. It reinforces the notion that social structure is justifiably gerontocratic. And for all its emphasis on social responsibility, discipline, and perseverance in the middle years, it encourages these as a means to a final state of spiritual freedom, ease, and universal belonging. . . . Here is a philosophy seemingly made for adulthood—giving it stature, movement, and optimism."

Even in the early history of the United States, before modernization shifted our interest from the old to the young, the elderly were the focus of great reverence. In the early 1840s, Reverend Cortlandt van Rensselaer captured this viewpoint in the following excerpt from a sermon: "What a blessed influence the old exert in cherishing feelings of reverence, affection, and subordination in families; in detailing the results of experience; in importing judicious counsel in church and State and private life."

According to Calvinist doctrine, which was profoundly influential during this period, living to a great age was taken as a sign of God's special favor. The more spiritually evolved elder was considered one of the elect, and therefore worthy of veneration. In reflection of this point of view, old age was highly honored and revered in all social rituals and on all public occasions. According to social historian David Hackett Fischer,

> The most important and solemn public gatherings in a New England town were the moments when the people met to worship together. In their meetinghouse they were carefully assigned seats of different degrees of dignity. The most honorable places did not go to the richest or strongest, but to the oldest.

As influential religious leader Increase Mather commented in the late eighteenth century, "If a man is favored with long life . . . it is God that has lengthened his days." The soul, the Puritans believed, grew like the body, reaching its highest earthly perfection in old age.

A GREAT AGE

If we are to live longer, on the average, than humans have ever lived before, and if our culture's center of gravity is to shift from youth to age, should this be regarded as good news or as bad?

As we have seen, the answer is "It depends." It depends on whether or not we can

- uproot the ageism and gerontophobia that cloud our hopes for the future and replace them with a new, more positive image of aging
- replace the limiting confines of the linear life plan with a flexible, cyclic plan, which is more appropriate to the shifting needs of a longer life
- create a new spectrum of family relationships that are matched to the sexuality, companionship, and friendship needs of adults
- discover ways to grow old well, in the absence of debilitating disease
- create products and services that will provide older men and women with comfort, convenience, and pleasure
- achieve cooperation among Americans of all ages in creating a social system that is fair and equitable for everyone

As individuals, whether an aged America turns out to be good or bad news will depend on whether we can grow beyond the values and expectations of youth to discover a positive and expanded vision of who we might become in our later years. Ultimately, it will not be the number of years that determine whether we live to a "great age," but the wisdom, richness, and quality that we bring to those years.

And, in the further discovery and expansion of the self that the precious extra years of life will make possible, we may realize that there is both more that we can be and more that we can give to society. We will have the maturity of vision and power that the young are too inexperienced to possess and that middle-aged adults are usually too busy to actualize.

In the past, older members of society were revered for their great wisdom and the mature perspective they could bring to social problems and crises. But historically, the children far outnumbered the few long-lived sages. We are now quickly heading toward a time when tens of millions of us will have experienced the depth and perspective of age.

The Age Wave will give us not merely the opportunity to live well and to live long, drawing much from life, but will also provide us with the time and energy to give more back, enriching society and ourselves with the special qualities and deep experiences of long life. When this happens, we will truly live to a great age.

Notes

1. The Rising Tide

4   Most of our historical figures come from the Census Bureau's *Historical Statistics of the United States: Colonial Times to 1970* or from Dr. Roy Walford's *Maximum Lifespan,* 1983.

5   The ages of average Americans in the last century were cited by Dr. Walford. The Ellis Island reference was confirmed by a National Park Service historian.

5–   The deadliness of various diseases, past and present, is detailed in James Fries
8   and Lawrence Crapo's *Vitality and Aging: Implications of the Rectangular Curve,* 1981. We also used information from the *Encyclopedia Britannica* and the federal Centers for Disease Control. The present and projected future median ages (as well as many other statistics in this chapter on the growth of the older population) are from *Aging America: Trends and Projections, 1987–88 Edition,* U.S. Department of Health and Human Services. The growth of the over-65 population can be traced in the Census Bureau's *Historical Statistics of the United States* and *Statistical Abstract of the United States, 1988.* The over-85 population in 2050 is from the U.S. Senate Special Committee on Aging report, *Aging America, Trends and Projections,* 1985–86. The rapid growth in centenarians is based on their numbers in the 1980 Census (25,000) and a projection for 1990 (50,000) by Stanley Kranczer, a statistician for Metropolitan Life, reported in the San Francisco *Chronicle,* March 3, 1987.

8–   The theoretical 120-to-140-year limit is based on experiments conducted by
10   Dr. Leonard Hayflick in 1960 and confirmed and extended many times since
      then. The life expectancy in Japan and other countries is reported in the annual
      "World Development Report," published by the World Bank. How much life
      expectancy would be increased if various diseases were conquered was es-
      timated by the U.S. Public Health Service.

11   The parenting habits of the boomers are outlined by the Census Bureau in its
      annual *Current Population Survey* by Landon Jones in his fascinating 1979 book
      on the boom, *Great Expectations*, and by Cheryl Russell, editor of *American
      Demographics*, in *100 Predictions for the Baby Boom*, 1987.

12–   The baby boom examples are cited by Landon Jones. The school figures are
16   from Leon F. Bouvier in *Population Bulletin, America's Baby Boom Generation: The
      Fateful Bulge*, vol. 35, no. 1, April 1980, p. 21.

21   The numbers marking Jane Fonda's success were provided by Karl/Lorimar
      Home Video. The increase in home gym equipment sales was provided by the
      National Sporting Goods Association The drop in smokers: according to the
      American Cancer Society, *1986 Cancer Facts and Figures*, in 1976, 42 percent
      of all Americans smoked; in 1986, 30 percent. The rise in exercise is from the
      Gallup Poll, comparing data from 1961 and 1986. The spiraling value of health
      club memberships is from the Association of Physical Fitness Centers' *APFC
      Quarterly*, Summer 1986.

2. Retiring the Myths of Aging

27   The Harris-NCA poll was conducted in 1981. Pat Moore made her comments
      to the authors.

30   Robert Wood made his comments to the authors.

32   The Bismarck story is related in the 1977 *Encyclopedia Britannica*

35–   We interviewed "Killer" Thompson and Jack LaLanne's assistant, and filled out
37   the LaLanne story from press accounts, including "LaLanne Staying Fit for
      Life," *Los Angeles Times*, 1988, and "Look, Ma, I'm an Institution," *Sports
      Illustrated*, 1981. Mavis Lindgren and Arabella Williams were profiled in
      Healthy Times, the newsletter of the Mori-Nu Tofu Company's "Health for Life
      Club," vols. 2 and 3, 1988. The Hulda Crooks story was taken from press
      accounts.

37–   The young medical students were interviewed by the author. The best informa-
38   tion on "senility" is reported by Robin Marantz Henig in the 1981 book *The
      Myth of Senility*.

38–   Beard's attack is chronicled by Tamara Hareven in her article, "The Last Stage:
39   Historical Adulthood and Old Age," in Erik Erikson's 1978 book *Adulthood*.
      Daniel Goleman reported on the state of current brain research in "The Aging
      Mind Proves Capable of Lifelong Growth," the *New York Times*, February 21,
      1984.

41   Robinson's article, titled "Research Update: The Older Worker," appeared in
      the summer of 1982. The studies on productivity include the article by D. P.
      Schwab and H. G. Heneman, "Effects of Age and Experience on Productivity,"
      Industrial Gerontology, 4:2, 1977; U.S. Department of Labor, 1965, *The Older*

American Workers: Age Discrimination in Employment; U.S. Senate Committee on Human Resources, 1977, *Findings on Age, Capacity and Productivity;* H. M. Clay, "A Study of Performance in Relation to Age at Two Printing Works," *Journal of Gerontology* 11, 1956; and S. H. Rhine, *Older Workers and Retirement,* The Conference Board, New York, 1978, The longevity of older workers was cited by Elliot Carlson in "The Plateau-Makers," *Dynamic Years,* March–April 1985. Turnover rates were reported by S. H. Rhine in *Older Workers and Retirement,* a report put out by The Conference Board in 1978. Great American First Savings' experience was reported by Lawrence S. Root, Ph.D., in "Corporate Programs for Older Workers," *Aging,* 1985, no. 351. Naugles' experience was related to the author by Anne Randsford, the executive director of the L.A. Council on Careers for Older Americans.

42   Injury rates were reported by N. Root in "Injuries at Work Are Fewer among Older Employees," *Monthly Labor Review,* March 1981; and in "Older Workers: Myths and Reality," Office of Human Development Services, Administration on Aging, U.S. Department of Health and Human Services Further sources backing these and other statements in this section can be found in Robinson's article in *Generations*

44–   The full names of the reports are: Bernard D. Starr and Marcella Bakur Weiner,
45   *The Starr-Weiner Report on Sex and Sexuality in the Mature Years,* 1981; and Harold Cox, *Later Life: The Realities of Aging,* 1984 The authors spoke with the Costains.

3. The Giant Wakes Up

52   The growth in the number of dissertations on aging was documented through Dissertation Abstracts Online, University Microfilms International. The growth in various societies and gerontology programs was provided by those societies and programs. Mr. Hansen was quoted in the January/February 1988, *NASLI News,* the newsletter of the National Association of Senior Living Industries.

53   The authors spoke to Mr. Hotchkiss.

55   The membership of advocacy groups was provided by those groups.

56   The authors spoke with John Rother, who (along with Director of Communications Peggy Hannon) provided the information about the activities of the AARP, and with Eric Schulman.

57   Figures on the growth of funding under the Older Americans Act come from Fred Luhmann of the Administration on Aging.

58–   The amount of the federal budget dedicated to the elderly was gleaned from
59   a comparison of figures in a report by the U.S. Department of Health and Human Services, *Aging America: Trends and Projections, 1985–86,* with those in the Census Department's *Statistical Abstract of the United States, 1987.* The Urban Institute's future projections were quoted in " 'Gray Power' Flexes Its Political Muscle," *U.S. News and World Report,* September 1, 1980. The details of Senator Gorton's defeat (and other NCSC involvements) were garnered from contemporary press accounts and the authors' discussions with Mr. Schulman.

59   Senator Graham spoke to the authors.

60   The voting trends showed up in the Health and Human Services' *Aging America* report and were confirmed by Peggy Hannon of the American Association of Retired Persons.

60–   Russel Edgarton spoke with the authors. Senator Moynihan was quoted by
61   Henry Fairlie in "Talkin' 'bout My Generation," *New Republic,* March 28, 1988. Dr. Binstock wrote in "The Elderly as an Electorate," *Aging Network News,* September 1986. Dr. Heclo was quoted by Elliot Carlson in "The Phony War," *Modern Maturity,* February/March 1987.

62   Mr. Jarvis was interviewed by Joe Flower during a 1980 political campaign for a profile that appeared in *San Francisco* magazine.

63   The AARP's political activities were outlined by Peggy Hannon. Dr. Cutler is quoted in " 'Gray Power' Flexes Its Political Muscle," *U.S. News and World Report,* September 1, 1980.

64   Henry Fairlie wrote "Talkin' 'bout My Generation," in *New Republic,* March 28, 1988.

65   AGE's original pamphlet was an exhibit of a hearing before the House Select Committee on Aging, April 8, 1986. Mr. Longman published his comments in "Taking America to the Cleaners," *Washington Monthly,* November 1982. Mr. Hewitt and Ms. Kuhn spoke with the authors. Mr. Brickfield wrote in "The Phony War," *Modern Maturity,* February–March 1987.

67   The current Social Security law was discussed in an interview with the commissioner of Social Security, Dorcas R. Hardy, and detailed in the 1987 Annual Report of the Board of Trustees of the Federal Old-Age and Survivors Insurance and Disability Insurance Trust Funds. The levels of OASDI, Medicare, and Medicaid funds for 1987 were provided by various federal agencies.

68   "Support ratios" were discussed by Mary Bourdette, Director of Government Affairs for the Children's Defense Fund, in testimony before the House Select Committee on Aging, April 8, 1986. Rahn was quoted in "Social Security at 50," *Modern Maturity,* August–September 1985.

69   Poverty-level statistics are taken from the Census Bureau's annual *Statistical Abstract of the United States.*

71–   The income figures for the oldest age groups are from Fabian Linden, "The
73      $800 Billion Market," *American Demographics,* February 1986. The charts are based on unpublished figures for 1986 provided by the Bureau of the Census.

74   The amount of the federal budget devoted to the elderly is given in HHS's *Aging America* report.

75   Throughout this discussion, the numbers attributed to the Social Security projections are taken from the annual reports of the Board of Trustees of the Federal Old-Age and Survivors Insurance and Disability Insurance Trust Funds.

77   The survey of actuaries is cited by Paul Light in "Currents and Soundings: Social Security and the Politics of Assumptions," *Public Administration Review,* May/June 1985.

77–   Henry Aaron, Robert Ball, and Dorcas Hardy spoke with the authors.
78

79   The percentage of health-care funds spent on the elderly is reported in *The Role of the Hospital in an Aging Society: A Blueprint for Action,* by Dr. Ken Dychtwald and Mark Zitter.

80   Daniel Callahan spoke with the authors. The specific examples are cited in his
        1987 book, *Setting Limits.*
81–   The Sun City schools story was recounted to the authors by school district
82   officials in the area.
82–   The rise in discrimination complaints is recounted in the 1986 AARP report,
83   "Workers 45+: Today and Tomorrow." Landon Jones is quoted from *Great
        Expectations.*
83   The LTV example was supplied by the LTV Steel Corporation.
84   Joseph King wrote in the April 14, 1986, issue of *Newsweek.*

4. The Cyclic Life

95   The quote is from Best's 1980 book, *Flexible Life Scheduling.*
96–   The marriage and divorce statistics are from the Census Bureau's *Statistical
98   Abstract of the United States, 1987,* and the *Wall Street Journal,* August 18, 1987.
        The school statistics come from the American Association of Junior and Com-
        munity Colleges.
98–   The surveys on retirement were conducted by Louis Harris and Associates, the
99   Roper Organization, and sociologist Fred Best; all were cited by Best in the
        Summer 1979 *Aging,* in his article "The Future of Retirement and the Lifetime
        Distribution of Work." The out-of-work executives were polled by Drake
        Beam Morin, Inc., and the figure was cited in "You're Fired!" *U S. News and
        World Report,* March 23, 1987.
100   The sources for the Mother Teresa profile include Courtney Tower, "Mother
        Teresa's Work of Grace," *Reader's Digest,* December 1987; *Life,* April 1988;
        and the *Encyclopedia Britannica's* 1980 Book of the Year.
102–   The stories of Gandhi, Schweitzer, and Matisse are told in standard reference
107   biographies.
104   Claude Pepper's story is told in many places. The authors referred to Ed
        Magnuson, "Champion of the Elderly," *Time,* April 25, 1983; Nancy Rica
        Schiff, "The Art of Aging," *Psychology Today,* January 1984; and Bonnie Jacob,
        "Pepper's Key: 'I Love What I'm Doing,'" *USA Today,* May 19, 1987.
105   Maggie Kuhn's story came from Jan Fisher, "Maggie Kuhn's Vision: Young
        and Old Together," *50 Plus,* July 1986; W. Andrew Achenbaum, "Stitching
        a Safety Net," *The Wilson Quarterly,* New Year's 1985; Maggie Kuhn, "For an
        End to Ageism," *Health And Medicine,* Summer/Fall 1984; "Maggie Kuhn: A
        Brief Biography," *Senior Citizen's Review,* August/September 1987; and the
        authors' interviews and personal acquaintances.
110   Louis and Reva were profiled in *People* magazine, February 1988, pp. 85–89.
112–   The authors spoke with Bagley and Flinn.
113

5. The New Leisure

116   The figures on the declining role of work were cited by Fred Best in "Recycling
        People: Work Sharing through Flexible Life Scheduling," *The Futurist,* Febru-
        ary 1978.

117   The NAB report was published in 1985. The history of pensions is related by Joseph Melone and Everett Allen in their 1972 book, *Pension Planning.* The figures on pension coverage were derived by comparing data from two Census Bureau publications, *Historical Statistics of the United States, Colonial Times to 1970* and *Statistical Abstract of the United States, 1985–86.* Data was provided by the Employee Benefit Research Institute.

118   The drop in the age of retirement and the percentage of people working past the age of 65 were reported by the American Association of Retired Persons in their 1986 publication, "Workers 45 +: Today and Tomorrow." Here, too, the figures on the declining role of work were cited by Best.

119   Max Kaplan is quoted from his 1975 book, *Leisure: Theory and Policy.* Donald Mankin is quoted from his article, "The Future of Leisure," in the 1981 book *Millennium: Glimpses into the 21st Century,* edited by A. Villoldo and K. Dychtwald.

123   The information on bowling came from the American Bowling Congress. The Mall-walker clubs were described to us by the National Council on Aging, which co-sponsors them, and Nancy Luttrop of the Fort Collins Park and Recreation Department, which sponsors the Foothill group. We interviewed Wright for the information on the National Senior Sports Association.

124   The number of senior golfers was provided by the National Golf Foundation.

124–   Stack was quoted by Lloyd Kahn in his 1986 book, *Over the Hill but Not Out*
125   *to Lunch.* Smitty's story was related in *Sports Illustrated* in the spring of 1986.

126–   United States National Senior Olympics provided information about its partici-
127   pants. The authors spoke with Helm, Lambert, and Gebhardt.

129   Information on discounts was provided by the companies and agencies named, and by "Senior Savings," *Travel-Holiday,* September 1985.

130–   American Youth Hostel, Mountain Travel, and Society Expeditions provided
131   the information on their respective operations.

133   The ages of customers at Epcot Center and Disney World were provided by Disney.

135–   The Sun City residents were interviewed by the authors. The racial composition
137   of Sun City is included in *Inside Phoenix 1984, 1984 Phoenix Market Study,* conducted by the Scarborough Research Corporation for the *Arizona Republic/ Phoenix Gazette.*

137–   The authors spoke with Wolfson and Wolfe.
138

139–   Royal Oaks provided the information on their fees. The fees at Villa Marin
140   were quoted by Tim Urbonya in "Room for Profits in Senior Housing?" *San Francisco Examiner,* June 8, 1986. The number of lifecare centers comes from "New Retirement Centers to Recreate the Past," *San Francisco Chronicle,* December 8, 1986, and an interview by the authors with Jim Sherman of Laventhol & Horwath, a Chicago-based CPA firm that specializes in the industry. Tom Curren spoke with the authors.

141   The number of age-segregated "retirement villages" comes from the 1984 AARP report "Housing Options for Older Americans," edited by Linda

Hubbard. The percentage of older Americans in retirement villages was reported by Golant in his article, "In Defense of Age-Segregated Housing," in *Aging.*

141–   The information on mobile homes was provided by Jim Mack, editor of *Mobile/*
142   *Manufactured Home Merchandiser,* and Ruth Walker of Foremost Insurance. The "slabs" story, reported by Richard Louv in his 1983 book *America II,* was augmented by the authors' interview with Sheriff Fox.

142–   The quotes from McCarthy and Longino, and the new retirement regions,
143   come from "State Populations Shift Unpredictably as Seniors Flock to Greener Pastures," *Los Angeles Times,* December 16, 1983.

6. Wisdom in Action

148   The authors interviewed Gabel.

149   The age of students at California colleges came from "They're Getting Older on Campus," *San Francisco Chronicle,* August 2, 1986. Information about learning programs for elders was provided by the institutions cited and by "Graying of America Changes Face of U.S. Higher Education," *John Naisbitt's Trend Letter,* February 4, 1988.

151   Elderhostel provided information about its operation.

152–   The Society Expeditions quote is from a letter to the authors, who also inter-
153   viewed van Zoelen.

153   The authors interviewed Powell.

155   Earthwatch provided the authors with information about its operations.

156–   The information and quotes on retirees moving to college towns were reported
157   by Richard Lyons, "Retirees Resettling in College Towns," *New York Times,* November 20, 1987. The information on intellectual retirement villages came from Dobkin.

159–   The AARP survey was conducted in 1981 by Hamilton and Staff, Inc., of
160   Washington, D.C., and published as "Older Americans and Volunteerism." The information on the federally sponsored volunteer agencies was provided by those agencies.

160   The information on ACTION comes from an "ACTION News" fact sheet, March 1986. The Peace Corps information was provided by Sinclair.

161   The authors interviewed Brosius, Crawford, and other Sun City volunteers. Boswell Memorial Hospital is a client of Age Wave, Inc.

162–   Dr. Perry's article, "The Willingness of Persons over 60 to Volunteer: Implica-
163   tions for the Social Services," appeared in *Journal of Gerontological Social Work,* vol. 5(4), Summer 1983. The authors interviewed Eaton.

164   Cahn's plan was detailed in "The Good Deed Account," *Miami Herald,* April 23, 1985; in "Earning More Than Money," *Washington Post,* June 12, 1985; and in 1985 testimony before the Florida Senate.

165–   Stambaugh's story was recounted in *People* magazine, May 1986. The authors
166   spoke to Lang's assistant.

167–   The Levi Strauss Foundation provided information about its work. The authors
168   interviewed Brune. Blue Cross/Blue Shield of Indiana is a client of Age Wave, Inc.

7. Reworking Work

175– 176	The polls on retired people who would rather be working were reported by the AARP in their 1986 report, "Workers 45 +: Today and Tomorrow." Kuhn made her comment to the authors. The authors interviewed Byrnes and Chapman. Ehrenhalt was quoted by Steven Greenhouse in the *New York Times'* article "Surge in Prematurely Jobless," October 12, 1986.
178	We interviewed Fisk.
179	Underwood made his comment to the authors.
180	Buffett was quoted in *Fortune*, April 11, 1988, in Carol Loomis' article "The Inside Story of Warren Buffett." For an overview of the impending labor shortage, see "Help Wanted," *Business Week*, August 10, 1987.
181– 182	Brickfield made his point in a speech before the American Express Corporation in 1987. The authors spoke with Curren. We also interviewed Mr. Capatosto. The age of board members was quoted from *Fortune* in the AARP's 1986 report, "Managing a Changing Work Force."
185– 186	Pifer was quoted by Elliot Carlson in "Longer Work Life?" in *Modern Maturity*, June–July 1985. The Carnegie Foundation's figure on training expenditures was cited in the 1985 report of the National Alliance for Business entitled "Invest in Experience: New Directions for an Aging Workforce." Carlson was also the source for IBM's training policy as discussed in "The Plateau-Makers," *Dynamic Years*, March–April 1985. Norwood was quoted by Tim Schreiner in "Big Problem for Business—Shortage of Young Workers," *San Francisco Chronicle*, October 28, 1986. Shugrue commented on IBM's policy in an interview with the authors.
186– 187	The information about company programs was provided by the companies.
188	The authors interviewed Atkins. Other examples of such programs were included in the NAB's report, "Invest in Experience."
189	Best wrote about sabbaticals in his 1980 book, *Flexible Life Scheduling*.
190– 191	Tandem's Patricia Becker was quoted by Dan Cody in "Time Out! How to Make Sabbaticals Work—for Yourself and for Your Company," *Republic*, December 1985. We interviewed Tandem's Jeri Flinn. Wells Fargo provided information about its sabbatical program. Community involvement sabbaticals were detailed in the AARP's "Managing a Changing Work Force."
192	Phased retirements and retirement rehearsals were described in the NAB's "Invest in Experience."
193– 194	The Polaroid experience was described by Lawrence S. Root, Ph.D., in "Corporate Programs for Older Workers," *Aging*, 1985, no. 351. The Aerospace policy was mentioned in the NAB's "Invest in Experience." The ISPRP provided its membership data.
195– 196	Toro provided the information about its policies, while the policies of Kentucky Fried Chicken were mentioned by Mark Memmott in "More Companies Are Calling on Retirees," *USA Today*, June 30, 1987. We interviewed Malcho; Rubenstein was quoted by Elliot Carlson in "Longer Work Life?" *Modern Maturity*, June–July 1985. We interviewed Greenberg.

197   Root cited Sterile Design in his *Aging* article. The percentage of companies using part-time help was uncovered in a study done by the Commerce Clearing House for the American Society of Personnel Administration.

198   The Challenger, Gray & Christmas survey was reported in "The World of Work," *Savvy*, October 1986. The projection concerning the percentage of individuals working at home was developed by Marvin Cetron, president of Forecasting International.

199–
200   The policies at General Motors and Mutual Life were mentioned by Alex Taylor III in "Why Women Managers Are Bailing Out," *Fortune*, August 18, 1986. Corning Glass Works was cited in the AARP's "Managing a Changing Work Force." The 1985 figure on companies offering flextime came from the Bureau of Labor Statistics; the 1987 figure and the percentage of companies still offering regular hours were provided from the Commerce Clearing House–ASPA study.

202   The authors interviewed Governor Lamm and Maggie Kuhn. The shift in the tax law was reported by Linda Demkovich in "Social Security at 50," *Modern Maturity*, August–September 1985 and in the *New York Times'* 1986 book, *The New Tax Law*. The personal savings rates of various countries are published by The World Bank in their annual "World Development Report."

203   Personal pensions are discussed in exhaustive detail by Emily S. Andrews in her 1985 report, "The Changing Profile of Pensions in America," written for the Employee Benefit Research Institute. Industry-wide portable pension plans are discussed in the Employee Benefit Research Institute's *EBRI Issue Brief*, July 1986.

204–
205   Peter Ferrara's study was published as "Social Security Rates of Return for Today's Young Workers," National Chamber Foundation, 1986.

8. Love in the Second Half

210   The figures on long marriages were provided by Arlene Saluter of the Census Bureau.

211   Atchley's book was published in 1977. An interesting analysis of golden marriages is found in Timothy Brubaker's *Later Life Families*. The Consumers Union survey was published in 1984 as *Love, Sex and Aging*, by Edward Brecher and the editors of Consumer Reports Books. Starr and Weiner published their findings in 1981 as *The Starr-Weiner Report on Sex and Sexuality in the Mature Years*.

214–
215   The number of marriages that end in divorce was derived from the Census Bureau's *Statistical Abstract of the United States, 1988*. Lee's comments were made in his article "Marriage and Aging," in *Society*, vol. 18(2), Jan./Feb., 1981. The divorce statistics were reported by *Newsweek* in "Portrait of Divorce in America," February 2, 1987. Elderly divorce rates are from *The Starr-Weiner Report*. "Nearly 10 million American households are already being run by remarried couples": the Census Bureau's 1980 Current Population Survey shows 9.2 million, and all indications reflect that the trend is up.

217–
218   The authors spoke with Chamberlain. The study of divorce in California was reported by Angela Heath, a program specialist with the American Association of Retired Persons, in "Research Findings: Late-Life Divorce." The "gray

divorcé" phenomenon was explored in "Late-Life Divorce," *Aging,* Fall 1983. The authors also interviewed Patty Clare. The dating ad ran in Marin County, California's *Pacific Sun,* July 4–10, 1986.

219   The number of people living alone was cited in the 1985 AARP report, "A Profile of Older Americans."

220   Bulcroft and O'Conner-Roden reported on their study in the June 1986 *Psychology Today.* The percentages of women over 65 who do not have a spouse, and of older men who do, were reported in *Aging America: Trends and Projections, 1987–88.* The percentage of males who are exclusively homosexual was reported by Alfred C. Kinsey et al., *Sexual Behavior in the Human Male,* 1948.

222–   The number of unmarried couples living together was provided by the Census
224   Bureau in "Marital Status and Living Arrangements," March 1985. The *Population Bulletin* quote is from "The Changing American Family," October 1983. The comparative numbers of men and women are recorded in the Census Bureau's *Demographic Aspects of Aging in the United States,* Current Population Reports, Series PC-23, No. 59, USGPO, 1976. The numbers of single men and women over 65 were provided by the National Center for Health Statistics. The marital status of older Americans is discussed in the AARP's 1985 report, "A Profile of Older Americans," and in Paul C. Glick's article, "Remarriage: Some Recent Changes and Variations," in *Journal of Family Issues,* December 1980.

225   According to the Census Bureau, in 1984, 2,984,000 American women were married to men a decade younger than themselves. Kassel made his remarks in "Polygyny after 60" in April 1966.

228   The authors interviewed Kline.

229–   The authors interviewed Bankster. Robinson wrote "A Sociologic Perspec-
230   tive" in the 1983 book *Sexuality in the Later Years,* edited by Ruth Weg, Ph.D.

9. Reinventing the Family

235   The movement of the median age between 1950 and 2050 is given in *Aging America: Trends and Projections, 1987–88,* U.S. Department of Health and Human Services. The quotes from Dr. Riley are taken from a speech given before the annual meeting of the National Council of Family Relations in October 1982, and published as "The Family in an Aging Society: A Matrix of Latent Relationships," in the September 1983 issue of the *Journal of Family Issues.*

237   *My Mother, My Self,* by Nancy Friday, was published in 1977; *Making Peace with Your Parents,* by Harold Bloomfield and Leonard Felder, in 1983; and *Nothing in Common,* by Barbara Bottner, in 1988.

238–   The actual and projected numbers of people over 85 are from Gregory Spen-
239   cer, U.S. Bureau of the Census, "Projections of the Population of the United States, by Age, Sex, and Race: 1983 to 2080," *Current Population Reports,* Series P-25, no. 952 (May 1984). The comparative numbers of parents and children is discussed in Samuel H. Preston's "Children and the Elderly in the U.S.," *Scientific American,* December 1984. The ratios of children to parents are shown by Cynthia Tauber in the Census Bureau's *America in Transition: An Aging*

Society, Current Population Reports, Special Studies, Series P-23, no. 128, revised December 1983.

239–
240
Jane Menken, a demographer at Princeton University, provided the comparison of years caring for children and for parents. The percentage of care given by relatives is mentioned in *Aging America: Trends and Projections, 1987–88,* U.S. Department of Health and Human Services.

240–
241
Troll made her remarks in "Parents and Children in Later Life," *Generations,* Summer 1986. Statistics about caregivers were reported by John Naisbitt in "Caring for Aged Relatives Falls on Woman in the Family," United Press International, September 12, 1986. Brody was quoted in *Newsweek,* "Who's Taking Care of Our Parents?" May 6, 1985. She gave a full exposition of her ideas in "They Can't Do It All: Aging Daughters with Aged Mothers," *Generations,* Winter 1982.

242–
244
Sources for this section on elder abuse include: Clare Ansberry, "Abuse of the Elderly by Their Own Children Increases in America," *Wall Street Journal,* February 3, 1988; Richard L. Douglass, M.P.H., Ph.D., "Domestic Mistreatment of the Elderly: Towards Prevention," Criminal Justice Services, American Association of Retired Persons, 1987; "Institutionalized Elderly Are Often Abused," *American Family Physician,* February 1986; Mary Bruno, "Abusing the Elderly," *Newsweek,* September 23, 1985; Ursula Vils, "The Abuse and Neglect of the Elderly," *Los Angeles Times,* March 29, 1985.

244–
245
The information about Partners in Care came directly from the company. The growth in home health agencies was provided by the Division of Ambulatory Care of the American Hospital Association. The Travelers Insurance survey was published as "The Travelers Employee Caregiver Survey: A Survey on Caregiving Responsibilities of Travelers Employees for Older Americans," June 1985. A number of care managing examples were mentioned in *Newsweek*'s "Growing Old, Feeling Young," November 1, 1982.

245–
246
Rothschild and Britt's program was described in the *San Jose* (California) *Mercury-News,* "Respite Program Helps with the Elderly," October 30, 1985. Other firms were mentioned by the *Los Angeles Times,* "A Little Help Lets Elderly Live at Home," June 25, 1986. The authors interviewed Barbara Kane.

247–
249
Roger Ricklefs of the *New York Times* reported on private care managers in "Adult Children of Elderly Parents Hire 'Surrogates' to Oversee Care," May 19, 1988. Elliot D. Lee of the *New York Times* reported on corporate involvement in "Firms Begin Support for Workers Who Look after Elderly Relatives," July 6, 1987. The Travelers survey was reported in *American Demographics* The number of Americans caring for a parent was mentioned by *Newsweek,* "Who's Taking Care of Our Parents," May 6, 1985. The authors interviewed Fisk.

253
The statistics on grandparents come from a 1986 study by Valley Forge Survey Company for *Grandparents* magazine. *Toy Trade News* reported its findings in August of 1986.

254
The results of the Cherlin and Furstenberg study were published in their article "Grandparents and Family Crisis," *Generations,* Summer 1986, and in their 1987 book, *The New American Grandparent.*

255
Kornhaber and Walker were quoted by the *New York Times* in "If It's Expensive, Grandparents Often Pay," May 22, 1986. The information on Duquesne University was provided by Duquesne.

256 The authors interviewed Flood.

257 Wylie told his story in "Grandfathers Aren't Supposed to Cry," *Grandparents* magazine, Fall 1987. Dan Woog wrote eloquently about grandparents' rights in "Grandma Who?" *American Way,* February 5, 1985.

258 David Diamond wrote about adopting grandparents in "Filling the Grandparent Gap," *50 Plus,* May 1988.

259– Hagestad wrote in "The Family: Women and Grandparents as Kinkeepers,"
260 in the 1986 book *Our Aging Society,* edited by Alan Pifer and Lydia Bronte.

261– The percentage of older people living alone is mentioned in *Aging America:*
262 *Trends and Projections, 1987–88,* U.S. Department of Health and Human Services. The estimate of the number of rooms available in California was made by Witkin. She was quoted in "A Solution to Housing for Seniors," *Los Angeles Times,* February 26, 1982. Himmel was quoted in "Wanted, a Roommate, Age 65 and Over Preferred," *Family Circle,* April 7, 1981.

262– Information on these alternative living arrangements came from a variety of
263 sources, including Linda Hubbard's AARP report; "Housing Needs: The Choices Increase," *U.S. News and World Report,* September 1, 1980; the testimony of the November 1980 hearings of the House Select Committee on Aging; "New Home-Sharing Options for Older People," *Changing Times,* December 1983; and "Memphis Share-a-Home Program," *Aging,* December 1983. Crown was quoted in the *Los Angeles Times* article. The *Challenge* article was "Shared Living for Elders: A Viable Alternative," September 1980. The Back Bay project was described in that article and in "Seniors Leave Loneliness for Life in a Co-op," *Los Angeles Times,* May 24, 1982.

264 The Shared Living Project was described in the *Family Circle* article. Gildea spoke with the authors.

10. The Maturing Marketplace

267– The television commercial study was published by J. Francher, "It's the Pepsi
268 Generation . . .: Accelerated Aging and the Television Commercial," *International Journal of Aging and Human Development,* 1973, 4:245–255. The magazine study, by Paula Englund, Alice Kuhn, and Teresa Gardner, was published as "The Ages of Men and Women in Magazine Advertisements," *Journalism Quarterly,* Autumn 1981.

268– The statistics on these pages are derived from a variety of sources. They
269 include: "A Marketing Guide to Discretionary Income," a joint study of the Census Bureau and the Conference Board, a private research firm; the Census Bureau's 1984 report, "After Tax Aggregate Income," series P-23, no. 147; "Mid-Life and Beyond," a 1985 report of the Conference Board's Consumer Research Center; the November–December 1985 report of the Direct Marketing Association; Peter Petre, "Marketers Mine for Gold in the Old," *Fortune,* March 31, 1986; and a speech by Robert Fallon, then executive director of Sears' Mature Outlook, presented at the American Society on Aging, Washington, D.C., September 29, 1987.

269 Gordon French wrote in "Old Money Is Smart Money," National Association of Senior Living Industries *News,* August 1985.

270–   The Yankelovich study was called "The Mature Americans," Fall 1987. Bal-
271   kite, Allen, and Sias spoke to the authors.

274   Gollub was quoted by Peter Petre in the *Fortune* article.

275   Poverty levels of elder age groups can be traced in the 1986 *Statistical Handbook on Aging Americans*, edited by Frank Schick.

276–   Russel wrote her comments in the December 1987 *American Demographics*. The
277   rise in the boomers' consumer spending—and the reasons for it—were noted by economist Frank Levy in *Dollars and Dreams: The Changing American Income Distribution*, published in 1987 by the Russell Sage Foundation. A *cohort* consists of all the people born within a narrow span of years.

280   Wood made his comment to the authors. Wolfe made his points in "The Ageless Market," *American Demographics*, July 1987.

281   The ad executive's comments (and Frances Lear's) were made to the authors.

283   Albin wrote in "Maturity Market," *50 Plus*, April 1985. Edmonds made his remark to the authors.

284   Pottasch was quoted by Paula Span in "The Pepsi Generation Grows Up," in *This World, San Francisco Examiner-Chronicle*. Berger wrote (and quoted Klein) in "Marketing Young to Reach the Old," *Food and Beverage Marketing*, September 1987.

285–   Black was quoted in "TV Grows Up," *Modern Maturity*, October–November
286   1987. Mandarino spoke to the authors.

287–   Jordan, Case and McGrath published their study in 1985 as "The 55+ Market:
288   The Marketing Opportunity of the 1980s." The Yankelovich Group published their study in 1987 as "The Mature Americans." Ogilvy wrote "The Experience Industry" in *American Demographics*, December 1986.

288–   Collins described his program in "Senior Programs—A Golden Opportunity
289   to Provide Bank-Centered Lifestyles," *Bank Marketing*, March 1988.

289   The amount of home equity owned by older Americans was reported by Bruce Jacobs, Ph.D., in "The National Potential of Home Equity Conversion," *The Gerontologist*, vol. 26, no. 5, 1986.

290   Data on home equity conversions were provided by Maurice Weinrobe, Professor of Economics, Clark University, Worcester, Massachusetts. Other information came from the authors' interview with Ken Scholen, director of the National Center for Home Equity Conversion. The estimate of the number of American elderly poor who could be supported by their equity was provided by Dr. Jacobs.

291   The authors spoke with Longino.

295–   The authors spoke with Varma. The development of the Lifeline was related
296   to Dr. Dychtwald by Dibbner.

296–   The beeper incident was reported in "Beeper Saves Woman, 93, Beaten Up
297   by Thieves," *San Francisco Chronicle*, June 26, 1986.

298   Carlisle spoke to the authors.

299–   Pellegrene spoke to the authors. Beck is an advisor to the board of Age Wave,
300   Inc. His experience with his father was related to the authors.

302   Baylor Medical Center is a client of Age Wave, Inc. This and other health-care examples can be found in *The Role of the Hospital in an Aging Society: A Blueprint for Action*, by Dr. Ken Dychtwald and Mark Zitter, Age Wave, 1986.

304   Lempert wrote in "The Store of 2000—A Fresh Look," *Advertising Age,*
       May 9, 1988.
306   The Gerber information was provided by Gerber.
307   Valenti and Goldberg were quoted in the *New York Times,* March 6, 1988.
308   Radabaugh was quoted in "TV Grows Up." Poltrack was interviewed by the
       authors. Porcino wrote "What Makes The Golden Girls So Hot?" in *50 Plus,*
       September 1987.

11. Redesigning America

312   McCarty made her remarks in the exhibition's catalog, "Designs for Modern
       Living," New York Museum of Modern Art, Spring 1988.
312–   The Gallup survey was conducted in 1983 under contract from Martech Asso-
313   ciates, Inc., of Portland, Oregon, funded by the Administration on Aging, and
       published by Gallup as "Survey of New Product Needs among Older Ameri-
       cans."
314–   A great deal of information about the physical aspects of aging was well set
336   out by Curtis Pesmen in the 1984 book *How a Man Ages;* by Robin Marantz
       Henig in the 1986 *How a Woman Ages;* by Schwartz, Snyder, and Peterson in
       Aging & Life, 1984; and by Joseph Koncelik in *Aging and the Product Environ-
       ment,* 1982.
315   Some of these specific ideas for car redesign came from Koncelik. Some are
       already in experimental or early marketing phases, as we discovered in a
       discussion with Ted Bohlen of General Motors' Human Factors Group;
       George Moon, executive designer with General Motors' Advanced Automo-
       tive Design Group; and Bill Carroll of Ford Motors.
318   The Donnelly study was published as "Insights into the Over-50 Market" in
       May 1987.
321   Mr. Eastlack's comments were made in an unpublished paper, "Trends in Food
       and Nutrition in the Mature Market."
322–   The Simplesse-Olestra war was reported in a Procter & Gamble press release
323   on June 2, 1987, and in *U.S. News and World Report,* February 1, 1988. Beef
       consumption was chronicled in "Trying to Make Beef Appetizing Again,"
       Fortune, November 25, 1985. The low-calorie trend showed up in *Calorie
       Control Commentary,* vol. 9, no. 1, Spring 1987.
324–   Architecture and interior design considerations are admirably covered in sev-
325   eral articles, including Lorraine G. Hiatt, "Architecture for the Aged: Design
       for Living," *Inland Architect,* November/December 1978; Hiatt, "Environ-
       mental Changes for Socialization," *Journal of Nursing Administration,* January
       1978; Hiatt, "Care and Design," *Nursing Homes,* July/August 1980; Joe Jor-
       dan, "Recognizing and Designing for the Special Needs of the Elderly,"
       American Institute of Architects' *Journal,* September 1977; and Jordan, "The
       Challenge: Designing Buildings for Older Americans," *Aging,* December
       1983–January 1984. The chair specifications are from Jordan.
326   The authors interviewed King. McCarty's comments here are also from the
       exhibition catalog.
327   The Jordan, Case and McGrath study was published in 1985 as "The 55+
       Market: The Marketing Opportunity of the 1980s."

329–   The authors spoke with Dr. Goin. Dr. Dinner was quoted in "Snip, Suction,
330   Stretch and Truss," *Time*, September 14, 1987. The number of hair transplants
         performed in 1986 is taken from data supplied by the American Society of
         Plastic and Reconstructive Surgeons, Inc.

331   Nordmann was quoted by William P. Barrett in the *Dallas Times Herald*, re-
         printed in the *San Francisco Chronicle* as "Hair Grower Boosts Upjohn," August
         24, 1985. Further information was provided by Upjohn. Artificial skin and
         other future directions of cosmetic surgery were explored by *Omni* in "Body-
         shop," by Viva, October 1986. Stambaugh was quoted by Curtis Pesman in
         How a Man Ages, 1984.

332   The costs of cosmetic dentistry—and Dr. Kurz' invention—were reported by
         Kay Williams in "The High Costs of Looking Young," *Money*, April 1985.

333   The number of coronary bypass operations performed in 1985 was provided
         by the American Heart Association. TPA was described in "FDA OKs New
         De-clotting Drug," Associated Press, November 13, 1987. Lovastatin was
         described by David Perlman in "Cholesterol Drug OKd," *San Francisco Chroni-
         cle*, September 2, 1987. The numbers of exercising Americans were arrived at
         by multiplying Gallup percentages by total population figures. Other informa-
         tion in this section came from: "Exercise Industry Sees Spurt in Sales to
         Homes," *New York Times*, May 21, 1984; Anastasia Toufexis, "Working Out
         in a Personal Gym," *Time*, February 10, 1986; "Numbers to Live By," Ameri-
         can Physical Fitness Clubs' *Quarterly*, Summer 1986; the American Federation
         of Physical Therapists; the American College of Sports Medicine; and the
         National Sporting Goods Association.

334   The Pritikin results were evaluated by the Department of Biostatistics and
         Epidemiology at Loma Linda University, Adventist Health System. The results
         were published in *The Journal of Cardiac Rehabilitation*, vol. 3, no. 12, Decem-
         ber 1983, pp. 839–846; vol. 1, no. 2, May 1981, pp. 99–105; and *Diabetes Care*,
         vol. 5, no. 4, July–August 1982, pp. 370–374.

336   The number of kidney and liver transplants performed is provided by the
         National Institute of Diabetes and Diagnostic Diseases.

338   The number of people who have received hip-joint replacements is provided
         by the National Center for Health Statistics. The number of people who have
         had heart-valve replacements is provided by the American Heart Association.
         The number of people with kidney machines is provided by data from the
         Health Care Financing Administration.

12. A Great Age

347   Monsignor Fahey is quoted from "The Third Age Center," *Pride*, Summer
         1987.

348   De Beauvoir made her comments in her 1972 work, *The Coming of Age*. Rohlen
         is quoted from "The Promise of Adulthood in Japanese Spiritualism," in *Adult-
         hood*, edited by Erik Erikson, 1978.

348–   Van Rensselaer's sermon was published as *Old Age: A Funeral Sermon*, Washing-
349   ton, D.C., 1841. Mather's "Dignity and Duty of Aged Servants" was quoted
         in *Growing Old in America*, by David Hackett Fisher, 1978.

Index

To communicate with Ken Dychtwald, or for more information about Age Wave, Inc.'s programs and products, contact:

Age Wave, Inc.
1900 Powell Street
Emeryville, CA   94608
(415) 652-9099